DRINK OF IMMORTALITY

DRINK OF IMMORTALITY

Essays on Distillation and Alcohol Use in Ancient India

Edited by

D. N. JHA

MANOHAR
2026

First published 2020

Reprinted 2026

ISBN 978-93-90035-21-2

Published by
Ajay Jain *for*
Manohar Publishers & Distributors
4753/23 Ansari Road, Daryaganj
New Delhi 110002

Typeset by
Ravi Shanker
Delhi 110095

Printed at
Replika Press Pvt. Ltd.

For

My teetotaller friends

अपाम सोमममृता अभूमागन्म ज्योतिरविदाम देवान्।
किं नूनमस्मान्कृणवदरातिः किमु धूर्तिरमृतं मर्त्यस्य।।

R̥gveda VIII.48.3

We just drank the Soma, we have become immortal, we have come to the light, we have found the gods. What can enmity do to us now, and what the mischief of a mortal, O immortal one?

Tr. Jan E.M. Houben

Contents

Introduction

The earliest textual reference to a heady drink, associated with the Aryans, is found in the *Ṛgveda*. It is called Soma to which the *Ṛgveda* devotes one full section (Maṇḍala IX). Soma was also the name of a Vedic god. Another drink, Surā, grain based unlike the plant based Soma, is also mentioned in the *Ṛgveda*. Soma was offered to Vedic gods; among them Indra was an inveterate imbiber and a dipsomaniac. Surā was used in the Sautrāmaṇi ritual. Unlike Soma, which was offered to the gods and which the brāhmaṇas/priests had the privilege to drink, Surā was popular among the ordinary people and was considered inferior to the former; it was also drunk at weddings, tournaments and other festive occasions. The Vedic and post-Vedic literature mentions other drinks as well, and some of them may have been substitutes for Soma which grew in the mountains and gradually became scarce as the Aryans moved into the plains. The name Soma, however, continued to be used in the general sense of an alcoholic drink. In subsequent times, greater variety of wine and other drinks were known and with the emergence of states, they tended to come under state control. Kauṭilya in his *Arthaśāstra*, assignable to the Mauryan period, provides for the appointment of a superintendent of liquor (*surādhyakṣa*) who controlled the sale and manufacture of liquor.

In the early centuries before and after Christ there was an unprecedented spurt in trade with the Western world; Rome exported a huge quantity of wine to India. Along with the brisk

Indo-Roman trade came the Graeco-Roman influence in different spheres, especially in art as is evident from the Bacchanalian group of sculptures from Mathura whose Dionysiac aspect has been a prominent theme of discussion among art historians and which is noticeable, in varying degrees, in later times too.

The literary texts of ancient India often describe drinking scenes in explicit detail. The *Rāmāyaṇa*, *Mahābhārata*, the works of Kālidāsa, etc., depict Rāma, Kṛṣṇa and other godly figures as engaging in drinking bouts. The twelfth-century work, *Mānasollāsa*, written by the Western Cāḷukya king Someśvara III, describes what a royal drinking party was like.

Religions of ancient India had varied attitudes to the use of liquor. The Vedic religion used Soma in rituals but early Buddhism did not favour drinking though the extent to which Buddhists abstained from it is a matter of speculation. However, there is evidence of wine making under the supervision of Buddhist monasteries in north-western India during the post-Mauryan period. Later, alcohol use became *de rigueur* with the rise of Vajrayāna Buddhism and other Tāntric sects like the Kāpālika and Kālāmukha; the *Mattavilāsaprahasana* (seventh century) by the Pallava king Mahendravarman parodies a Kāpālika who is heavily drunk.

II

It is evident from the above that the history of alcohol use goes back to very early times. The first article on the theme was written by Rajendralal Mitra and was published in the *Journal of Asiatic Society of Bengal* in 1878. Since then no full length and comprehensive study has been undertaken of the subject so far and, as a result, there has been a vacuum in the area of alcohol studies. The present volume is not intended to fill that vacuum but only to create an awareness of the need to study the history of liquor consumption in early India. Mitra's paper provides an overview of liquor use in ancient India, but like all pioneering work it has its shortcomings. Mitra uses the term distillation in a loose sense and does not discuss its antiquity. This forms the subject matter of Part I which includes articles by F.R. Allchin, M.S. Oort, James McHugh, and Irfan Habib; the last one draws mainly on medieval sources (Chs. 1, 2, 3 and 4). In Part II Rajendralal Mitra (Ch. 5) deals with drinking habits of ancient Indians. Articles by Rajesh Kochhar and Jan Houben (Chs. 6 and 7) deal with the various issues related to the identity and historiography of Soma; and Pentti Aalto (Ch. 8) surveys the evidence of drinking in ancient India and focuses on the types of intoxicating drinks that were used. The article by Martha Carter (Ch. 9) discusses how the drink culture permeated in Indian art in the wake of India's interaction with the West during the early centuries AD, especially the Kuṣāṇa period. The last section (Ch. 10) is a translation by David Lorenzen of the one-act farce, *Mattavilāsaprahasana* (seventh century), whose protagonist Kāpālika is suitably tipsy and provides a fitting finale to this volume on alcohol. In a collection like this overlapping is inevitable; for this I crave the indulgence of the reader.

I thank Professor Niraj Kumar Jha (Princeton), and Dr Jyotsna Arora and Malvika Gulati of the Indian Council of Historical Research, New Delhi, for their help. I am grateful to Ramesh Jain and Siddharth Chowdhury for expediting the publication of the book.

7 October 2019 D.N. Jha

PART I

CHAPTER 1

India: The Ancient Home of Distillation?

*F.R. Allchin**

It is generally believed that the art of distillation was known to the Greeks of Alexandria before the opening of the Christian era, and later used by the Arabs for obtaining essential oils; but that the distillation of alcohol only developed in western Europe from the twelfth century AD. In this article the author refers to the identification of certain pots as parts of stills. The pots are found in archaeological excavations in north-west Pakistan, and together with the contexts in which they occur, lead to the conclusion that the distillation of alcohol was common in that region between *c.* 150 BC and *c.* AD 350. This type of still resembles one of the two main types surviving in popular use throughout South Asia into this century. A fresh look at references to alcoholic drinks in Indian literature suggests that certain terms, hitherto not clearly understood, may refer to distillation, permitting us, in India and Pakistan, to take its history back to *c.* 500 BC.

Considering the importance of alcohol for mankind, and the diverse uses to which it is put, it is surprising that comparatively little is known of its early history or of the stages of its discovery and exploitation. There seems to be fairly general agreement that a knowledge of fermentation is so elementary and so widely diffused

* Reprinted from *Man*, New Series, vol. 14, no. 1 (March 1979).

throughout human society that it must have been discovered at a very early date and probably in many different places. Even so, definite evidence is hard to come by. On the all-important step of the discovery of the concentration of alcohol by distillation there are widely divergent views. Forbes (1948) in one of the very few books devoted to the subject traces the discovery back to the Alexandrian Greeks at the beginning of the Christian era. At that time the process was apparently used mainly for chemical purposes. The onward development seems to have been at the hands of the Arabs who used it for the extraction of essential oils for perfumes. Although there are rare Arab references, towards the end of the first millennium, to the distillation of wine, it seems probable that for religious reasons they did not exploit it (Forbes 1948: 41). According to Forbes, distillation of alcohol for drinking seems first to have developed in Europe in the twelfth century and thereafter. He dismisses the thesis advanced by some ethnographers (Maurizio 1933) that the very wide distribution of simple stills among primitive peoples in Africa, Asia and middle America indicates the antiquity of distillation, and believes that all such modern occurrences may be traced to the recent diffusion of the technique. Thus, there appears to be an unresolved contradiction between the historical view, supplied by a critical reading of textual evidence, and the ethnographic, deriving from modern observations of primitive peoples. Because of the fugitive nature of much of the material evidence involved, archaeology has hitherto had little to say on this question. Recently, however, archaeological evidence from north-west India and Pakistan has led me to re-examine the problem in the light of local textual and ethnographic evidence, and this has produced encouraging results. It leads to the conclusion that only an inter-disciplinary approach can provide a convincing hypothesis in the present state of knowledge.

Viewed in the light of textual references the Indian picture at first sight seems to coincide with Forbes's view. On the other hand, the ethnographic evidence is plentiful and suggests that in South Asia distillation was certainly much older than the texts appear to indicate. When the first distilleries on European lines were established in India around 1835 there was already in many parts of the subcontinent a local cottage industry distilling spirits from a variety of fermented liquors, including unrefined sugar, palm juice, rice and the flowers of the *mahuā* tree (*Bassia latifolia*). The apparatus they used was extremely simple, consisting most commonly of a globular pot, covered by an inverted terracotta bowl with a hole cut in one side to admit a bamboo pipe connecting it to a second, receiving pot. The joints were sealed with clay and the still-head was usually covered with a wet cloth, while the receiver was stood in a basin of cold water to promote condensation (Fig. 1.1). A second type of still is also widely reported in South Asia. Here a large pot has a smaller placed over its mouth, having perforations in its base. A small bowl is set inside the perforated pot whose mouth is in turn closed by a third pot with a rounded or conical base and filled with cold water

Figure 1.1: Indian tribal still from Andhra Pradesh (copyright C. von Fürer-Haimendorf 1943). This is a modern example of the type of apparatus which has been found in ancient Gāndhāra.

(Fig. 1.2). The fermented liquid is boiled in the lower pot and the steam rises through the perforations, condensing on the base of the uppermost pot and dripping down into the receiving bowl. Both these methods have been recorded in South Asia among tribal groups, rural agriculturalists and specialist castes whose products are sold to an urban population.

The custom of taking alcoholic drinks, including the products of distillation, was certainly current among Indians in early British times, and leads one to believe that the native distilleries were then patronized not only by tribal peoples, but also by princes. Some Rajput princes jealously guarded the secret formulae of

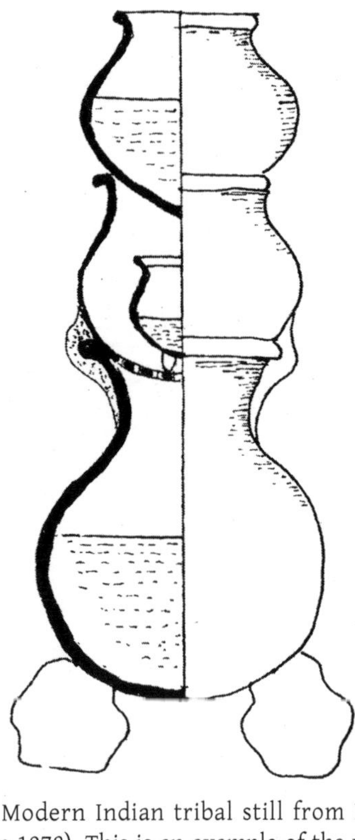

Figure 1.2: Modern Indian tribal still from Bihar (after Mahdihassan 1972). This is an example of the vertical type of still sometimes referred to as the Mongol still.

their palace stills and their products formed an important item of hospitality. About the Sikh prince Ranjit Singh, Burnes tells us, that he was 'immoderately fond' of strong drinks, and that his favourite beverage was a spirit distilled from the grapes of Kabul (Burnes 1834: I.30). However inconclusive such evidence may be, it suggests that the drinking of spirits was common among Rajputs and Sikhs in the period when direct European influence can only have been slight, and therefore that at least in the Punjab and Rajputana may be far older than that influence.

By comparison the textual evidence from India and Pakistan is not very helpful. Both the major types of still are mentioned as being in the still-room of the Mughal emperor Akbar in the sixteenth century, along with a third variety which Joseph Needham has identified as a Chinese type, otherwise unrecorded in South Asia. The earliest explicit reference to distillation is in a medical text *Bhaiṣajya Ratnāvalī* of Govinda Dāsa, datable to around the seventeenth century, where it is used in the preparation of a medicinal drink known as *Mṛtasañjīvanī surā*, i.e. spirits to raise the dead! Apparatus resembling the first type of still is described in the chemical text *Rasaratnasamuccaya* of Vāgbhaṭa (c. twelfth century), under the name of *tiryak pāṭana yantra*, the 'oblique falling' apparatus. Its use is for chemical purposes and there is no mention of concentrating alcohol in this context.

The paucity and lateness of references to early Indian distillation are in contrast to the explicit references to the preparation of drinks and medicines by fermentation. From the time of the *R̥gveda* (c. 1200 BC) *surā* is mentioned as an intoxicating drink, used in certain rituals alongside the more prestigious *soma* about whose nature and manufacture there is still controversy and which Wasson (1969; 1972) has identified as the product of the fly-agaric mushroom, *Amanita muscaria*. According to the commentators *surā* was a ferment of rice or barley. The *Arthaśāstra* (in part perhaps from the third century BC) gives recipes for several fermented drinks including those whose ingredients are rice, sugar cane juice, grapes and various spices. The early medicinal texts (early centuries AD) have sections on intoxicants and intoxication, recommending their use for certain conditions and supplying many recipes, including some to combat alcoholic remorse! They describe several categories of drink, both medicinal and other, all produced by fermentation. But there is no indication that any of the ferments were concentrated by distillation. The ingredients are again very varied and include grains, sugar cane juice, honey, grapes and other fruits, and *mahuā* flowers (which as we noticed above are still favourites of modern tribal distillers). The critical historian, basing himself on textual evidence, can hardly be blamed for concluding that while fermentation was commonplace from very early times in India, distillation was 'unknown' (the infelicitous term often used by textual scholars when they mean 'not mentioned in texts') before the twelfth century; and that it was only after the Muslim invasions that it became common. There is thus an unresolved difference between the textual evidence and the inferences which may be drawn from ethnographic observation.

It is on this paradoxical situation that I believe archaeology may be able to throw some light. In his excavations at Taxila, now in Pakistan, Sir John Marshall (1951: 420) discovered, some fifty years ago, a group of vessels which he reconstructed as apparatus for condensing water. The apparatus consisted of an iron tripod and a group of terracotta vessels – a globular pot, covered by an inverted bowl or cowl, having a short spout on one side, and joined by a terracotta tube to a receiver in the form of a distinctive pot, entirely enclosed except for a short wide spout on the domed top. Marshall supposed that the receiver would have been placed in a basin of water to assist condensation (Fig. 1.3). After making this bold reconstruction he hesitated to express a view on the actual use to which the apparatus may have been put. Others, less cautious, have since not failed to see its obvious suitability for the distillation of alcohol (Ray 1956: 80; Mahdihassan 1972: 164). If we accept this conclusion it would provide evidence of distillation in ancient India in the first century BC-AD. But so long as the Taxila

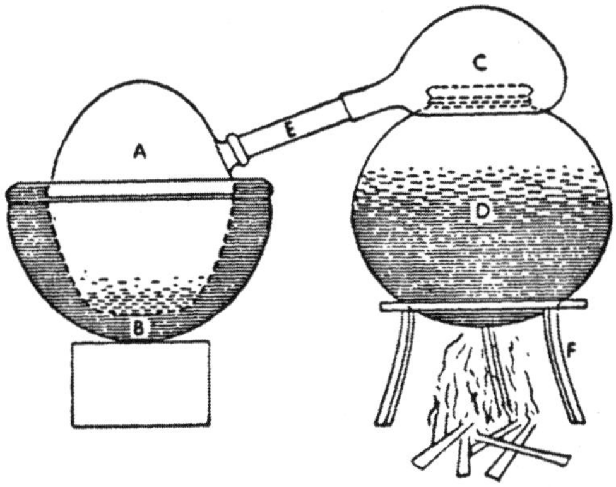

Figure 1.3: Still reconstructed from finds at Taxila, Punjab (after Marshall 1951). This apparatus dates from first century BC-AD

evidence remained unique it could scarcely be sufficient basis for so major a conclusion.

Plentiful supporting evidence, however, was discovered in the Cambridge-Peshawar Universities collaborative excavations at Shaikhan Dheri, Charsada, in 1963, although it barely finds any mention in the preliminary report (Dani 1966). Shaikhan Dheri, the second city of Charsada, was founded by the Indo-Greeks soon after 200 BC and occupied until the fourth-fifth century AD. From the first century AD the city was ruled by the Kuṣaṇas who had followed the Greeks into north-west India from Afghanistan and Central Asia. The ancient name of the city was Puṣkalavatī and it was the capital of the Gāndhāra region. In one part of the excavated area large numbers of characteristic receivers were found, occurring without a break from *c.* 150 BC to the end of the occupation. More than a hundred examples were recovered in an area of 350 sq. m. From the first century BC some of the receivers were marked during manufacture with a stamped impression. One of the earliest marks took the form of a wine jug. With the arrival of the Kuṣaṇas the stamped marks are generally monograms similar to those found on the Kuṣaṇa coins and generally regarded

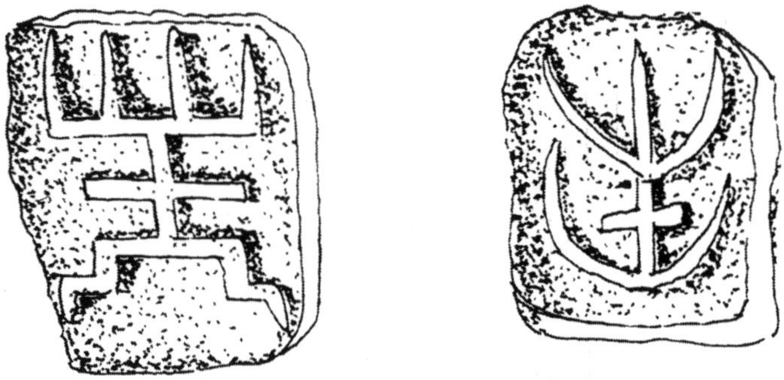

Figure 1.4: Examples of Kuṣaṇa royal monograms stamped on receivers from Shaikhan Dheri, North West Frontier Province, Pakistan (first-third centuries AD)

as royal insignia (Fig. 1.4). The custom of stamping pottery with decorative or auspicious marks, and more rarely with royal marks, goes back in India to the third century BC, but no comparable series has hitherto been recorded. One is at once reminded of the common practice of stamping the handles of the amphorae used in the Mediterranean world for the carriage and export of wine from Rhodes and elsewhere during Greek and Hellenistic times. It seems reasonable to infer a similar role for the stamped marks on these receivers in the Gāndhāra region.

The part of Shaikhan Dheri where the finds were made also contributes to the picture. Throughout the life of the city it took the form of an open area surrounded by houses and on the side of a main road; many shallow drinking bowls were fouhd there. In the last period of occupation many were discovered stacked up in heaps on the ground. There was much ash scattered about, and many fragments of globular pots with sooty exteriors, some of which could well have served as one of the elements in the distilling apparatus. There were also several hearths. A single terracotta tube, made to imitate bamboo, and fragments of one or two typical cowls were also found. Putting these various elements together we can reconstruct an apparatus surprisingly similar to that postulated by Marshall (Fig. 1.5). Reviewing the evidence from Shaikhan Dheri we conclude that it is consistent with the yard

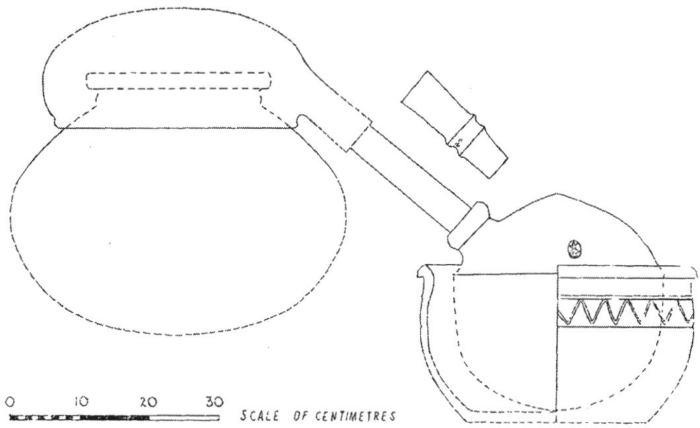

Figure 1.5: Still reconstructed from finds at Shaikhan Dheri. The receivers here occur.repeatedly from second century BC-fourth century AD

having been used as a small-scale distillery and drinking shop, where the receivers, both marked and unmarked, were used in the production, storage and subsequent sale of spirits.

The distinctive receivers may well provide a clue to the extent of the practice at that date, but ethnographic observation warns that even common water pots may be used as receivers, when covered with a suitable cloth. None the less, the form of the receivers appears to be deliberately adapted to their special function. The distribution of sites where they have been found is shown in Fig. 1.6.

With the new perspective provided by archaeology we may look once more at early Indian literature and try to discover whether some of the references to drinks may not conceal implicit evidence of distillation, even though there are no explicit references. Over a century ago one Indian scholar wrote a paper on the occurrence of spirituous drinks in ancient India in which he maintained that 'all the liquors noticed in Sanskrit works were likewise first fermented and then distilled; none were manufactured as European wines by mere fermentation' (Mitra

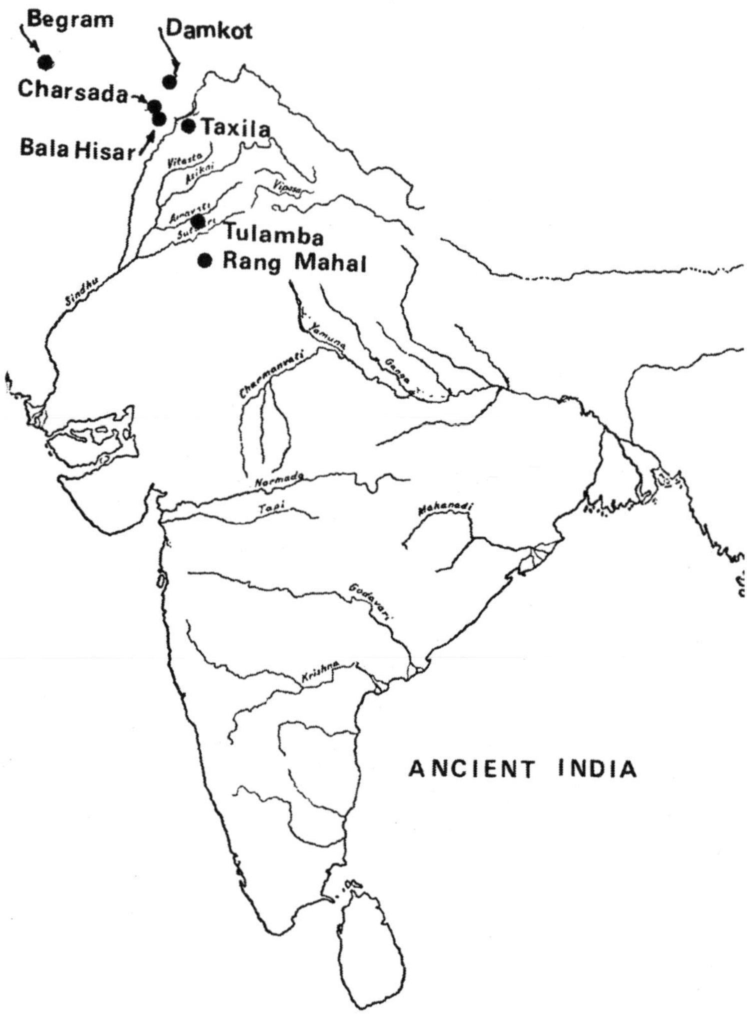

Figure 1.6: Map of sites where the distinctive receivers have been found.

1873: 18). Unfortunately he offered little evidence to support his view, and indeed its source remains unclear. The belief that distillation was known and practised anciently in India is followed by several modern Ayurvedic scholars. They identify a group of Sanskrit words, including *pariśrut* and *pariśravaṇa*, having meanings associated with trickling, with distillation. European Vedic scholars have generally favoured a different meaning for these words, involving the straining or filtering of wine. But conclusive proof is not forthcoming. Our archaeological evidence would permit us to accept the former interpretation, although it cannot offer any proof. More certainty attends a second group of words, deriving from Sanskrit *śūṇḍa*, elephant's trunk, and associated with the manufacture and sale of, and addiction to, strong drinks. These words occur in literature from *c.* 500 BC. It has been pointed out that the cowl and pipe of the Taxila still, or for that matter of the modern Indian still, bear a strong resemblance to the head and trunk of an elephant. The analogy of the intoxicating rut trickling down the trunk of the elephant to the concentrated alcohol running down the pipe of the still is obvious. Even in the much later *Bhaiṣajya Ratnāvalī* the term *gajakumbha*, elephant's forehead, is used as a simile for a part of the distilling apparatus, and in an early nineteenth-century dictionary the term *śūṇḍa yantra*, trunk apparatus, is translated as alembic or retort. Thus there seems to be good reason to see in this group of terms, occurring from the fifth century BC onwards, reference to the use of stills similar to those we have described. The conclusion is that Indian literature does, after all, contain numerous references to distillation, although one could scarcely have recognized them until the archaeological evidence was available.

It is interesting to speculate on the circumstances which led to the apparent contradiction between the textual evidence and that of archaeology or modern observation. First, it must be admitted that throughout early Indian texts references to the production of alcohol, even by fermentation, are at best oblique. In the medical texts, for instance, one is told the ingredients to be added to a quantity of water for a specific recipe, and that the mixture should be sealed in a pot and buried in the fire-room for so many days. But we are not told that this is fermentation, or that the net result is alcoholic. References to the use of yeast or other fermenting agents are very rare. Second, there is a general reluctance in early Indian literature to discuss craft practices (compare, for example, iron or bronze working), particularly when these were regarded as of questionable respectability. A third reason for secrecy is that the consumption of alcohol seems to have had from the beginning a ritual and sacramental aspect, and this is preserved till today in its use in certain Tantric rituals, including its role among the five *makāras* of the *cakra pūjā*. All these things combine to make it less probable that references to distillation should have found their way into literature, at least until some new element was introduced, such as perhaps the importation of new and technically improved apparatus during the past three centuries.

If I am right in thinking that the *śūṇḍa-śauṇḍika* words derive from the elephantine appearance of the still and were in particular associated with the fermenters and distillers of alcohol, then the series of derivative occupational caste names which survive from the Punjab, Uttar Pradesh, Madhya Pradesh, Bihar, Bengal, Assam and Orissa, may provide supporting evidence. In view of the way in which modern prohibitionist legislation in both India and Pakistan is cutting off links with their traditional occupations, there is a real urgency in investigating this aspect of the question. I have a feeling that much important information might still be gathered by questioning such people.

To conclude: the type of still discovered at Shaikhan Dheri between *c.* 150 BC and *c.* fourth century AD has a distribution which fully entitles us to name it the Gāndhāran still. Its form permits us to identify the 'elephant's trunk' associations with drinking in Indian literature from the fifth century BC, and to see it as the direct ancestor of the village stills which, until recent years, were to be found in almost every province of India, Pakistan and Bangladesh. Mahdihassan (1972), whose contribution to the discussion has been of great importance, has ventured even farther into the past and suggests that certain pottery types which are by no means rare in the peninsula of India from *c.* 2000

BC may also be regarded as the precursors of the still-head of the Gāndhāran type still. He may well be right, but without further research and consideration I hesitate to follow him so far. Even without this addition, the conclusion is sufficiently striking. India appears on present evidence to have been the first culture to exploit widespread distillation of alcohol for human consumption; and it may well be that the art of distillation was India's gift to the world!

NOTE

This article is a summary of the evidence put forward in a longer paper read at the Fourth International Conference of South Asian Archaeologists in Naples in July 1977, and to be published in the proceedings of that conference. The author invites comments and criticisms from scholars working in allied disciplines, particularly anthropologists and chemists, on the different aspects of the problem.

REFERENCES

Burnes, A., 1834, *Travels into Bukhara,* 3 vols, London: John Murray.

Dani, A.H., 1966, 'Shaikhan Dheri Excavations, 1963 and 1964', *Ancient Pakistan*, 2: 17-214.

Forbes, R.J., 1948, *A Short History of the Art of Distillation,* Leiden: E.J. Brill.

Mahdihassan, H., 1972, 'The Earliest Distillation Units in Indo-Pakistan', *Pakistan Archaeol.*, 8: 159-68.

Marshall, J., 1951, *Taxila*, 3 vols., Cambridge: Cambridge University Press.

Maurizio, A., 1933, *Geschichte dergegorenen Getränke,* Berlin.

Mitra, Rajendralal, 1873, 'Spirituous Drinks in Ancient India', *J. Asiatic Soc. Bengal*, 43: 1-23.

Needham, J., *Science and Civilisation in China,* vol. 5, pt. 4, Cambridge: Cambridge University Press.

Ray, P.C., 1956, *History of Chemistry in Ancient and Medieval India*, ed. P. Ray (2nd edn), Calcutta: Indian Chemical Society.

Wasson, R.G., 1969, *SOMA: Divine Mushroom of Immortality*, New York.

———, 1972, *Soma and Fly-agaric,* Cambridge, Mass.: Botanical Museum of Harvard University.

CHAPTER 2

Surā in the *Paippalāda Saṁhitā* of the *Atharvaveda*

*Marianne S. Oort**

Two recently published hymns of the *Paippalāda Atharvaveda* afford insight on the nature, preparation, and effects of the intoxicating beverage *surā* and may give evidence for the technique of distillation in early Vedic times.

There are only a few references in the *Ṛgveda*[1] to *surā*, an alcoholic beverage. The connection of *surā* and *viṣa* (poison) is mentioned, as well as *dṛtiṁ surāvato gṛhé* (the leather bag hanging in the house of the possessor of *surā*) (I.191.10). The Aśvins have a particular relation to *surā*, primarily in their function as healers along with Sarasvatī in a verse (X.131.5) which could be an abstract of the opening myth of the Sautrāmaṇi sacrifice in the *Śatapatha Brāhmaṇa*.

With the publication of the critical edition of the *Paippalāda Saṁhitā* of the *Atharvaveda* by Dipak Bhattacharya,[2] *kāṇḍas* 1-15 are finally available to the scholarly public in printed form. *Kāṇḍas*

*Reprinted from *The Journal of American Oriental Society*, vol. 122, no. 2 (2002).

[1] *Ṛgveda* I.116.7; I.191.10; VII.86.6; X.131.4,5.

[2] Dipak Bhattacharya, *The Paippalāda-Saṁhitā of the Atharvaveda*, vol. 1, Calcutta: The Asiatic Society, 1997.

5 and 8 of the *Paippalāda Atharvaveda* contain two *sūktas* dealing entirely with the preparation and effects of *surā*. The use of *surā* in a ritual context is connected with the Sautrāmaṇi and the Rājasūya where it is offered instead of *soma*. It is also an integral part of some *gṛhya* rites. In order to explicate the content of the two *sūktas* presented in this paper, I will give a short summary on beer and the preparation of *surā* as given in Brāhmaṇic texts.

Beer can be defined as an alcoholic liquor made from malted grain. It was widely used in Egypt and Mesopotamia in ancient times, and papyri of the period around 1300 BC refer to the regulation of beer shops. Barley, corn, and millet were some of the early grains used to make beer. In India rice was later introduced as one of the ingredients. In all the cultures producing beer, the beverage was not only meant to be an intoxicant but was also considered medicinal. To brew beer the malted grain is crushed and mixed with hot water. The resulting infusion produces starch which is converted into a sugar to start the fermentation process. In the simplest form of brewing, the mash is allowed to ferment in a warm place for one or more days. The resulting liquid is strained. Sometimes honey, fruit, or herbs such as hops are added. The Russian summer beverage *kvas*, made from rye bread, sugar or honey, and water is an example of this simple process.

In her book *Surā the Liquor and the Vedic Sacrifice*,[3] Madhavi Kolhatkar describes the use and preparation of *surā* with copious references to passages in *Śatapatha Brāhmaṇa* and other Brāhmanic texts. The two versions of the Sautrāmaṇī are the principal subjects of her publication. The preparation of *surā* according to the Brāhmanic texts[4] is a bit more complicated than brewing beer. Much of the ritualization of the process attempts to follow the rituals pertaining to the preparation of *soma*. I will restrict my description to the ingredients and a few implements mentioned and to the procedure, with little reference to the ritual

[3] Madhavi Bhaskar Kolhatkar, *Surā the Liquor and the Vedic Sacrifice*, New Delhi: D.K. Printworld, 1999.

[4] *BaudhŚS* XVII.31, *KātyŚS*, *ŚB*.

paraphernalia and *mantras*. The ingredients mentioned are *śaṣpa* (malted grain), *tokma* (malted barley), *lājā* (parched or fried grain), and *nagnahu* (a powder made of pulses and spices). The main implements are three pots made of the wood of different trees, a *kārotara* (filtering vessel), the hair of three different animals, a lion, a wolf, and a tiger, *iṇḍva* (a covering for the hands or head made of grass), *śatātṛṇṇā* (a pot with a 'hundred' holes), a *sata* (pot or pan), and a strainer made of hair. In the ritual context the *surākāra* is the Adhvaryu[5] who mixes the ingredients, often reciting the verse *svādīṁ tvā svādunā*. . . . Some of the ingredients are pounded, and two mashes of rice and millet with water are made, which are then cooked separately until they boil over. The scum is often collected for sealing the cover of the pot later during the fermentation process. A portion of malted rice, barley, parched rice, and spice mixture, which is called *māsara*, is added to the separate pots. The contents of each pot is then dried and pounded and finally added to the remaining grain in a large vessel which is covered and placed in a hole. This mixture, called *pariśrut*, in this case raw liquor, is fermented for one to three days. In some texts[6] milk and additional powdered malted barley are added each day, resulting in a beverage I could define as a cow-milk based *koumiss*. The *surā* is then filtered through a strainer made of hair, which is sometimes interpreted as using an animal hide.[7] Surā Devī arose from the foam produced through the churning of the ocean by the *devas* and the *asuras*; our *surā* arises from the scum of boiling rice and barley.,

Descriptions of the preparation of *surā* have only been transmitted in ritual texts. The beverage resulting from the process resembles beer. The addition of milk makes it another kind of drink. The word *surā* seems to refer to different kinds of alcoholic drinks depending on the context. In the *gṛhya* texts *surā*

5 *KāṭhS* XII.9.
6 *KātyŚS* XIX.1.21; *ŚB*, XII.8.2.12.
7 *KātyŚS* XIX.2.6; *VājS*, XIX.8.

functions at weddings and rites for the dead, often mentioned as a part of the payment in *natura* to the women taking part in these ceremonies.[8] It was probably quite common to brew *surā* as beer for daily consumption or festive occasions, and it is highly unlikely that only an Adhvaryu could be a *surākāra*.

I should now like to turn to our two *sūktas* on *surā* from the *Paippalāda Saṁhitā*. A. Lubotsky has graciously allowed me to use his translation of 5.10 which is included in his unpublished critical edition and translation of *kāṇḍa* 5. The text of the two hymns generally follows Bhattacharya's edition with only a few exceptions, where emendations are marked with an asterisk.

AVP 5.10. To the liquor (*Surā*)

iyaṃ yā muśalāhatā, dr̥ṣatpiṣṭā viṣāsutā
*tapur agnis +tapur d̦yaus, *tapus t$_u$vam sure bhava* |1|

This one, which is crushed by a pestle, ground by a grindstone, is a poison-brew.
Agni is burning heat; Heaven is burning heat. Become, O liquor, burning heat yourself.

viṣaṁ te tokma rohayanto '$_a$bruvan, viṣaṁ kumbhe '$_a$va srava
*viṣaṁ ta *āmanaṁ sure, viṣaṁ tvaṁ hasta āhitā, viṣaṁ pra-tihitā bhava* |2|

'Poison is your malted barley,' said those who were raising [you]. Being poison, flow down into the pot.
Poison is your disposition, O liquor; poison are you when taken by hand. Become poison when put to [the lips].

siṃhas te astu taṇḍulo, v̦yāghraḥ par̦yodanam
**pr̥dākūr astu nagnahur, vr̥kasya hr̥di saṁ srava* |3|

Let your rice grain (*lājās*?) be a lion, [your] gruel (*māsara*?) a tiger.
Let the ferment be a panther. Flow into the heart of a wolf.

*iyaṁ yā pātra āsutā, +śaṣpasrakvā *vighasvarī*
varāhamanyur ajan̦y, uttānapādam ardaya |4|

This [liquor], brewed in a cup, is, with [the taste of] malted grain in the mouth, nutritious.

[8] *Āśvalāyana Gr̥hyasūtra* 5.5.

Boar's ardor has arisen: shake the one with stretched legs (= earth).

+udardanī pracyavanī, pāṁsupiṅgā vighasvarī
utkhātamanyur ajani, yat paścāt tat puras kr̥dhi | 5 |

[The liquor] is agitating, shaking, dust-yellowish, nutritious.
The ardor of the uprooted one (= earth) has arisen: what is behind, make in front.

viṣaṁ te pavane sure, rudhiraṃ sthāne astu te
*mathnant$_{u}$v anyo anyasmā, iṣudhīṁs *tvad dhanus t$_{u}$vat* | 6 |

O liquor, let poison be in your strainer, the blood-red [substance] in your pot!
Let them destroy the quivers and the bow of each other.

viṣapāvāno rudhirāś caranti, pātāro martās tavase surā ime
*hatāso anye yodhayant̥y *anyāṁs, tam ic chaṁsa mahimānaṁ surāyāḥ* | 7 |

The red poison-drinkers walk around, these mortals drinking for strength, O liquor.
Those who are hit set each other to fighting: praise that power of liquor.

tān vīrudho vi sravo balena-, -ut pātaya mādaya yodhanāyai
bhinnāratir bhinnaśīrṣṇā sam r̥cchatāṁ, ārtacelo visravan te surāpaḥ | 8 |

Flow out with the strength of the plant to them, make [them] fly up, make [them] drunk so that they set each other to fighting.
Let the one with a broken elbow fight the one with a broken head! With afflicted garment, (blood-) dripping is your drinker, O liquor.

viṣāsutāṁ pibata +jarhr̥ṣāṇā, asnā saṁsr̥ṣṭāṁ rudhireṇa miśrām
chinnahastaś carati grāme antar, vairahatyāni bahudhā paṇāyan | 9 |

Drink you, who are excited, the poison-brew, [which is] united with blood, mixed with red.
He who has his hand cut off walks around the village, praising all kinds of men-killings.

asimatīm iṣumatīm un nayāmi satād adhi
māday$_{a}$ābhi mādaya-, -ahir^{i}vainān pra ropaya-, -anyo '$_{a}$nyasya mocchiṣan | 10 |

The knife-sharp, arrow-sharp [liquor] do I raise up from a pan.
Make [them] intoxicated, make [them] tipsy. Like a snake, cause them racking pain, let them leave nothing of each other.

AVP 8.12. To *Surā*

svādvīṁ tvā mitrāvaruṇā, svādvīṁ devī sarasvatī
svādvīṁ tvā aśvinā sure, kr̥ṇutām puṣkarasrajā |1|

Let Mitra and Varuṇa make you tasty, let Goddess Sarasvatī make you tasty.
O *Surā*, let the lotus-garlanded Aśvins make you tasty.

yām asiñcan saudhanvanā, viśve devā marudgaṇāḥ
yām aśvinā $_{a}$siñcatāṁ, sā surā bahu dhāvatu |2|

That (*surā*) whom the Saudhanvanas, the All Gods, together with the troop of Maruts, sprinkled,
Whom the Aśvins sprinkled, let that *surā* run abundantly.

svādos svādīyasī bhava, madhor madhutarā bhava
yathā r̥śyasyeyam āriś$_{i}$y, evā tvaṁ subhage bhava |3|

Be tastier than tasty, be sweeter than sweet.
As the roe(?) is to the roebuck, so be you, O fortunate one.

abhrāj jātaṁ varṣāj jātam, atho jātaṁ divas pari
ath$_{a}$o samudrāj jātaṁ, tat surā daraṇaṁ bhava |4|

Born from a cloud, born from the rain, born from the sky,
Then born from the sea, you become *surā*-rending.

nāḍi nāmāsi januṣā, sā surādaraṇī bhava
sakhā hi bhadras ta āsīd, vr̥kṣas svāduvikaṅkataḥ |5|

From birth (onwards) you are called reed, so become *surā*-rending,
Because you had an auspicious friend, the sweet *vikaṅkaṭa* tree.

asuras tvaurdhvanabhasaś cakāra prathamas sure
sure dāsasya tvā gr̥he, śiraś cāndhaś ca cakratuḥ |6|

O *surā*, the *asura* Aurdhvanabhasa (going upwards cloud?) made you first.
O *surā*, in the house of a *dāsa* the head and the stalk have produced you.

nıṣ puṣpakam kaśıkaya, nır dharayas suram uta
ud ehi vājinīvati, kim añkatiṣ$_{u}$v icchasi |7|

Dis[till] the mucus out of the ferret, and dis[till] the *surā* out of the stream.
Move up, strength bestowing; why do you linger in the curves(?).

ime te janyā āsate, gambhirā abhidhṛṣṇavaḥ
sure devi pari prehi, mādayantī janaṁ-janam ।8।

Your people sit here, profound, overpowering.
O divine *surā*, circumambulate, making each person exhilarated.

yasyā gṛhṇanti sthālena, gām aśvaṁ dhānyam vasu
sā surā bahu dhāvatu ।9।

For a pot of which they get a cow, a horse, grain, goods,
let that *surā* run abundantly.

ācarantīḥ parvatebhyaḥ, khanamānā anabhrayaḥ
yāsāṁ samudre saṁsthānaṃ, yāsāṁ nāsti niveśanaṃ
tās te dadatu budbudam ।10।

They come here from the mountains, digging without a spade;
Their abode is the ocean, they have no resting place.
Let these give you bubbles/foam.

**udarīkod*[9] *acemāṁ surāṁ, yāṁ hṛdā kāmayāmahe*
*tāṁ me bhagas tā aśvinā, tāṁ mā *āvāṭ sarasvatī* ।11।

O bucket, bail up this *surā*, which we heartily desire.
Let Bhaga, the Aśvins, Sarasvatī not carry away that (*surā*) which is mine.

ayaṁ devo mayūlaśas, +sa surādaraṇaṁ dadat
saṁsravaṇāt prasravaṇād, giribhyas paryābhṛtaḥ
*madhye *śatasya*[10] *+mastiṣko, anaḍvān iva mehatu* ।12।

This [is] the divine *mayūlaśa* fetched from the mountains that will give the *surā*-rending
From the spout, the flow.
May the brains/skull piss like an ox in the middle of the *sata* pot.

Some obscure points in both hymns remain open to other interpretations. However, many of the ingredients used in *surā*, as well as some of the implements, are mentioned in a way that indicates the preparation of the alcoholic drink. The negative passages found in 5.10 and the more positive passages in 8.12 certainly portray recognizable effects of drinking alcoholic

9 A. Lubotsky and M. Witzel independently arrived at this emendation.
10 Cf. above 5.10.10.

beverages. The view of the subject in 5.10 recalls the fact that other cultures also use 'poison' as a slang expression for liquor.

The first six verses provide a good description of the ingredients and the process of making *surā* according to the ritual texts. In 5.10.3 the terms 'malted barley' and 'malted grain' and the reference to 'grinding' echo the descriptions in these texts, as well as the reference to the 'lion' as a grain of 'rice', a 'tiger' as the 'gruel', and the 'spice mixture' as a 'panther'. A strainer made of wolf-hair may be meant by 'the heart of the wolf'. All these images, combined with the element of heat, can refer to the simple process of making beer.

The last four verses comment on the social life of the ancient Aryans, reading like a temperance tract on the evils of strong drink. A large quantity of weak beer would be necessary to result in the drunken aggression described in these passages. In 5.10.10 we find 'the knife-sharp, arrow-sharp [liquor]' and the simile of the bite of a snake. It appears that a beverage with a stronger alcohol content than beer is the cause of bloodthirsty violence.

The initial verse of 8.12 begins with the first two words of the formula *svādvīṁ tvā svādunā* used when mixing the ingredients at various stages of the preparation process. Although gods are mentioned in some of the verses, the description later implies a secular use. In 8.12.4 the heavenly waters or vapours and the earthly waters become *surādaraṇa*, the means of separating sure. Again in 8.12.5 we find *surādaraṇī* (*surā*-rending). 8.12.6 and 8.12.7 allude to one substance being taken out of another and moved upwards. The repetition of the verb *dṛ̥*, meaning to 'tear apart, rend', i.e. to separate, and the use of the prefix *nis* here in conjunction with heat, boiling up and over in both hymns, suggests another phase in the process of making alcohol, namely distillation.

Surā has been used to describe many types of alcoholic beverage, and even in modern times in some parts of India it is the word for *toddy* (palm liquor). There has been some speculation that *surā* is a loan word. The beginning of a distilled liquor is always a simple fermented pulp of malted grain or fruit that is subjected to a further process in order to strengthen the alcohol content. On the basis of remnants of pottery found in areas of the Harappa culture by Marshall, Allchin also speculated on the possibility of the use of a simple distillation apparatus in ancient India.[11] At a Soma Workshop at Leiden University in July 1999, the Russian archaeologist Sarianidi working on excavations in the area of the Bactria-Margiana Culture, third to second millennium BC, described a room in a temple complex for the preparation of 'alcoholic drink'. Remnants of distillation assemblies were also found at the site.

Distillation is generally described as having its roots in alchemy and medicine. Sometimes texts of a later period can give information that may reflect practices used in the past. In the *Suśruta Saṁhitā surā* is listed under the *rasāyanas*, along with a number of other alcoholic spirits. Distilled spirits called *ariṣṭa* are a form of *surā* called *surāsava*, prepared with *pippalī*, *piper longum*, and piper niger. Other forms of distilled *surā* are also mentioned.

Not only in the papyri of Egypt can we find references to the regulation of beer shops. Kauṭilya's *Arthaśāstra* contains a section on 'The Controller of Spirituous Liquors' (chap. 25).[12] Distilled liquor is mentioned in connection to the amount of duty to be paid to the state by persons 'dealing with wines and ferments'. It is even stated that 'Householders should be free to manufacture white liquor on festive occasions'. We are now entirely out of the ritual sphere and into the mundane life of weddings and festivals.

What is the basis of the distillation? Distillation is defined as 'the process of vaporizing a liquid and subsequently recovering it by condensation.'[13] In the specific case of distilling alcohol "it

[11] F.R. Allchin, 'India, the Ancient Home of Distillation?', *Man: The Journal of the Royal Anthropological Institute* (n.s.), 14 (1979): 55-63.

[12] R.P. Kangle, *The Kauṭilīya Arthaśātra*, vol. 2, Delhi: Motilal Banarsidass, rpt. 1986.

[13] *Chamber's Encyclopaedia*, London: George Newnes, 1959.

is based on the fact that alcohol has a lower boiling point than water. The apparatus required for distillation (the still) consists, in its simplest form, of (1) the retort or distilling flask, (2) the condenser and (3) the receiver, arranged as indicated in the figure' (Fig. 2.1). A mash of fermented grain or fruit is processed under constant heat, water being added so that steam is passed through the fermented liquor. The alcohol leaves the top of the receptacle to be collected at the bottom.

S. Mahdihassan reconstructs a simple still from pottery found by B.B. Lal at Hastinapura dating to 300 BC.[14] I have included his reconstruction (Fig. 2.3) and his drawing (Fig. 2.2) of 'a distillation assembly of pots of common domestic use as among the hill tribes of Bihar, India'.

Can we apply this information to some of the verses found in our two *sūktas* on *surā*? We return to the imagery of rending = separation. In the myths connected to the Sautrāmaṇi sacrifice, Indra's body is torn asunder after drinking the *soma* forbidden him by Tvaṣṭṛ. Indra's *vīrya* flows into fruit, plants, animals, metals, as well as *pariśrut*, raw liquor, and *surā*. In the Namuci passage of the

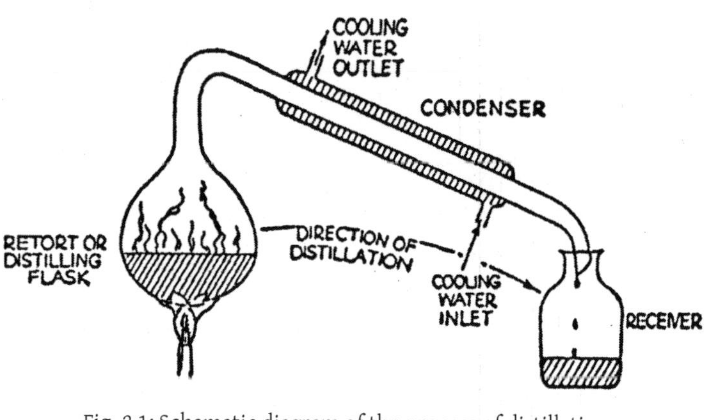

Fig. 2.1: Schematic diagram of the process of distillation.

[14] S. Mahdihassan, 'Distillation Assembly of Pottery in Ancient India with a Single Item of Special Construction', *Vishveshvaranand Indological Journal* 17 (1979): 34.

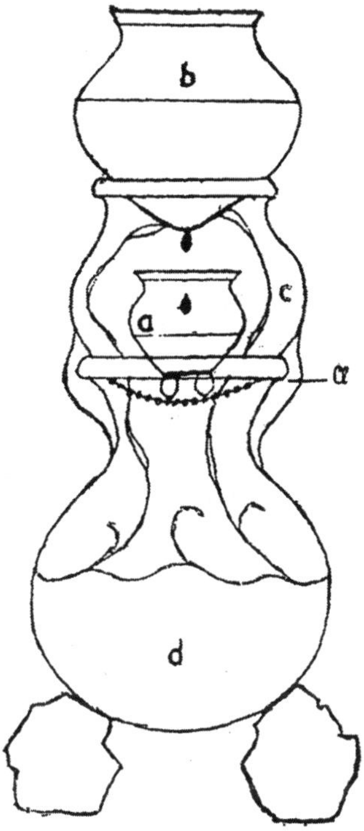

Fig. 2.2

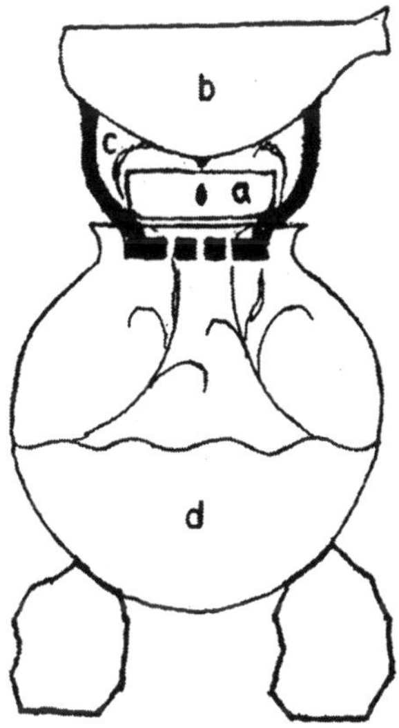

Fig. 2.3

myth a mixture of *soma*, *surā*, and blood in the demon's severed head is drunk, but with a method which separates the blood from the other mixture.

In the two descriptions of the making of *surā*, the imagery of heat, water, and malted grain in *AVP* 5.10.1, 2 depicts a process that could be a description of making the initial mash for distillation as well as beer. *AVP* 8.12.5, 6, 7, and 12 also can be interpreted as referring to the pots and spout of a still. The flow of liquid from one receptacle to another, the vapour or bubbles, *budbudam*, all seem to indicate a different type of procedure from that used for just brewing a beer-like beverage. Let us turn back to Figs. 2.2 and 2.3. The pot-still in Fig. 2.2 used by hill tribes in Bihar has the fermented mash in pot d, which is then boiled, the alcohol vapors rising through perforated pot c; pot b acts as a cover which is filled with water. The alcohol vapours hit the cold bottom surface and drop down again into pot a. In Fig. 2.3 we see that in the reconstruction the pottery fragments are stacked similarly. The implements described in the texts could easily be assembled to form the same kind of structure. In 8.12.4 we find water images being called *surādaraṇa* (*surā*-rending). In 8.12.6 the name of the *asura*, Aurdhvanabhasa, can be translated as 'going upwards cloud', vapour. *Śiras* as 'top' could refer to the upper pot. *Nāḍī* and *cāndhas* are problematic but perhaps refer to something hollow, such as the holes in the bottom of the perforated pot. In 8.12.7 the image of upward movement out of something lower also fits the process of the alcohol rising up out of the mash. In 8.12.10 we have the *budbudam*, the bubbles or foam of condensation adhering to the cooling pot before they drop down into the collecting vessel. Finally 8.12.12 gives a vivid description of liquid coming from the top and flowing down into the middle of a pot.

I hope, by presenting these two *sūktas* from the *Paippalāda Saṁhitā* in the light of what might be called cultural history, to stimulate discussion about the non-ritual information that can be gleaned from the text.

CHAPTER 3

Too Big to Fail

The Idea of Ancient Indian Distillation

James McHugh

When did distillation of alcoholic drinks begin in South Asia, and when did the process become common? Very early South Asian texts do not mention distillation of alcoholic drinks, but we possess clear references to alcoholic distillation in both Sanskrit and Persian texts from approximately the thirteenth century CE onwards.[1] However, scholarly writing on alcohol in pre-modern South Asia is often characterized by translations that imply drinks were distilled. Sometimes this is because of the content of Sanskrit dictionaries and previous translations, and sometimes it is connected to a lively debate as to whether distillation was practised at an early date in South Asia, depending

[1] The first clear description of distillation and a still in Sanskrit is from approximately 1200 CE, in the medical text *Gadanigraha* where we read of a copper device used to distill (*niṣkāśayet*) an '*arka.*' *Gadanigraha Prayogakhaṇḍa Āsavādhikāra* 269 BC-272 (p. 388). On this text, including the date, see Meulenbeld 1999-2002, vol. IIA, 218-19. For a translation of this description of distillation, and other examples of this verbal form used for distillation see McHugh, *An Unholy Brew: Alcohol in Indian History and Religion* (forthcoming). For Persian sources that suggest a similar date of introduction of alcoholic distillation, see Irfan Habib's work. Habib 1985: 205. Also Habib 2011: 55-6.

largely on archaeological evidence that I discuss in this article. So did alcoholic distillation begin in South Asia in the thirteenth century CE, or many centuries earlier? In this article I criticize the arguments for ancient distillation, considering also why the idea is so widespread and enduring. I present the positive evidence for how ancient drinks actually were made (i.e. only fermented) elsewhere.[2]

Let us start with how dictionaries contribute to the notion that there was ancient distillation. In his *Sanskrit-English Dictionary*, composed in the late nineteenth century, Monier Williams translates *madya* as 'any intoxicating drink, vinous or spirituous liquor, wine' and he translates a term meaning 'a jar for *madya*' as 'a vessel for intoxicating liquors, brandy jar'.[3] Another important dictionary, that of Apte (1892), also translates *madya* as 'spirituous liquor, wine, any intoxicating drink'. Apte even foregrounds the term 'spirituous'. These are both excellent dictionaries, and thus some readers and translators of Sanskrit texts might well think words such as *surā* in texts from all times and in all places refer to distilled drinks.

Why did these scholars translate Sanskrit with English words that suggest distilled drinks? Words in ancient, 'dead' languages are not in fact stable in meaning when the language in question is still in use. Thus for traditional scholars educated in Sanskrit in India in the nineteenth century, *madya* and other words for intoxicants might well have referred to distilled drinks, as such drinks were available in India and had been so for many centuries. For example, Rajendralal Mitra in 1873 routinely used the term 'spirituous drinks' to refer to drinks in very early sources.[4] Indian users and scholars of Sanskrit could well have understood *madya* to designate a distilled drink such as arrack for quite a long time, as

[2] McHugh, forthcoming.

[3] The St. Petersburg Lexicon of Boehtlingk and Roth, a major source for Monier-Williams' dictionary, only gives 'an intoxicating drink' (*einberauschendesGetränk*) in this sense of *madya*.

[4] Mitra 1873: 1-23, 58.

distilled alcoholic drinks had been produced since approximately the thirteenth century CE. So, in Sanskrit texts *as composed or as read* in the nineteenth century, words such as *madya*, *surā*, etc. could indeed refer to a distilled drink. Compare to how the English word 'corn' changed reference over time, from a cereal grain to maize, especially in American English.

This updating of Sanskrit is separate from the vigorous discussion concerning the origins of distillation in South Asia based on archaeological finds. We can mostly trace this debate to John Marshall's publication in 1951 of an illustrated account of archaeological excavations at the ancient city of Taxila, in what is now Pakistan.[5] Here, he reported finds of some pottery vessels dating from around a century before or after the turn of the Common Era, which he lists as 'water-condensers'. About these vessels he wrote: 'The precise use made of these vessels is not certain, but it seems probable that the condensing was done as shown in the sketch.' In the related page of plates, three vessels are illustrated both separately and also in a diagram that shows two of them assembled into a still that involves other types of vessels.

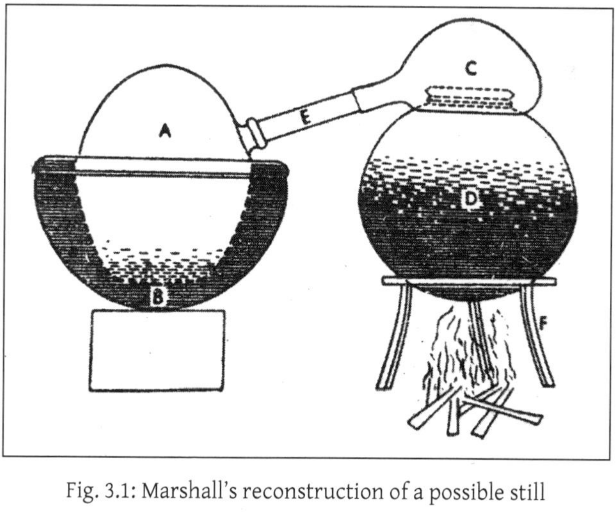

Fig. 3.1: Marshall's reconstruction of a possible still

[5] Marshall 1951, vol. 2: 420-1; vol. 3, pl. 125.

In his description Marshall does not mention alcohol, and instead mentions steam distillation, a process that could, of course, have many other applications. On first appearances it seems quite clear that we have an excavated still here. But on closer examination it is clear that the three vessels illustrated were *not* all found together, rather they were found in quite different places at different strata.[6] Thus, given his own notes on the finds, Marshall did *not* excavate the 'water condenser' *as illustrated*, with all the components present in one place, as an *assemblage* of distillation equipment. He says nothing of the find contexts, but one assumes if the parts were all found in different areas yet always in similar brewery-like settings of some sort he would have mentioned it, as that would strengthen a case for the vessels as a distillation-assemblage. Instead, wishing to understand the purpose of the vessels, and probably basing his theory on contemporary but traditional technology he had seen

[6] Marshall writes that the 'whole apparatus' consists of five separate vessels. He presents these *hypothetically assembled* (not as found) to look like a still in the volume of illustrations (vol. III, pl. 125). Some elements of this 'still', say the bowl to contain water, are very common and unremarkable types of vessels, and the key elements of the 'water condenser' for Marshall are the vessels numbered 127-9. Numbers 127 and 128 are what Marshall calls condensers, and 129 is what he called the condensing cowl. The two condensers were found in separate areas of the excavation. Was either of the 'condensers' found with the 'condensing cowl'? It seems not. All the vessels were excavated at the site called Sirkap:

'condenser' (127) in Block C, square 47.77′, stratum III;
'condenser' (128) in Block K, square 159.110′, stratum II;
'cowl' (129) in Block C, square 50.47′, stratum II.

Thus they are all from different locations and/or strata. Examination of the plan of the site of Sirkap (vol. III, pl. 10), shows that condenser (128) was found in a different part of the city than the other objects. The condenser from block C was found at a different stratum and across a main street, at a distance of approximately 300 ft from the so-called condensing cowl.

in other contexts, Marshall assembled (i.e. created) the so-called 'condenser'. To reiterate: the 'still' in his well-known illustration (and subsequent museum reconstructions) is *not* an assemblage he excavated with all the parts together in one place. Rather this 'still' is the product of his imagination, as informed by what some types of still look like today. Thus, of course, Marshall's grouping of vessels looks like a still – that is because it is based on a modern still![7] So, at that point in the history of this research, no one had

[7] Some more reflections on Marshall's still: the 'condensing cowl' part of the 'still' does not have a particularly unusual form and could be used for all sorts of straining, funneling, or drainage. Thus I assume it was the 'condenser' that needed to be assigned a function, and prompted the distillation hypothesis, as that vessel is unusual in having a spout towards the top of the vessel yet at one side. Presumably in reflecting why a vessel would have a spout at such an angle it occurred to Marshall that this was to allow a pipe to enter the pot from the side, which would evoke the image of certain types of still. However, that is far from the only explanation of the form of these vessels. Indeed, as one sees in the traditional production of perfume *itr*s in north India today, a better design for immersing the condenser fully in water is a vessel with a long neck, such that the whole body of the vessel can be submerged, and only the neck protrude to join the tube from the boiler. Moreover, such a vessel need not have the spout at the side, as it can simply be placed at an angle in the cooling water. I might also add that I have observed these *itr* stills and the large tanks of water become extremely hot, such that Marshall's tiny bowl of cooling water is not ideal for condensing – in making such *itr*s quite large tanks of water are used, and in making mahua liquor the still is often taken to a source of running water. Another explanation for this form of pot is that it had something to do with storage and transportation, or that the spout, being at the side, could always remain moistened by fluids, keeping any sort of 'stopper' swollen and well-sealed. A good way to move forward would be to conduct an analysis of the residues inside them. I remain agnostic about the purpose of these vessels, but as we shall see below there is evidence that suggests they contained a liquid that was traded and perhaps also drunk by humans, and given the relative prominence of wine imagery in the cultural sphere (broadly speaking) where they were found, they may have contained grape wine, or a grape derived liquid.

'found' a still, or even anything that looks conclusively like it was part of a still. And none of the early texts point to distillation. We should look at the next developments with this in mind.

In 1979 the late F.R. Allchin, a famous archaeologist of early South Asia, published a paper entitled 'India: The Ancient Home of Distillation' in which he considerably expanded Marshall's theory of such vessels as water condensers.[8] This paper draws on his conclusions in a paper published in 1977, 'Evidence of Early Distillation at Shaikhān Dherī'.[9]

Over a hundred vessels of Marshall's 'condenser' type were discovered at the site called Shaikhān Ḍherī, and these vessels were dated from *c.* 150 BCE until the end of the occupation of the site in the fourth-fifth century CE.[10] Allchin reports that many of the vessels of the so-called 'condenser' form bear stamps (as many amphoras do), which suggests they contained a valuable commodity, something that needed to be marked for the purposes of trade. These stamps date from the Śaka-Pahlava period and the middle and late Kuṣāṇa period.[11] Allchin writes: 'That they [the vessels] were designed for the reception of some sort of liquid seems certain. The unusualness of the form suggests some special function.'[12] Allchin notes of some of the vessels that they seem to have been treated in such a manner that increases (cooling) porosity, which would make them good condensers.[13] Yet if these same vessels are indeed stamped for *trade* such porosity would render them useless for that purpose, and it would be better to use a separate vessel for condensing the vapour and another for

[8] Allchin 1979.

[9] Allchin 1977.

[10] I might note that neither of the receivers in the 'primitive' contemporary stills illustrated by Allchin and also Mahdihassan (see below) resemble these 'condenser' receiver-vessels. Instead these modern receivers are simple vessels of no special design.

[11] Allchin 1977: 755-66.

[12] Allchin 1977: 773.

[13] Allchin 1977: 769.

trade. Note that it is not common practice anywhere today to trade distillates in the vessel in which they are received-condensed, which tends to be a special vessel, and the vessels used for trading or storage are usually regular containers, suited to the liquids in question: see the whisky or *itr* trades (barrels, bottles; skin-*kuppis*, small bottles). Allchin also explains that the finds at this site show that the supposed 'condenser' vessels developed in form, with the earlier ones being taller and more ovoid, and the later ones closer to a spherical shape.

Where Marshall tells us almost nothing of the find contexts of his vessels, Allchin describes the find site at Shaikhān Ḍherī in some detail. These vessels were used in a context where people probably used to drink something.[14] The site was an open or partly open area in the heart of the city, by a narrow street, with houses at the north and south. There were two hearths, one inside a single room structure. A large number of shallow bowls were found stacked up here, impressed with the design of an ear of corn. There was also much wood ash, and several large jars and bowls of the variety Marshall incorporated into his 'still' (though bear in mind that these are common shapes for vessels, even today). One terracotta tube was found which Allchin suggests connected the parts of the still, though at a length of approximately 15 cm this is a poor candidate for a condenser tube. And one spout was found that may have belonged to the 'condenser cowl' type vessel. So these other parts of the hypothetical 'still' are proportionally underrepresented. More significantly this site contained many of the larger 'condenser' vessels with the side-spout.

If Marshall had never presented his imaginary/hypothetical 'still', would Allchin, on the basis of these liquid-storage vessels, cups, bowls, jars, and evidence of fire have concluded that this assemblage might be a site of distillation? The finds are easily compatible with this being a drinking-ground of some sort where drinks were perhaps prepared, and likely stored and served from

[14] Allchin 1977: 773-9.

the jars, drunk in bowls, and food cooked. In another site, a house which may have been some sort of Buddhist shrine, there was a storage room containing five large storage jars on an earth bench against one wall, several stamped 'condensers', and, in the middle of the room, a basin and a large flat stone with a grindstone on top. Again it is uncertain what people did in this place, and what these vessels contained, but it is possible that some sort of drink was stored or fermented here. Allchin notes that the average volume of the condenser vessels is around one-fifth of the Attic amphora.[15]

In Allchin's account of the site he repeatedly uses the word 'condenser', which, despite his use of inverted commas, gives the impression that there are condensers everywhere. I am perhaps guilty of the same usage, and maybe had I referred to this object as, for example, 'Taxila amphora' the impression conveyed by my discussion would also be different.

Yet Allchin is at times cautious in his conclusions. He writes that

> we are inclined to conclude that the open space with its accumulated ash and debris, and its piled up drinking bowls, was used either for the manufacture or sale of alcoholic beverages, or for both, and that the 'condensers' were either simply wine vessels, *or more particularly* were used as receivers for the process of distillation ... [the stamp marks are] indicative of the *rājāmudrā* or royal stamp of license, or even ownership of the liquor the vessels contained.[16]

And then he suggests that the Buddhist shrine site may 'regretfully' have been associated with these drinks (ibid.). Of course, this is not so shocking. There are many possible explanations of why such a place might have had wine present if that is what was drunk here: this was medicinal wine or a form of drink processed such that it was not considered intoxicating, or simply syrup? Or maybe monks, nuns, or lay using this site did indeed drink whatever was in these vessels and this was not considered an enormously

[15] Allchin 1977: 772-3.

[16] Allchin 1977: 778-9. My emphasis.

serious infringement of morality or the rule. I agree with Allchin that these vessels may have contained a drink that was traded in these places, and that this may have even been wine, but I see nothing to support the distillation theory here beyond the shape of the 'receivers' as interpreted in the light of Marshall's earlier (in my opinion unjustified) arrangement of vessels as a still.

Then, abandoning this caution, Allchin provides some extra arguments for an ancient South Asian still. First he suggests that the presence of a type of technology among so-called primitive people in a given area suggests its great antiquity there, and he notes the abundance of ethnographic evidence for distillation technology among 'primitive people' in South Asia today. Presumably he holds that it is unlikely that such people might ever learn a new technology, and therefore this technology for distilling alcohol must be quite ancient. Yet he notes that there are no references to this sort of distillation in ancient and medieval Indic textual sources. And so he writes 'There is thus an unresolved difference between the textual evidence and the *inferences* which may be drawn from ethnographic observation.'[17] His reasoning is as follows: 'primitive' people nowadays in India distill alcohol. Therefore distillation is an ancient (= primitive) practice in South Asia. But there are no early textual references to this process. In order to resolve this contradiction we should look to archaeology. Furthermore, Allchin thinks there possible *are* textual references to distillation that scholars have overlooked.

He therefore examines the textual record, noting there are indeed descriptions of distillation in some much later Sanskrit texts, but that these do not support a case for earlier distillation. Although, as noted, his conclusions concerning archaeological evidence are at times stated very cautiously he then writes that we 'have now reached a perplexing position, that while there is no clear literary evidence in support of [Rajendralal] Mitra and the other scholars who believe . . . that distillation was practiced

[17] Allchin 1979: 58; 1977: 783-5. My emphasis.

in ancient India, the archaeological evidence *appears to lend them strong support*'.[18] Mitra falls into the category of scholars working in a world where these Sanskrit words did indeed refer to distilled drinks. Allchin now looks for distillation in earlier texts.[19] He considers two verbal roots whose derived forms (e.g. *āsava*) definitely do not refer to distillation or distilled products in earlier periods.[20] He also considers the word *śūṇḍa*. This word means 'elephant's trunk', but *śūṇḍa* and cognate forms are connected to drink and drinking. Observing that the condenser in Marshall's reconstructed still somewhat resembles an elephant's head and trunk, he concludes that the use of this term (elephant's trunk) in contexts related to intoxicating drinks did in fact refer to the products of distillation made with a still that looked like the one both Marshall and Allchin wish to reconstruct: an *elephant's head shaped* still. He thus concludes that 'Indian literature does, after all, contain numerous references to distillation, although one

[18] Allchin 1977: 787-8. My emphasis.

[19] Kolhatkar (1987, 44), who studied *surā* in detail, notes that the vessels named in Vedic texts on *surā* brewing that Allchin postulated as still-components are never all mentioned together in one text, and that the recipes for *surā* clearly describe fermentation alone. I entirely agree.

[20] I explore the nature of early *āsavas* and *pariśrut* in McHugh (forthcoming). The roots Allchin considers are *pari* √*sru*, *ā* √*su*, as well as the word *śūṇḍa* and connected forms. *Ā* √*su* (as in the derived form *āsava*), though translated by Monier-Williams as 'to distil' is associated more with the processing of *soma* (as Allchin notes). Confusingly, English 'distill' has an older sense of 'to trickle down' or 'to let fall minute drops' which may also inform some of the older dictionary entries. As for the drinks called *āsavas* we have many early recipes for these in medical texts and these are definitely *not* distilled, and even today Āyurvedic *āsavas* are not distilled. On *āsavas*, which were not, historically limited to medical contexts, see McHugh (forthcoming). The same applies to the drink called *parisrut*, associated with the production of *surā* in Vedic sources which appears to be the fermented, liquefied slurry of grains prior to filtration. On this drink see the section on Vedic *surā* in McHugh (forthcoming).

could scarcely have recognized them until the archaeological evidence was available.'[21] But the two senses of *śūṇḍa* need not be in any way connected, polysemy is quite common, and if we are looking for a connection between drinking and elephant trunks in ancient texts, then the leather-covered bamboo-spout called a 'trunk-outlet/mouth' (*śūṇḍamukha*) attached to a device (the *kārotara*) used for brewing *surā* according to one Vedic ritual texts perhaps more plausible a link than the secret ancient practice of distillation.[22] Allchin then attributes the reluctance of authors of Sanskrit texts to furnish explicit descriptions of distilled alcohol to three facts. First, he writes that Sanskrit texts are generally reluctant to discuss alcohol, even fermentation – which is utterly untrue. Second, he says such sources do not discuss craft practices – again, totally incorrect. And third, he claims there was a general secrecy surrounding alcohol owing to its 'ritual and sacramental aspect' which I abundantly (even tediously) demonstrated not to be the case elsewhere.[23] In fact, we have abundant detailed descriptions of making all sorts of drinks, from grains, sugar cane, and other sources, over a long period from the Vedic *Śrautasūtra*s until the early modern period, even later. These recipes, such as the *surā* in the *Baudhāyana Śrautasūtra* (approx. fifth century BCE), or the drinks described in the *Mānasollāsa* (twelfth century CE) only describe fermentation.[24] When people start distilling they are quite explicit about it, as one sees in the *Gadanigraha* (see

[21] Allchin 1979: 62.

[22] *Āpastamba Śrautasūtra* XIX.6.2-5. It is into/in this spout that the liquified-grain substance, the *pariśrut*, flows. Allchin notes that a much later Sanskrit text does refer to part of a still as shaped like a trunk, but that text is so much later that it does not change my argument.

[23] Allchin 1979: 62. Also see McHugh (forthcoming) for many examples of texts that are quite open about alcohol.

[24] This is not the place to present the positive evidence for drinks as fermented. I translate and explore the recipes from these texts and several more in McHugh (forthcoming). For ancient *surā* brewing see also Kolhatkar 1999.

above). Thus these three points are quite incorrect. To conclude: the archaeological evidence is at best very weak, and the textual evidence/theory of a conspiracy of silence Allchin provides is no good either. We still have no still.

Finally, another scholar, S. Mahdihassan, discussed the Marshall 'still' and suggested that other styles of distillation may also have been practised in South Asia in ancient periods. His basic method is to look for any vessels from earlier periods that are analogous to those used for Marshall's still. He discusses another type of still that consists only of a large jar for boiling the fermented drink, a perforated jar placed above this into which vapour passes, a dish placed above that perforated jar containing cold water on the base of which water condenses, and a small dish placed *inside* the perforated jar, into which condensed vapour drips (i.e. what is sometimes called a Mongolian style still). Now the components for this sort of still can be found all over the archaeological record, and they are also to be found in my own kitchen. Faced with so many still components, which Mahdihassan knows full well are quite ambiguous in function, he writes '. . . such abundance would easily support its primary use as a kitchen vessel'.[25] Yet despite these ambiguities, by repeatedly comparing a number of ancient vessels to modern primitive stills he builds to a conclusion that 'distilled alcoholic drinks are mentioned in Rig Veda and archaeological finds of some of the units constituting distillation can be assigned the earliest date of 300 BC' – all on the most flimsy evidence. Mahdihassan's methodology is at fault here, and there is no need to examine each of his claims about vessels in detail. In short, if we have distillation in all these early contexts, future archaeologists will find my own house to be a veritable moonshine factory.

[25] Mahdihassan 1972: 166. Also see Mahdihassan 1979, 265. Readers should take care to remember that the stills illustrated in his articles are all either modern stills or hypothetical reconstructions, not assemblages as excavated. Yet, as with the 'Taxila still' these (arguably misleading) images are memorable and powerful.

Needham, in *Science and Civilization in China*, reviews these materials, taking a balanced view of the matter, though ultimately he is cautiously convinced by Allchin's 'elephant trunk theory' and Marshall's reconstruction.[26] Thus, although by no means all scholars are convinced by this material, the thesis that archaeologists have found an ancient Indian still while distillation is *strangely* absent in early texts persists in some quite respectable scholarship on the history of technology in Asia.

More recently, Brancaccio and Liu, in an article on Gāndhāran art and culture, accept the distillation theory dating back to Marshall and developed by Allchin.[27] They add a rationale for the use of distillation: that it inhibits the degeneration of wine in a hot climate, which is indeed the case. But distillation is not essential to trade wine. There was a vast trade in non-distilled wine in the also very hot southern Mediterranean, extending to south India.[28] Brancaccio and Liu rightly point out the connections between Hellenistic wine culture and certain aspects of the urban culture of the Gāndhāra region. Yet it is strange that there would be such a sudden shift from a love of wine, coloured, sweet, and flavourful, to a 'Hellenized-Gāndhāran' culture of rough white brandy, ancient pisco. For a grape wine distilled in Marshall's still would have been clear (colour comes from wooden barrels) and probably extremely harsh (as making a smooth distillate is a fine art).

In fact Brancaccio and Liu present a far better explanation of Allchin's vessels, which involves not distillation, but the cooking, concentration and (effectively) pasteurization of wine, when they describe a method that might possibly tie Gāndhāran wine culture to that of Europe, better supporting their general argument. They cite a passage in an Indian Buddhist monastic code, the *Mūlasarvāstivāda Vinaya*, where the Buddha and some monks are

[26] Needham 1980: 85-6; 131-2.

[27] Brancaccio and Liu 2009: 225-7.

[28] On the various ancient Greek techniques for preserving wine in amphoras for trade see Koehler 1995: 328-30.

travelling in the north-west and a supernatural being called a *yakṣa* gives them some grapes. The grapes, and other fruits are said to be sent from Kashmir, suggesting the connection – also seen later – between grapes and this region even at an early stage.[29] The Buddha explains of this novel fruit that 'These are fruits from the northern region. They are called grapes. One can eat them after having purified them with fire.' After touching them with a burning ember to purify them, they have some grapes leftover and the Buddha tells the monks 'The grapes should be pressed to extract the juice, and then the fluid should be heated and removed from the fire before it is completely cooked. . . . To store the syrup and serve it to the samgha out of the proper time [for meals], one should heat the juice until it is completely cooked.'[30] What process do we see in this text? We have heat, so is this distillation? Although attitudes towards alcohol in early India are more complex than often assumed, one assumes that the Buddha is not telling the monks how to make brandy (also a distilled drink contains no sugar and cannot be further reduced to syrup). The first stage here involves cooking, but not entirely reducing the grape juice, then if one cooks it some more one can make what is translated as 'syrup', and both of these are apparently permitted to monks – the more concentrated version being the sort of sugary 'medicine' that was indeed permitted to Buddhist monastics after mealtimes. Cooking the juice like this would arrest fermentation, and if the cooking was taken further the concentrated syrup would store extremely well, like grape 'mollases' today. Making syrup is a good thing to do with grapes, for one finds oneself with a lot of grapes at harvest season. These can be made into wine of course, or dried to make raisins. Or the

[29] See Przyluski (1914: 506) for this text in translation. As discussed in Brancaccio and Liu (2009), though in my account here I have added some extra details from Przyluski.

[30] *Mūlasarvāstivāda Vinaya Oṣadhivastu*, ch. 9. Translation as provided in Brancaccio and Liu (2009: 226). I also thank Jeffrey Kotyk for mentioning this text to me.

juice can be made into syrup, which would not only be sweet but also richly flavoured and coloured, different to sugarcane syrup, and an excellent source of storable sugar, perhaps the most important source of sugar in certain regions (wild honey never being enormously abundant). Wine too can be cooked, both before and after fermentation, and if Allchin's vessels were indeed used for a drink, I think some sort of wine or cooked grape juice is a good candidate for this. As Koehler writes of the ancient Greek wine trade, 'Perhaps more concentrated wine, and the syrupy syraeum and defrutum, made by boiling down must to one-third or one half of its original volume, respectively . . . would have survived transport more readily.'[31] Such concentrates (e.g. *mostocotto*) could be consumed as they are, or diluted, or added to wine to concentrate and stabilize it. Thus Brancaccio and Liu, though they mention distillation, have made a far more plausible connection between surviving texts and archaeological evidence. The textual evidence they provide points to complex processing of grape juice at an early period in the north-west, and Allchin's stamped jars are compatible with that sort of product.

Making a related textual argument, Marianne Oort has suggested two hymns of the Paippalāda recension of the *Atharvaveda* actually describe a distillation process for making the ancient grain drink, *surā*.[32]As background to her discussion she refers among other things to Allchin's work at Taxila which she incorrectly connects to the 'Haṛappā Culture'. She also quotes a misleading translation of the *Arthaśāstra* where Kangle renders the 'Superintendent of *Surā*' (in the sense of alcoholic drinks in general) as the 'Controller of Spirituous Liquor', this being an example of the sort of loose, possibly anachronistic translation also found in dictionaries, as discussed above.[33] Accepting this sort of evidence for distillation in ancient India she reads the two Atharvavedic hymns in a manner

[31] Koehler 1995: 330.

[32] Oort 2002. On *Atharvaveda Paippalāda* 5.10 and 8.12. Also see Lubotsky's (2002: 43) comments on and translation of hymn 5.10.

33 Oort 2002: 358. Citing Kangle's translation of *Arthaśāstra*, Ch. 25.

that suggests they too support a case for ancient distillation. For example, the 'knife-sharp, arrow-sharp' *surā* in one hymn that causes violence must apparently be distilled to have such effects. But of course drink, including old English ale, was commonly associated with social disorder in many cultures before distillation became common.[34] More central to her argument is a reading of some aspects of the hymns (especially hymn 8.12) as referring to parts of stills and the processes of distillation: bubbling, fluid-separation, vapours, and dripping down in some manner. Now of course these descriptions are *consistent* with distillation, but they by no means strongly imply it, especially when we have somewhat later descriptions of *surā* brewing (e.g. *Baudhāyana Śrautasūtra* 17.31-2), which involves various processes, including cooking/boiling, drainage/dripping, and filtration, and which also involves lifting up liquids and letting liquids drip down at some points – just as we see in various forms of making coffee! Additionally, it seems that the *surā* in one of these hymns called 'blood red' (5.10.6), and a freshly distilled alcoholic drink would be white/transparent, like vodka, in the absence of additives or significant barrel ageing. All considered, the contents of these Atharvavedic hymns do not require us to postulate ancient distillation in order to make sense of them. They are quite consistent with brewing and all that this process involves.

To conclude this part of the article: the evidence for ancient alcoholic distillation in South Asia is hardly compelling. We have very meagre evidence, especially if we ignore anything that could be said to be circular (e.g. Oort's interpretation of a hymn that itself relies in part on archaeological evidence). This is not to say there may not have been some vapourizing-condensing processes used in some contexts in early India, but the Taxila vessels are probably not parts of a still, and we know very well how alcoholic drinks were made in early India, and that *did not*

[34] For many examples of rowdy, ale-fuelled behaviour at the English alehouse see Clark 1983.

involve distillation until a later period.[35] Also, consider how distilled drinks require extra fuel, more time, more vessels and labour to make. In South Asia, where grain-based or sugar-based drinks were quite easy to produce in most regions such that few people needed to trade alcohol long distances (prestigious wine excepted), what is in most need of explanation is why alcoholic distillation did flourish after a certain period.

The three archaeologists above presented some at best ambiguous data along with a very strong interpretation of the finds, not supported by textual sources. Some other scholars have then uncritically incorporated the archaeological, distillation hypothesis into the study of texts and cultural history. Textual data have been somewhat clumsily aligned with data deemed more scientific and authoritative to support a rather ambitious thesis – interesting but shaky, yet unusually memorable.

So why are so many people attached to the idea of ancient Indian distillation? With the archaeologists above the matter is relatively simple: their research locates very early distillation in South Asia – possibly distillation was *discovered* in South Asia – and this important shift in the history of technology is derived from *their* finds and *their* interpretation. With the 'stills' as reconstructed in museums in South Asia there is an intersection of the history of nations with the history of technological discovery, whether this be in India or Pakistan. Yet this is a complex issue – milestones in the history of technology are one thing, but a hypothetical golden age of brandy making in South Asia quite another.

Things are different with the Western humanists. By evoking the distillation theory, Oort is able to make better sense of quite difficult Vedic texts. She can ground her argument elsewhere, in a field that uses different types of data (note I

[35] We must separate the question of 'Who first did any sort of distillation anywhere in the world? (mercury? medicinal? alchemical?)' from 'Who first did something we would class as some sort of distillation in South Asia?' from 'Where and when did alcoholic distillation for retail and consumption become a common practice?'

am *extremely* open to this sort of work, though materials from other fields must be handled with great caution). But why else might the theory keep rearing its head both in academia more generally, and in the popular imagination? Katherine Foxhall has discussed a similar phenomenon where scientific data was aligned with the humanities: the twentieth-century theory that the visions of medieval mystic Hildegard of Bingen were actually migraine auras, an idea that has proved attractive and enduring.[36] She highlights 'the methodological problems that can result from the decontextualization and accumulation over time of . . . "interdisciplinary borrowings"'. As with Hildegard of Bingen's migraines, I believe we also see with 'ancient Indian distillation' what I might call the scholarly appeal of the striking interdisciplinary anecdote: 'The visionary paintings of Hildegard of Bingen – you know it was all just migraines!' Medieval migraines, *soma*-as-hallucinogenic mushroom, distillation-technology hiding in the Vedas – these are all quite fascinating intrusions of a somewhat surprising idea from another discipline, ideas that have a different epistemological gravity to the historian, or to a more general audience, and reflect an accessible excursion into unplumbed and novel intellectual depths. Such flourishes might not always be expected to serve an argument. Instead, as incongruities placed in the middle of writing in the humanities they are an almost aesthetic phenomenon of scholarship. In a similar vein, Foxhall mentions the 'parlour game' of retrospective diagnosis, King George III's madness-as-porphyria and so on.[37] These sorts of ideas linger in the memory of many a student, and even sometimes get humble professors in the newspapers, much to the delight of their employers.

In conclusion, we have abundant positive textual evidence for early alcoholic drinks in South Asia being only fermented, not distilled. We also have clear textual evidence for alcoholic

[36] Foxhall 2014.
[37] Foxhall 2014.

distillation in the region as of around the thirteenth century CE, which neatly matches Irfan Habib's approximate estimate of when alcoholic distillation became common, based on Persian sources from India.[38] Yet the notion of very ancient Indian distillation is still commonly encountered both in academia and beyond.[39] Sometimes this is simply a matter of secondary sources relying on certain dictionaries and previous translations (sometimes based on said dictionaries . . .), yet Marshall's invention, the 'Taxila still' informs most more considered work on the topic, being invoked in both Allchin's and Oort's works (and being displayed in many a museum, reaching a more popular audience). Yet on close examination this archaeological evidence (and inference) is very weak at the best, and not at all supported by the clear textual record. There was probably no alcoholic distillation in ancient India.

Nevertheless, I have entitled this article 'Too Big to Fail' for a good reason. For I am confident that the idea of ancient Indian distillation is so deeply engrained in secondary scholarship and even in the popular imagination, for reasons briefly discussed above, that this epistemological momentum, shared among a quite diverse group of people, will override any arguments I or others make *against* the idea, perhaps indefinitely.

[38] See above.

[39] At almost every lecture I have given on alcohol in India someone has mentioned the Taxila 'still' in the question and answer session. Quite often their knowledge of the 'still' is based on having seen it in a museum.

BIBLIOGRAPHY

Primary Sources

Āpastamba Śrautasūtra. Ed. R. Garbe, *The Śrautasūtra of Āpastamba. Bibliotheca Indica*. Calcutta: Asiatic Society of Bengal, 1882-92.

Āpastamba Śrautasūtra. Tr. Ganesh Umakant Thite. *Āpastamba-Śrautasūtra: Text With English Translation and Notes*. Delhi: New Bharatiya Book Corp., 2004.

Arthaśāstra of Kauṭilya. Ed. and trans. R.P. Kangle. *The Kauṭilīya Arthaśāstra*. Bombay: University of Bombay, 1963.

Atharvaveda Paippalāda, Kāṇḍa Five. Ed. and trs. Alexander Lubotsky, Harvard Oriental Series, Opera Minora, vol. 4. Cambridge, MA: Department of Sanskrit and Indian Studies, Harvard University, 2002.

Baudhāyana Śrautasūtra. Ed. Willem Caland, 1904-24. *The Baudhāyana Śrauta Sūtra belonging to the Taittirīya Saṁhitā*. *Bibliotheca Indica* 163. Calcutta: Asiatic Society of Bengal.

Gadanigraha of Śrī Vaidya Soḍhala. Kashi Sanskrit Series, vol. 182. Varanasi: Chowkhamba Sanskrit Series Office, 1968.

Secondary Sources

Allchin, F. Raymond. 1977. *Evidence of Early Distillation at Shaikhân Dherî*. South Asian Archaeology.

_____. 1979. 'India: The Ancient Home of Distillation', *Man*, New Series 14: 1 (1979), 55-63.

Apte, V.S. 2003 (1912). *The Practical Sanskrit-English Dictionary*. Revised and enlarged edition. Delhi: Motilal Banarsidass.

Böhtlingk, Otto von, and Rudolph Roth, 1855-75. *Sanskrit-wörterbuch-heraugegeben von der Kaiserlichenakademie der wissenschaften, bearbeitet von Otto Böhtlingk und Rudolph Roth*. St. Petersburg: Buchdr. der K. Akademie der wissenschaften.

Brancaccio, Pia, and Liu Xinru, 2009. 'Dionysus and Drama in the Buddhist Art of Gandhara'. *Journal of Global History* 4: 219-44.

Clark, Peter. 1983. *The English Alehouse: A Social History, 1200-1830*. London; New York: Longman.

Foxhall, Katherine. 2014. 'Making Migraine Medieval: Men of Science, Hildegard of Bingen and the Life of a Retrospective Diagnosis'. *Medical History* 58.3: 354-71.

Habib, I. 1985. 'Medieval Technology: Exchanges Between India and the Islamic World'. *Aligarh Journal of Oriental Studies* 1.2: 197-222.

_____. 2011. *Economic History of Medieval India, 1200 1500*. History of Science, Philosophy, and Culture in Indian Civilization. Vol. VIII: *Economic History of India*, pt. 1. New Delhi: Pearson Education.

Koehler, Carolyn G., 1995. 'Wine Amphoras in Ancient Greek Trade', In *The Origins and Ancient History of Wine*, ed. Patrick McGovern and Solomon H. Katz, pp. 323-37. London: Gorden and Breach.

Kolhatkar, Madhavi, 1987. 'The Method of Preparing Surā According to the Vedic Texts'. *Bulletin of the Deccan College Research Institute* 46: 41-5.

______. 1999. *Surā, the Liquor and the Vedic Sacrifice*. New Delhi: D.K. Printworld.

Mahdihassan, S. 1972. 'The Earliest Distillation Units of Pottery in Indo-Pakistan'. *Pakistan Archaeology* 8: 159-68.

______. 1979. 'Distillation Assembly of Pottery in Ancient India'. *Vishveshvaranand Indological Journal* 17: 264-6.

Marshall, John Hubert. 1951. *Taxila: An Illustrated Account of Archaeological Excavations Carried Out At Taxila Under the Orders of the Government of India between the Years 1913 and 1934*. Cambridge: Cambridge University Press.

McHugh, James. Forthcoming. *An Unholy Brew: Alcohol in Indian History and Religions*.

Meulenbeld, G. Jan. 1999-2002. *A History of Indian Medical Literature*. Groningen: E. Forsten.

Mitra, Rajendralal. 1873. 'Spirituous Drinks in Ancient India'. *Journal of the Asiatic Society of Bengal* 42.1: 1-23.

Monier-Williams, M. 2000 (1899). *A Sanskrit-English Dictionary*. New Edition. Oxford: Oxford University Press.

Needham, Joseph. 1980. *Science and Civilisation in China*, vol. 5: *Chemistry and Chemical Technology*, pt. IV *Spagyrical Discovery and Invention: Apparatus, Theories and Gifts*. Cambridge: Cambridge University Press.

Oort, Marianne S. 2002. 'Surā in the Paippalāda Saṁhitā of the Atharvaveda'. *Journal of the American Oriental Society* 122 (2): 355-60.

Przyluski, M.J. 1914. 'Le nord-ouest de l'Indedans le Vinaya des Mula-Sarvastivadin et les textesapparentés'. *Journal Asiatique* Series 11, vol. 4, November-December 1914: 493-568.

CHAPTER 4

Distillation

*Irfan Habib**

It is a tribute to the attraction offered by the potentially intoxicating powers of such products of agriculture as sugar, grape, barley, toddy, coconut, *mahuā*, etc., that the production of liquor by distillation should have benefited from the helping hands of so many civilizations.

P.C. Ray's *History of Hindu Chemistry* had, by its citations of Sanskrit texts on distillation, suggested an early medieval date for it in India. None of this, however, even the linguistic curiosity inherent in the double meaning of *śūṇḍa* (elephant's trunk, side-tube), gave any certainty to India's role in the early history of alcohol production. But the archaeological evidence of ancient stills from Taxila, first brought to light by John Marshall and A. Ghosh, has now been heavily reinforced by the excavations of Raymond Allchin, who has unearthed numerous remains of stills recovered from Shaikhān Ḍherī (Charsadda, NWFP, Pakistan). Needham gave these stills (Fig. 4.1) the name of 'Gāndhāra stills', compared them with the Western or Hellenistic type of his still classification, and then propounded that they were essentially 'retorts' and, because of their early date (150 BC-AD 150), might well

* Extracted from Irfan Habib, *Technology in Medieval India*, New Delhi: Tulika Books, 2016, pp. 23-6.

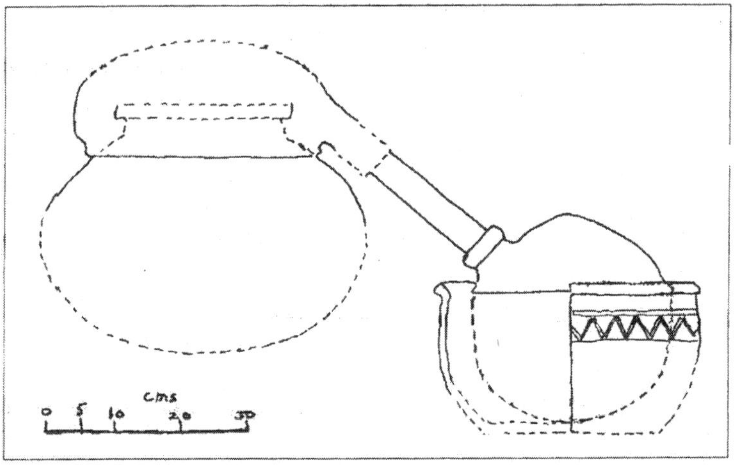

Fig. 4.1: Gāndhāra still (F.R. Allchin's reconstruction)

be 'the origin of all such forms of still'. The pottery remains at Shaikhān Ḍherī were so extensive, viz., one alembic, 130 receivers, and many possible still bodies ('with soot on them'), and the receivers so capacious that one must assume alcohol (and not, for example, mercury) was the intended product. This would give precedence to India over other countries in liquor distillation. However, since alcohol evaporates at very low temperatures, the Gāndhāra stills could have produced only heavily diluted alcohol; and, if the fire was kept low to reduce dilution, the pace of collection must have been very slow.

The modification that were introduced in Italy in the twelfth century (possibly in close exchange of ideas with the Arab world, as some terms tend to show) were designed to improve cooling in the still so as to increase pure alcohol collection at a low level of heat. The 'Moore's head' was a water container set over the alembic (main still), which had a concave inverted spoon-like roof and annular rim for collection of the liquid, thence conveyed by a tube to the receiver. This undoubtedly led to the achievement of a much higher degree of purity in the distilled alcohol than under any other device. Travelling through the Islamic world, the new stills soon reached India. The fresh wave of alcohol extraction, then, which India seems to have witnessed by the late thirteenth century, probably obtained its impetus from the improved still now received. The historian Ẓiya Baranī, writing in 1357, speaks of the occupation of obtaining liquor 'made to fall drop by drop' (*chakānīdana*) from stills (*bhaṭṭīs*) established as an industry in Delhi and surrounding towns already by 1290. The same word, *chakānīdana*, is also used for distillation in the *Miftāḥu'l Fuẓalā* (1469). The significance of this word is that it was only in the Italo-Arab still that the receiver was not only separate from the main still, but also received not the vapours (as in the Gāndhāra still) through a covered pipe but the liquid itself, which could be seen to fall into it drop by drop from the pipe. The word thus implies the presence of that special kind of still.

By this time there were two other forms of liquor stills also in use: one, what Needham calls the 'Mongol still' (condensation in a catch-bowl within the still), and the other, the 'Chinese stills' (with the catch-bowl connected by a side-tube with the receiver outside), the former is depicted on the wall of a cave of the period 1031-1227, and the latter in a drawing of 1163 in China. But neither of these devices could have probably competed successfully with the improved stills from the Mediterranean.

The famous passage on liquor distillation in the *Ā'īn-i Akabarī* of Abū'l Faẓl (1595) describes three kinds of still, the first being the 'Mongol' and the second, the 'Gāndhāran', of Needham's classification. Abū'l Faẓl expressly states that in the second the condenser was the receiver itself, being placed in cold water. The third is the most interesting, since it clearly has the Moore's head (water at the top and still head shaped like a 'spoon'). It was, in other words, the medieval Italian-Arab still (see Fig. 4.2). In 1800 Buchanan examined a rough version of it in southern India, so that the still was now widely diffused over the country.

In medieval times the process of distillation was extended to produce perfumes and essences. Gode points out that rose (*gul*) was unknown to Sanskrit literature before the mid-fifteenth

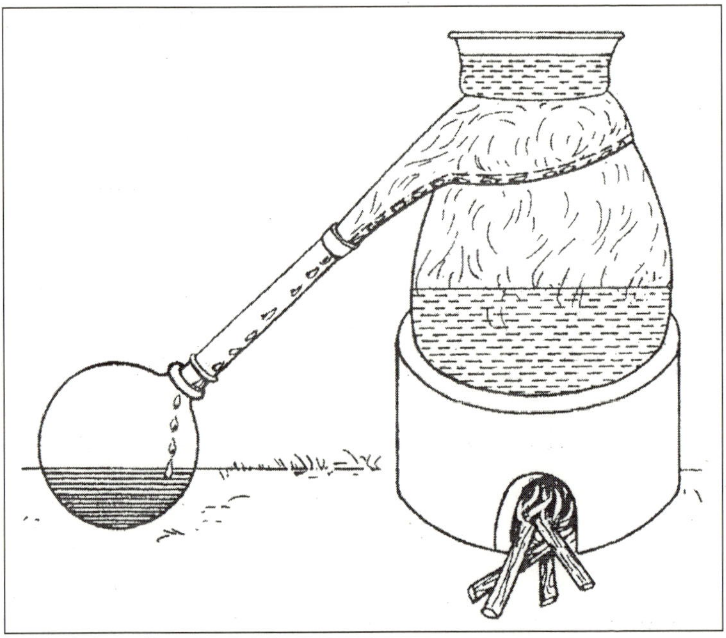

Fig. 4.2: Italo-Arab still, as described by Abū'l Faẓl (artist's drawing)

century. Different kinds of roses are, however, mentioned by Baranī (1357), as being planted in newly laid-out gardens in the area irrigated by Firoz Tughluq's canals. 'Rose water' (*julāb = gulāb*) was being sold in the 1340s in Bengal, when Ibn Baṭṭūṭa visited it. It was obtained by the simple method of putting pressed roses with water in the alembic, with the vapours conveyed by pipe to the receiver, from which the rose water was collected. While still warm, a fine film formed on the surface of the rose water. Emperor Jahāngīr (d. 1627) says that the mother of his queen, Nūr Jahān, had this film carefully collected and found it to have a very fine, strong scent. It received the name '*iṭṛ-i jahāngīrī*, and began to be produced extensively in the course of the seventeenth century. Abū'l Faẓl also describes for us the rather complex mode of distillation by which the essence of aloe-wood oil was obtained.

PART II

CHAPTER 5

Spirituous Drinks in Ancient India

*Rajendralal Mitra**

Sages and moralists have, in all ages and in every clime, expatiated in strong terms on the impropriety of indulgence in spirituous drinks, and some physiologists have recently discovered that such drinks do not possess any of the virtues which tradition has all along ascribed to them. We are told that they do not add to our strength, or power of digestion; they have no influence on the heart's action; they are powerless to increase the temperature of the body; they cannot help us to resist the chilling effect of cold; and are inert as aliments, failing alike in affording fuel for the lungs and material for the formation of the tissues. But neither the anathema of sages and moralists, nor the dicta of the professors of science, have anywhere sufficed to suppress their use. They prevail in some form or other in almost every part of the world; and those primitive races which have no knowledge of them, seize them with the greatest avidity the moment they find them; for, like tobacco, spirituous drinks have a peculiar charm which enables them, if not to defy, at least to hold their own alike against the deductions of science and the mandates of religion. In the eye of reason, voluntary inebriation may appear in the most offensive light; but there seems to be a craving in human nature to elevate the spirit above the dull routine of everyday existence,

* Reprinted from the *Journal of Asiatic Society of Bengal*, vol. 42 (1878).

and to produce a temporary frenzy during which the cares and troubles of life are forgotten, and trains of delightful ideas fill the mind, which nothing can completely eradicate.

The history of Muhammadan civilization affords a most striking illustration of the truth of this assertion. None condemned the use of wine more emphatically than the Prophet of Arabia, and yet there is no Muhammadan country where the consumption of wine is other than considerable, or as the great historian, Gibbon, has aptly expressed it, 'the wines of Shiraz have always prevailed over the laws of Muhammad'.

The annals of the Indo-Aryans yield a no less remarkable illustration. The earliest brāhmaṇa settlers were a spirit-drinking race, and indulged largely both in *soma* beer and strong spirits. To their gods the most acceptable and grateful offering was *soma* beer, and wine or spirit (for in connection with India the two words may be used synonymously, there never having been any such thing as pure wine), was publicly sold in shops for the use of the community. In the *R̥gveda Saṁhitā* a hymn occurs which shows that wine was kept in leather bottles,[1] and freely sold to all comers. The said wine was, likewise, offered to the gods, and the Sautrāmaṇi and the Vājapaya rites, of which libations of strong arrack formed a prominent feature, were held in the highest esteem. Doubts have been entertained as to the nature of the *soma* beverage, and people are not wanting who repudiate its intoxicating nature; but none will venture to deny that the *surā* of the Sautrāmaṇi and the Vājapaya was other than arrack manufactured from rice-meal, and that will suffice to show that the Vedic Hindus did countenance the use of spirit. As to the *soma*, if any reliance is to be placed in the directions given for its preparation, and on the Vedic descriptions of its effect on the gods, it is impossible to take it to have been other than a fermented intoxicating beverage. Of this, however, I shall treat lower down.

[1] 'I deposit the poison in the solar orb, like a leather bottle in the house of a vendor of spirits', Wilson's *Rig Veda*, II, p. 204.

In the hot plains of India, over-indulgence in spirituous drinks, however, gradually bore its evil consequences, and among the thoughtful a revulsion of feeling was the result. The later Vedas accordingly proposed a compromise, and, leaving the rites intact, prohibited the use of spirit for the gratification of the senses, in language very similar to Sydney Smith's 'Think not, touch not, and taste not,' saying 'Wine is unfit to be drunk, unfit to be given, and unfit to be accepted,'[2] and denounced drinking to be heinous in the last degree, quite as bad as the murder of a brāhmaṇa. The Smṛtis, following in their wake, included, the sin of winebibing among the five capital crimes or *mahāpātakas,* and ordained the severest punishment against the offender.

It is said that the prohibition was first promulgated by Śukrāchārya, the high priest of the *asuras*, who was disgusted by the remembrance of certain excesses to which he himself had been led by over-indulgence in strong drink. The *Mahābhārata* has euphuised the story in the 76th chapter of its first book. According to it, Kacha, son of Bṛhaspati, had become a pupil of Śukrāchārya with a view to obtain from him the charm of reviving dead men, which none else knew. The *asuras* came to know of this, and, dreading lest the pupil should obtain and afterwards impart the great secret to the *devas*, assassinated him, and mixed his ashes with the wine of his tutor, and thus transferred him to the bowels of Śukrāchārya. It happened, however, that during his pupilage Kacha had won the affection of Devayāṇi, the youthful and charming daughter of Śukrāchārya, and that lady insisted upon her father to restore the youth to her, threatening to commit suicide if the request was not complied with. Śukra, unable to decline the favour to his daughter, repeated the charm, and anon, to his surprise, found the youth speaking from his own belly. The difficulty now was to bring the youth out, for this could not be accomplished without ripping open the abdomen of the tutor. Śukrāchārya thereupon taught the youth the great

[2] मद्यमपेयमदेयमग्राहं। श्रुतिः।

charm, and then allowed himself to be ripped open, and Kacha, in grateful acknowledgement of his restoration to life, revived his tutor. Now Śukrāchārya, seeing that it was the influence of drink which had made him insensibly swallow the ashes of a brāhmaṇa, and that brāhmaṇa, his own pupil, prohibited the use of wine by brāhmaṇas, 'From this day forward,' said he, 'the brāhmaṇa, who through infatuation will drink arrack (*surā*) shall lose all his religious merit; that wretch will be guilty of the sin of killing brāhmaṇas, and be condemned in this as well as in a future world. Let all pious brāhmaṇas, mindful of their duty to their tutors, as also to the *devas* and mankind in general, attend to this rule of conduct for brāhmaṇas ordained by me for all the regions of the universe.'[3]

Śukrāchārya was followed by Kṛṣṇa, who also cursed the wine-bibber because his kith and kin, the Yādavas, proved the most intractable and unruly of drunkards.

The legends on which these prohibitions are founded may be, for ought we know, after-thoughts, designed to illustrate the heinousness of excessive indulgence, and to give weight to the prohibitions, by invoking the authority of great men against over-indulgence. But the fact remains unquestioned that, from an early period, the Hindus have denounced in their sacred writings the use of wine as sinful, and two of their greatest lawgivers, Manu[4] and Yājñavalkya[5] held that the only expiation meet for a brāhmaṇa who has polluted himself by drinking spirit, is suicide by a draught

[3] यो ब्राह्मणोऽद्यप्रभृतीह कश्चिन्मोहात्सुरां पास्यति मन्दबुद्धिः।
अपेन धर्म्मा ब्रह्महा चैव स स्याद्स्मिन् लोके गर्हितः स्यातपरे च।।
मया चतां विप्रधर्म्मो कृसीर्मा मर्य्यादां वै स्थापितां सर्व्वलोके।
सन्तो चिप्रा शुश्रुचांसो गुरूणां देवा लोकाश्चोपूटखन्तु सर्व्वे।।
आदिपर्व्वणि 76 अ.

[4] Manu XI, 91 to 96.

[5] सुराम्बुघृतगोमूत्रपयसामग्निसन्निभं।
सुरापोन्यतमं पीत्वा मरणाच्छुद्धिमृच्छति।।
याज्ञवल्कीये 3 अ.।

of spirit or water, or cow's urine, or milk in a boiling state, taken in a burning hot metal pot. Aṅgirās, Vasiṣṭha and Paiṭhīnasi restricted the drink to boiling spirits alone.[6] Devala went a step further, and prescribed a draught of melted silver, copper or lead as the most appropriate.[7] Even in cases of accidental drinking of spirits through ignorance on the part of any of the three twice-born classes, nothing short of a repetition of the initial sacramentary rites, effecting a complete regeneration, is held sufficient to purge the sin.[8] The brāhmaṇa woman who transgresses this law, is denied access to the region of her husband, and is doomed to be born a slut, or a cow, or a vulture.[9] Manu likewise provides for judicial cognizance of such offence by brāhmaṇas, and ordains excommunication and branding on the forehead the figure of a bottle as the most appropriate punishment.

237. For violating the paternal bed, let *the mark of* a female part be impressed *on the forehead with hot iron;* for drinking spirits, a vintner's flag;[10] for stealing sacred gold, a dog's foot; for murdering a priest, the figure of a headless corpse.

238. With none to eat with them, with none to sacrifice with them, with none to read with them, with none to be allied by marriage to them, abject and excluded from all social duties, let them wander over the earth.

239. Branded with indelible marks, they shall be deserted by their

[6] सुरापश्चार्द्रवाससा चाग्निवर्णां सुरां पिवेत्।

[7] सुरापाने ब्राह्मणो रूप्यताम्रसीसकानामन्यमतग्निकल्पं पीत्वा शरीरत्यागात्पूयते।

[8] अज्ञानात्तु सुरां पीत्वा रेतो विण्मूत्रमेव वा।
पुनः संस्कारमर्हन्ति त्रयो वर्णा द्विजातयः।।

[9] पतिलोकं न सा याति ब्राह्मणी या सुरां पिवेत्।
इहैव सा शुनी गृध्रो शूकरी चोपजायते।।

[10] The words are सुरापाने सुराध्वजः।। 'For drinking, a liquor-flag', but as there is no flag known as peculiar to arrack, or arrack-sellers, commentators take the term *surādhvaja* to mean the particular kind of jar or flagon which was formerly used to hold liquor. What the shape of this jar was, I cannot ascertain.

paternal and maternal relations, treated by none with affection, received by none with respect: such is the ordinance of Manu.(IX.)

Even drinking of water kept in a wine bottle is held sinful, and various expiations are recommended for removing the sin.[11]

Other authorities on law and religion are in no respect less stringent. And yet it would seem that at no time in their history have the Hindus as a nation altogether abstained from the use of spirituous drinks as a means of sensual gratification. Elders, anchorites, sages and learned men, forming the bulk of the priestly race, doubtless scrupulously abstained from them, as they do now in this and other countries; and a good number of pious and respectable householders, and men of rank and position of the other classes followed their example, even as they do now; but as they constituted but a fraction of the sum total of the community, their abstinence could not lead to abstinence on the part of the whole nation, or the bulk of it. There was probably also a considerable amount of hypocrisy, or outward expression of horror against wine on the part of the higher orders of the people, such as we know does prevail in the present day; but Sanskrit literature, both ancient and modern, leaves no room for doubt as to wine having been very extensively used in this country at all times, and by all classes.

Manu, notwithstanding his stern anathema, found the public feeling or practice so strong against him as to be under the necessity of observing in one place that 'there is no turpitude in drinking wine', but 'a virtuous abstinence from it produces a signal compensation'.[12] Elsewhere he provides that the soldier and the

[11] मद्यभाण्डस्थितं तोयं यदि कश्चित पिवेद् द्विजः।
पद्मोदुम्बरबिल्वानां पलाशस्य कुशस्य च।।
एतेषामुदकं पीत्वा त्रिरात्रेण विशुध्यति।

[12] न मांसभक्षणे दोषो न मद्ये न च मैथुने।
प्रवृत्तिरेषा भूतानां निवृत्तिस्तु महाफला।।

merchant should not deal in spirituous liquors, leaving the śūdras to follow the trade at their pleasure.[13] The prohibition in the case of the soldier and the merchant refers to arrack only, so they were at liberty to take all other kinds of liquor, and accordingly the Mitākṣarā comes to the conclusion that brāhmaṇas alone have to abstain from all kinds of spirituous drinks, the kṣatrīya and vaiṣya from arrack or *paiśṭi,* leaving the śūdras to indulge in whatever they liked.[14]

Coming from the age of the Vedas to that of the Sūtras, I find that not only the *soma* and the *surā* of the Saṁhitās and the Brāhmaṇas retained their firm hold on the people, but several new candidates for public favour appeared in the forms of *mādhvīka* or *mowā, gaudī* or rum, *tāla* or toddy wine, and so on. They could not have been manufactured had there been no demand for them, and the conclusion becomes irresistible, that they were used to a considerable extent as a means of sensual gratification, though they seem never to have found a footing in religious ceremonies.

Turning now to the *Mahābhārata* we have abundant evidence to show that most of the leading characters in that great epic were addicted to strong drinks, and no picnic or pleasure party was complete in which wine did not hold a prominent part. The extract from the *Harivaṁśa* published in the last volume of this journal (p. 340 et seq.) affords a very graphic account of the manner in which such distinguished personages as Baladeva and Kṛṣṇa and Arjuna indulged in drink in the company of their wives, sisters and daughters, and other extracts equally precise and full, might be easily multiplied, if needed. The description of Arjuna's picnic on the Raivata mountain given in the Ādi Parva, offers a remarkable instance in point. Elsewhere Kṛṣṇa and Arjuna are described as 'having wine-inflamed eyes'. 'Both Kṛṣṇa and Arjuna have been

[13] X. 89.

[14] त्रैवर्णिकानामुत्पत्तिप्रभृति पैष्टीप्रतिषेधः। ब्राह्मणस्य तु मद्यमात्रप्रतिषेधोऽप्युत्पत्ति-प्रभृत्येव। राजन्यवैश्ययोस्तु न कदाचिदपि गौड्यादिमद्यनिषेधः। शूद्रस्य तु न सुराप्रतिषेधो नापि मद्यप्रतिषेधः। इति मिताक्षरा।

seen by me, both lying on a cot, or in their cars, besprinkled with sandal paste, and having their eyes reddened by *mādhvi* and *āsava*.'[15] Sudeṣnā, the queen of Maharājā Virāṭa, in the Virāṭa Parva, feeling thirsty, sends her maid, Draupadī, to her brother, Kīcaka, to obtain from him a flagon of good wine for her use.[16] In the Mausala Parva, the Yādavas are described to have been so overcome by drink at the sea-side watering-place of Prabhāsa as to have destroyed each other in sheer drunkenness.

According to the *Bhāgavata Purāṇa*, when questioned by his brother Yudhisthira as to how the Yādavas were doing, Arjuna is reported to have said:

> O king, our friends, of whom you are inquiring, losing, through a brāhmaṇa's curse on the house of our well-wishers, their senses by over-indulgence in Vāruṇi liquor, have, without recognizing each other, exchanged blows and destroyed themselves. Now only four or five are left alive to tell the tale.[17]

The *Rāmāyaṇa* also frequently notices wine and drinking. In one place no less a personage than the great sage, Viśvāmitra, who is the author of a considerable number of the hymns of the *Ṛgveda*, is said to have been entertained with *maireya* and *surā* by his host, Vasiṣṭha.[18] Bharadvaja another great sage, offered wine to Bharata

15 उभौ मध्वासवक्षीवौ उभौ चन्दनचर्च्चितौ।
उभौ पर्य्यङ्करथिनौ दृष्टौ मे केशवार्जुनौ।।

16 पर्वणि त्वं समुद्दिश्य सुरामन्नं चकारय।
तचैनां प्रेषयिष्यामि सुराहारी तवान्तिकं।।
उत्तिष्ठ गच्छ सैरिन्ध्रि कीचकस्य निवेशनं।
पानमानय कल्याणि पिपासा मां प्रबाधते।।

17 राजंस्तथानुपृष्टानां सुहृदां नः सुहृत्पुरे।
विप्रशापविमूढानां निघ्नतां मुष्टिभिर्मिथः।।
वारुणीं मदिरां पीत्वा मदोन्मथितचेतसां।
अजानतामिवान्योन्यं चतुःपञ्चावशेषिताः।।
श्रीमद्भागवते 1 स्कन्ध 15 अध्यायः

18 *Rāmāyaṇa*, Carey's edition, I, p. 462.

and his soldiers when they spent a night under his hospitable roof. 'O ye drinkers of spirits,' said the sage, 'drink spirituous liquors; O ye hungry, eat; fill yourselves with frumenty and various kinds of juicy meats.'[19] This sage welcomed Rāma by slaughtering 'the fatted calf', but he is not reported to have offered the exile liquor for his regalement. Two passages, however, occur in the second book of the *Rāmāyaṇa* which afford the most conclusive proof of wine having been extensively used, and held in considerable estimation as a favourite drink in former days. The practice of making vows at times of danger and misfortune to offer something choice to the gods, was universal in former days, and is common enough now in most parts of the world. The nature of the offering doubtless differs under different circumstances; but the offering is made all the same. The candles for the Madonna of Roman Catholic countries is in Bengal represented by milk, or frumenty, or richer offerings, and rarely is a child sick in the house, or a cow suffering from the pains of parturition, for which some milk is not vowed to the lares and penates. Sītā, the model of feminine grace and virtue, was not above this custom, and when crossing the Ganges in her way to the wilderness of the south, is said to have made a similar vow; but instead of mentioning milk or frumenty, she pledged herself to offer a plentiful supply of arrack. Addressing the river, she said: 'Be merciful to us, O goddess, and I shall, on my return home, worship thee with a thousand jars of arrack and dishes of cooked flesh-meat.'[20] When crossing the Yamunā she said, 'Be thou auspicious, O goddess; I am crossing thee. When my husband has accomplished his vow, I shall worship thee with a thousand head of cattle and a hundred jars of arrack.'[21] Again, Bharata, returning from his ineffectual mission to bring back Rāma, mourns

[19] *Rāmāyaṇa*, Carey's edition, III, p. 297.

[20] सुराघटसहस्रेण मांसभूतौदनेन च।
यक्ष्ये त्वां प्रीयतां देवि पुरीं पुनरुपागता।।

[21] स्वस्ति देवि तरामि त्वां पारयेन्मे पतिर्व्रतम्।
यक्ष्य त्वां गोसहस्रेण सुराघटशतेन च।।

the lost glories of the capital: 'No longer the exhilarating aroma of arrack, nor the enchanting scent of garlands, of sandalwood, and of agallochum now wafts through the city.'[22] After these, the presence of wine in the palaces of Rāvaṇa and Sugrīva, and the greatest glory of the streets of Kiṣkindhā having been the aroma of arrack[23] are not matters of wonder, seeing that those persons were not included in the pale of Hinduism and the city belonged to a race of monkeys.

Buddhism must have contributed much to check the spread of drunkenness in India, as it did in putting down the consumption of flesh-meat, but it never was equal to the task of suppressing it. The Jātakas and Avadānas abound in stories of drunkenness, and among the sculptures of Sāñchī, several ladies of high rank, standing in the verandas of the upper storeys of their mansions to behold religious processions in the street, are represented with attendants holding forth tazzas and flagons, which evidently were intended to contain something more potent than water or sharbat. In three love-scenes, the lovers are represented offering overflowing goblets to their mistresses, certainly not with a view to smother the flames of Cupid with a cooling draught. In a Buddhist drama, entitled *Nāgānanda,* lately translated into English by Ralph Boyd, a scene occurs, the plot of which depends upon the vagaries of a drunkard, who had for his lady-love a maid of honour of the queen.

In the time of Kālidāsa drinking seems to have been very common, for we find in the Śakuntala, the Superintendent of Police, who was no other than the king's brother-in-law, proposing, like an English policeman, or cabby, to spend the

[22] वारुणीमद्गन्धश्च माल्यगन्धश्च मूर्च्छितः।
चन्दनागुरुगन्धश्च प प्रवाति समन्ततः।।
114 अ. 20 श्लो.

[23] चन्दनागुरुपद्माभ्यां गन्धैः सुरभिगन्धिभिः।
मैरयाणां मधूनाञ्च समावृतमहापथाम्।।
किष्किन्धाकाण्डे 33 सर्ग

present offered him by the fisherman who recovered the lost ring, at the nearest grog shop.

FISHERMAN—Here's half the money for you, my masters. It will serve to purchase the flowers you spoke of, if not to buy me your goodwill.

JĀNUKA—Well, now, that's just as it should be.

SUPERINTENDENT—My good fisherman, you are an excellent fellow, and I begin to feel quite a regard for you. Let us seal our first friendship over a glass of good liquor. Come along to the next wine shop, and we'll drink your health.[24]

In his graphic description of the triumphal march of Raghu, Kālidāsa specially notices drinking-booths set up by the soldiery at Rājamundri, to drink the famous cocoanut liquor of the place.[25] The proper way to drink it was in betel leaf cups. So profusely was this liquor partaken of, that, in the hyperbolical language of the poet, the water of the Cauvery was tainted by the smell.[26] In a subsequent part of the description, the same soldiery appear to have in Persia drunk grape-wine, seated on leather cushions spread under umbrageous vineyards.[27] A passage in the *Kumāra-sambhava,* of the same author, extols a crystal palace on the Himalaya as so exquisite as to be best adapted for a drinking hall.[28] Drinking must have been common in high circles to justify this comparison. Elsewhere drinking halls, as specially reserved apartments in a palace, are frequently mentioned.

[24] Williams's *Śakuntala*, p. 153.

[25] ताम्बूलीनां दलस्तत्र रचिता पानभूमयः।
नारिकेलासवं योधाः शाचवञ्च पपुय्शः।।४.४२।।

[26] स सन्यपरिभागने गजदानसुगन्धिना।
कावरीं सरितां पत्युः शङ्कनीयामिवाकरोत।।४.४५।।

[27] विनयन्ते स्म तद् योधा मधुभिर्विजयश्रमम्।
आस्तीर्णाजिनरत्नासु द्राक्षावलयभूमिषु।।४.६५।।

[28] यत्र स्फटिकहर्म्येषु नक्तमापानभूमिषु।
ज्योतिषां प्रतिविम्बानि प्राप्नुवन्त्युपहारताम्।।
६ सर्गे ४२ श्लोकः

Kālidāsa is also lavish in his references to drinking by women of quality. In the *Raghuvaṁśa*, he makes Aja bemoan the loss of his wife, Indumatī, by this apostrophe: 'How will you, dear one of wine-reddened eye, who have quaffed delightful liquor from my mouth, drink the mist-befouled water which I offer with my tears."[29] Adverting to a practice of making *vakula* trees (*Memusops elengi*) flower by gargling wine on them, the same author says: 'Sprinkled over with arrack from charming faces, the blossoms partook of the character of the liquor.'[30] Again: 'Liquors, which excite delightful recreation, overcome by their bouquet the aroma of *vakula* flowers, never break the current of enjoyment, and are friendly to Cupid, the ladies drink with their husbands.'[31] Again, 'The ladies in private drank highly exhilarating liquor from the mouth of Agnivarṇa, and he on his turn blossomed like the *vakula* by drinking of arrack from their mouths.'[32]

In the *Kumārasambhava,* Rati, mourning the loss of her lord Cupid, says: 'Rice liquor, which causes the reddened eyes to roll, and speech to get disjointed at every step, has, in thy absence, become a torture to loving women.'[33]

[29] मदिराक्षि! मदाननार्पितं मधु पीत्वा रसवत् कथं नु मे।
अनुपास्यसि बाष्पदूषितं परलोकोपनतं जलाञ्जलिम्।।
रघु. 8 सर्गे ६८ श्लोक:

[30] सुवदनावदनासवसम्भृतस्तदनुवादिगुणः कुसुमोद्गमः।
मधुकरैरकरोन्मधुलोलुपैर्वकुलमाकुलमायतपङ्क्तिभिः।।
रघु. ९ सर्गे ३० श्लोक:

[31] ललितविभ्रमबन्धविचक्षणं सुरभिगन्धपराजितकेसरम्।
पतिषु निर्विविशुर्मधुमङ्गनाः स्मरसखं रसखण्डनवर्जितम्।।
रघु. ९ सर्गे ३६ श्लोक:

[32] सतिरेकमदकारणं रहस्तेन दत्तमभिलेषुरङ्गनाः।
ताभिरप्युहृतं मुखासवं सोऽपिवद्वकुलतुल्यदोहदः।।
रघु. १९ सर्गे १२ श्लोक:

[33] नयनान्यरुणानि घूर्णयन वचनानि स्खलयन् पदे पदे।
असति त्वयि वारुणीमदः प्रमदानामधुना विडम्बना।।
४ सर्गे १२ श्लोक:

In the 7th book of that work, when describing Śiva's approach to the palace of Himālaya, the poet says that 'the faces of the ladies who rushed to tbe windows in great haste and with half finished toilettes, to behold the procession, evolved the odour of the arrack they had drunk, and their dark eyes appeared like black bees on charming lotuses.'[34]

Māgha, in the *Śiśupālavadha* describing Baladeva, says 'when he spoke, the aroma of liquor which had obtained sweetness by lodging in the mouth of Revatī, issued from his mouth'.[35]

The Purāṇas abound in descriptions of wine and drinking, and, though the object of many of them is to condemn the use of wine, the inference is clear, that there was a widespread malady which they proposed to overcome. In some instances, moreover, the object was not reprobation, but mere description, and no less an authority than the *Bhāgavata Purāṇa* enjoins the use of spirit by brāhmaṇas at the Sautrāmaṇi rite. So does Bṛhaspati, the high priest of the gods, whose Saṁhitā is a standard authority on law.[36] In the *Mārkaṇḍeya Purāṇa,* the great goddess Durgā is represented as particularly addicted to strong drinks. Kubera serves her with overflowing goblets of strong liquor, and she drinks and drinks till her eyes become flaming red, and she bursts out in wild laughter. When girding herself to prepare for her combat with the fierce demon Mahiṣa, she says: 'Roar, roar, you fool, for a moment only, till I finish my drinking.'[37]

[34] तासां मुखैरासवगन्धगर्भैर्व्याप्तान्तरासान्द्रकुतूहलानाम्।
विलोलनेत्रभ्रमरैर्गवाक्षाः सहस्रपत्राभरण इवासन्।।
९ सर्गे ६२ श्लोकः

[35] ककुद्मिकन्यावक्त्रान्तर्वासलब्धाधिवासया।
मुखामोदं मदिरया कृतानुव्याधमुद्वमन्।।
समाघस्य २ सर्गे २० श्लोकः

[36] सौत्रामण्यां तथा मद्यं ऋतौ भक्ष्यमुदाहृतं।
Apud Viramitradaya.

[37] ददावशून्यं सुरया पानपात्रं धनाधिपः।
ततः क्रुद्धा जगन्माता चण्डिका पानमुत्तमम्।

Other instances may be quoted *ad libitum,* but they are not wanted. I shall abstain also from extracting more passages from the poetical literature of the last fifteen or sixteen hundred years to show how frequently references are made to drinking among the higher classes of the community. But I can not omit noticing the Tantras, which afford the most indubitable proofs of a strong attachment on the part of a large section of the Hindus to over-indulgence in spirituous drinks. These works profess to be revelations made by Śiva to his consort Pārvatī, and constitute the life and soul of the modern system of Hinduism. In the way of religious rites, nothing is done in the present day, and nothing has been for the last fifteen hundred years in Bengal, which does not, or did not, borrow its main characteristics from the Tantras. They govern alike the conscience of the followers of Śiva, the worshippers of Śakti, and the adorers of Viṣṇu. In the present day, some few ceremonies are called Vedic, and Vedic *mantras* are used in a great many others; but in most instances, the *mantras* used have been transmitted through a Tantric medium, and it may be said with very little exaggeration that the life of a Hindu from birth to burning-ground is one eternal bondage to the ordinances of the Tantras. Doubtless the Tantras are of various kinds, some Vaiṣṇavite, others Śaivite, and others designed for the glorification of Śakti, or the female energy, and the last two classes of works are described by the Vaiṣṇavas, and very justly, as *sanmohini* or 'delusive', designed with a view to mislead mankind in this sinful iron age; but even the most bigoted Vaiṣṇava dares not question their character as revelations by Śiva, and most faithfully owns his allegiance to such Tantras as are of a Vaiṣṇavite tendency. The Śaivite and Śakta Tantras are, however, much more numerous, and their followers in the present day may be reckoned by hundreds of thousands. Before the advent of Caitanya, four hundred years ago, their influence was much greater; and

---

पपौ पुनः पुनश्चैव जहासारुणलोचना।।
गर्ज गर्ज क्षणं मूढ़ मधु यावत् पिवाम्यहं।

the great bulk of the Hindus professed the faith inculcated in those works. The doctrine of equality which Caitanya and his successors preached, won over to their side the major portion of the lower orders of the people, and the Vaiṣṇavas, therefore, now prevail in Bengal; but the brāhmaṇas could never brook the idea of owning equality with low caste men, so most of them stuck to, and still follow, the doctrines of Śaiva or Śakta worship, and the Tantras which inculcate them give free liberty to their votaries to indulge in drinking spirits. The Śakta Tantras go further, and insist upon the use of wine as an element of devotion. According to them no worship of the Devī can be complete which is not celebrated with the five great essentials, 'fish, flesh, wine, fried grain, and female society', technically called the five Ms, from the circumstance of the initial letters of their Sanskrit names being M. To describe the details of the worship would be so shocking that I cannot venture upon the task. Suffice it to say, that the Kaulas, who are the most ardent followers of the Śakta Tantras, celebrate their rites at midnight in a closed room, where they sit in a circle round a jar of country arrack, one or more young women of a lewd character being in the company; they 'drink, drink, and drink until they fall down in utter helplessness, then rising again they drink, in the hope of never having a second birth'.[38] In such circles (*bhairavi cakra*) Kaulas of all castes are admissible, for, say the Tantras, when once in the mystic circle, all castes are superior to brāhmaṇas, though on coming out of it, they revert to their respective ranks in civil society.[39] It is true that this 'left-handed' or secret worship (*vāmācāra*) is observed by a few of the most ardent votaries of the sect, at long intervals; and the Tantras

[38] पीत्वा पीत्वा पुनः पीत्वा पुनः पतति भूतले।
उत्थाय च पुनः पीत्वा पुनर्जन्म न विद्यते।।
महानिर्वाणतन्त्रं।

[39] आगता भैरवीचक्रे सर्व्वे वर्णाः द्विजोत्तमाः।
निर्गता भैरवीचक्रात् सर्व्वे वर्णाः पृथक् पृथक्।।

inculcate absolute secrecy in its performance, and disclosure is condemned as calculated to frustrate all its merits, and prove highly disreputable; but the use of wine is enjoined at the ordinary daily prayers or *sandhyās*, and on particular occasions it is a *sine qua non.* I knew a highly respectable widow lady, connected with one of the most distinguished families in Calcutta, who belonged to the Kaula sect, and had survived the 75th anniversary of her birthday, who never said her prayers (and she did so regularly every morning and evening), without touching the point of her tongue with a tooth-pick dipped in a phial of arrack, and sprinkling a few drops of the liquor on the flowers which she offered to her god. I doubt very much if she had ever drunk a wine-glassful of arrack at once in all her life, and certain it is that she never had any idea of the pleasures of drinking; but, as a faithful Kaula, she felt herself in duty bound to observe the mandates of her religion with the greatest scrupulousness. That thousands of others do so, I have every reason to believe. In some parts of Bengal, where arrack is not easily accessible, such female votaries prepare a substitute by dropping the milk of a cocoanut in a bell-metal pot, or milk in a copper vessel, and drink a few drops of the same. Men are, however, not so abstemious, and the Tantras ordain a daily allowance of five cupsful, the cup being so made as to contain five *tolās*, or two ounces,[40] i.e. they are permitted to take ten ounces or about a pint of arrack daily.

The most appropriate way of drinking liquor is in the mystic circle above noticed; but as this cannot be got up every day, the devotee takes the bulk of his potation alone after the evening prayer. He is also at liberty to drink wherever he likes, and in whatever company chance may throw in his way, provided he faithfully observes one condition, and that is, never to drink without neutralizing the curse of Śukrācārya and purifying the drink. This is done by drawing a triangular figure on the ground with the right index finger dipped in liquor, placing the flagon

[40] पानपात्रं प्रकुवीर्त नपञ्चतोलकाधिकं।

thereon, and repeating over it three *mantras* which say—

(1) "Oṁ! The great Brahmā is one alone; verily, he is both material and immaterial. Through him I destroy the sin of Brāhmanicide which has originated in (the murder of) Kacha (son of Bṛhaspati. (2) Oṁ! O goddess, dweller in the orb of the sun, born in the abode of waters, and consisting of the sacred mantra of Ama, remove the curse of Śukrāchārya. (3) Oṁ! If the Praṇava be the source of the Vedas, and essentially and solely the felicity of Brahmā, by it, the truth, O goddess, cast away the sin of killing brāhmaṇas.[41]

After repeating the mantras, the word vaṁśa is to be muttered several times, and then repeating his own especially bījamantra, the votary should meditate on the form of his favourite divinity, which is generally a manifestation of Kālī, and then on that of Śiva who is described as 'blood red in complexion, four-handed, three-eyed, benign, beneficent, bearing a mass of matted hair on his head, a necklace of snakes round his neck, a diminutive tomtom, a skull, a club, and a noose in his hands, and arrayed in a tiger skin.'[42] Ten repetitions of the Gāyatrī after this and of the words hūṁ and phaṭ effect the complete purification of the grog, and the neutralization of the curse. At the formal mystic circle, several other mantras are repeated, and some formulas gone through;

[41] ॐ एकमेव परं ब्रह्म स्थूलसूक्ष्ममयं ध्रुवं।
कचोद्भवां ब्रह्महत्यां तेन ते नाशयाम्यहं।।
ॐ सूर्य्यमण्डलसम्भूते वरुणालयसम्भवे।
अमावीजमये देवि शुक्रशापाद्विमुच्यतां।।
ॐ देवानां प्रणवो वीजं ब्रह्मानन्दमयं यदि।
तेन सत्येन ते देवि ब्रह्महत्यां व्यपोहतु।।
कैवल्यतन्त्रे २ पटलः

[42] रक्तवर्णं चतुर्वाडं त्रिनेत्रं वरदं शिवं।
जटाजूटधरं देवं वासुकीकण्ठभूषितं।।
डमरुञ्च कपालञ्च मुद्गरं पाशमुक्तमं।
धारिणं नं यजेद्देवं ब्याघ्रचर्म्माम्बरं शिवं।।
कैवल्यतन्त्रे २ पटलः

but they are not absolutely necessary for the ordinary every day ritual, or for the purification of the drink. In practice the ritual above set forth, or a modification of it, including of course the three important mantras, does not take much time, and I have seen it completed in two or three minutes. But whether an epitome is adopted, or the whole ritual be gone through, some ceremony is imperatively necessary, for the Kaula who drinks wine without purifying it, becomes a criminal of the worst class. According to the Utpatti Tantra, 'the brāhmaṇa who drinks unpurified liquor is guilty of killing a brāhmaṇa; drinking purified arrack he becomes as pure as a flaming fire. At the Sautrāmaṇi rite and in the Kaula circle, a brāhmaṇa should always drink arrack; but by drinking elsewhere for the mere gratification of his senses, he loses his brāhmaṇahood'.[43]

The *Mātṛkā-bheda Tantra* is most eloquent in praise of drinking. It makes Śiva address his consort thus:

O sweet-speaking goddess, the salvation of brāhmaṇas depends on drinking wine. I impart to you a truth, a great truth, O mountain-born, (when I say) that the brāhmaṇa who attends to drinking and its accompaniments forthwith becomes a Śiva. Even as water mixes with water, and metal amalgamates with metal; even as the confined space in a pot merges into the great body of surrounding space on the destruction of the confining vessel, and air commingles with air, so does, dear one, a brāhmaṇa melt in Brahmā, the great soul. There is not the least doubt about this, O mountain-born. Similitude with the divinity, and other forms of liberation are designed for kṣatriyas and others; but true knowledge can never be acquired, goddess dear, without drinking wine; therefore should brāhmaṇas always drink. No one becomes a brāhmaṇa by repeating the Gāyatrī, the mother of the Vedas; he is called a brāhmaṇa only when he has a knowledge of Brahmā. The ambrosia of the gods is their Brahmā, and on earth it is arrack; and because one

[43] असंस्कृतां सुरां पीत्वा ब्राह्मणो ब्रह्महा भवेत्।
संस्कृतान्तु सुरां पीत्वा ब्राह्मणो ज्वलदग्निवत्।।
सौत्रामण्यां कुलाचारे ब्राह्मणः प्रपिवेत् सुरां।
अन्यत्र कामतः पीत्वा ब्राह्मण्यादेव हीयते।।

attains the character of a god (*surātva*), therefore is arrack called *surā*.[44]

The work, nevertheless, will admit of no drinking without the purification aforesaid.

The three *mantras* for the neutralization of the curse of the brāhmaṇa (Śukrāchārya) should always be repeated. Then only does arrack become full of Brahmā. Even as a fire flames up when clarified butter is poured on it, so does arrack become the giver of salvation on the neutralization of the curse. Therefore should brāhmaṇas always drink (after purifying his grog). Such a drinker, is a true brāhmaṇa; he is proficient in the Vedas; he is truly an Agnihotri; he is thoroughly initiated; what more can I say, O noblest of goddesses, when I add that he rises above the three qualities (inherent in matter). This is the true path to salvation; but it should be kept a secret from bestial people (*pāsu*, men who do not drink wine), for disclosure leads to want of success, and is highly disreputable.[45]

44 ब्राह्मणस्य महामोक्षं मद्यपाने प्रियंवदे।
ब्राह्मण: परमेशानि यदि पानादिकं चरेत्।।
तत्क्षणात् शिवरूपोऽसौ सत्यं सत्यं हि शैलजे।
तोये तोयं यथा लीनं तैजसं तैजसे यथा।।
घटे भग्ने यथाकाशं तापौ वायुर्यशा प्रिये।
तथैव मद्यपानेन ब्राह्मणो ब्राह्मणि प्रिये।।
लीयते नाच सन्देह: परमात्मनि शैलजे।
सायुज्यादि महामोक्षं नियुक्तं क्षत्रियादिषु।।
मद्यपानं विना देवि तत्त्वज्ञानं न लभ्यते।
अतएव हि विप्रस्तु मद्यपानं समाचरेत्।।
वेदमाता जपेनैव ब्राह्मणा न हि शैलजे।
ब्रह्मज्ञानं यदा देवि तदा ब्राह्मण उच्यते।।
देवानाममृतं ब्रह्म तदेव लौकिकी सुरा।
सुरत्वं भोगमात्रेण सुरा तेन प्रकीर्त्तिता।।

45 हविरारोपमात्रेण वह्निकर्दीप्तो यथा भवेत्।
शापमोचनमात्रेण सुरा मुक्तिप्रदायिनी।।
अतएव हि देवेशि ब्राह्मण: पानमाचरेत्।
स ब्राह्मण: स देवज्ञ: सोऽग्निहोत्रौ स दीक्षित:।।
बञ्ड किं कथ्यते देवि स एव निर्गुणात्मक:।

The *Kāmākhyā Tantra* speaks very much in the same vein. 'Whoever,' it says, 'after being initiated in the salvation-giving *mantra* of Kālikā, fails to drink wine, is a fallen man in this iron age. He has no right to the performance of Vedic and Tāntric ceremonies; he is called unbrāhmaṇa, ignorant as an elephant; and whatever oblations he offers his manes, becomes as impure as the urine of a dog. Having obtained the mantra of Kālī or Tārā, he who conducts not himself as a Vīra (or hero, i.e. drinker of wine), unmistakeably acquires in his person the degradation of a śūdra.'[46]

It will be naturally supposed that those who wrote the above panegyric must have had various kinds of liquor for their use; and the Śāstras afford the most convincing proof on this head. Pulastya, an ancient sage and author of one of the original Smṛtis, enumerates twelve different kinds of liquor besides the *soma* beer, which is not usually reckoned under the head of *madya,* and his successors have added largely to the list. The twelve principal liquors of this sage are 1. *pānasa,* or jack liquor; 2. *drākṣa,* or grape liquor; 3. *mādhūka,* or honey liquor; 4. *khārjjura,* or date liquor; 5. *tāla,* or palm liquor; 6. *aikhṣava,* or cane liquor; 7. *mādhvika,* or mowa liquor; 8. *saira,* long pepper liquor; 9. *ariṣta,* or soap-berry liquor; 10. *maireya,* or rum; 11. *nārikelaja,* or cocoa-nut liquor; 12. *surā,* or arrack, otherwise called *vāruṇi* or *paiṣṭi.*[47] This verse, as

---

मुक्तिमार्गनिदं देवि गोप्तव्यं पशुसङ्कटे।
प्रकाशात् सिद्धिहानिः स्यान्निन्दनीयो न चान्यथा।।

46 कालिका तारिणी दीक्षां गृहोत्वा मद्यसेवनं।
न करोति नरो यस्तु स कलौ पतितो भवेत्।।
वैदिके तान्त्रिके चैव जपहोमवहिस्कृतः।
अब्राह्मणः स एवोक्तः स एव पितृष्वपि।
काली तारामनुप्राप्य वीराचारं करोति न।
शूद्रत्वं तच्छरीरेण प्राप्नुयात् स न चान्यथा।।
कामाक्षातन्त्रे ५ पटलः

47 पानसं द्राक्षमाधूकं खार्ज्जूरं तालमैक्षवं।
माध्वीकं सैरमारीष्टं मैरेयं नारिकेलजं।।
समानानि विजानीयात् मद्यानेकादशैव तु।

quoted in the *Śabdakalpadruma,* gives *ṭāṅka,* or wood apple liquor, and the *Viṣṇu Saṁhitā koli* or jujube liquor in lieu of *saira.*

The mode of preparing these liquors is briefly described in the *Matsyasūkta Tantra.* It says, 'Place unripe jack, mango, and plums, in a jar, and pour on it daily a quantity of unboiled milk, and add some flesh meat; put therein hemp leaves and sweet lime on alternate days, and when duly fermented, distil, and this is jack wine.'[48]

For the 2nd, the grape juice is to be fermented with curds, honey and ghi, distilled in the usual way, and flavoured with *manjit,* and *ciretta.*[49] This is of course brandy-bitter, pure and simple, dyed with *manjit* instead of burnt sugar. The 3rd has honey for its principal ingredient, and with it is to be associated *viḍaṅga* (a bitter drug), salep misri, long pepper, and salt.[50] The 4th has ripe dates for its basis, and with it is mixed jackfruit, ginger and the juice of the *soma* vine.[51] The 5th is made with the ripe palm fruit spiced with *danti* (*Croton polyandrum*) and the leaves of the *kakubha* plant.[52] The 6th has sugar cane for its basis, and black pepper, plums, curds, and salt for adjuncts.[53] The 7th is made of

---

द्वादशन्तु सुरामद्यं सर्वेषामधमं स्मृतं।।

48 अपक्कं पनसञ्चैव आम्रञ्च वदरं तथा।
स्थापयित्वा घटे नित्यं दद्यादामपयःफलम्।।
त्रैलोक्याविजयाञ्चैव मातुलङ्गं तथैव च।
समेऽहनि ततो दद्यात् सन्धानात् सत्त्वमीरितम्।।

49 दधिमधुघृतञ्चापि मञ्जिष्ठं तिक्तकं तथा।
अनुपाने तु देवेशि द्राक्ष-मद्यं सुनिश्चितं।।

50 विडङ्गं शालवो मूलं।
मधुना सह संस्थाप्य शेषे पाकं समाचरेत्।
पिप्पली लवणं दत्वा मधुना मद्यमीरितं।।

51 पानसं पक्वखार्ज्जूरं आर्द्रं सोमलतारसं।
एकोकृत्याग्निसन्धानात् खज्जूरं मद्यमीरितम्।।

52 पक्वतालं दन्तिशाकं ककुभञ्च तथैव च।
एतैरेव सुसन्धानात् तालमद्यं प्रकीर्त्तितम्।।

53 इक्षुदण्डं मरीचञ्च वदरञ्च तथा दधि।
शेषे तु लवणं दत्वा इक्षुमद्यं प्रकीर्त्तितम्।।

the blossoms of the *Bassia latifolia,* mixed with sugar and ripe *bel* fruit.[54] The 8th is made of molasses and long pepper. The Tantra follows the reading of Rājā Rādhākānta Deva, and has *ṭanka* instead of *saira,* and it should be made, according to it, with the root of the *Asparagas racemosus,* the root of the wood-apple-tree, a drug called *lakṣmaṇa,* lotus flowers, and honey.[55] The 9th, according to the reading of the Mitākṣarā, is a liquor made from soap-berry plant with molasses, but according to the Tantra, of the root of the fugle marmelos, plums, and sugar.[56] The 10th of the above list occurs in the Tantra under the name of *gauḍī,* or rum, made from molasses, the adjuncts during fermentation being curds, hemp leaves, and a drug called *karikaṇā.*[57] The 11th is made of the milk, or toddy, of the cocoa-nut, mixed with plantains, ripe emblic myrobolans, and the drug Indrajihvā.[58] The 12th has half-boiled rice, barley, black pepper, lemon juice, ginger, and hot water for its ingredients. The rice and barley are to be digested in hot water for two days, then boiled, then spiced with the other ingredients, and allowed to ferment thoroughly, and lastly distilled.[59]

The arrack described in the Vedas was somewhat differently

[54] नवं मधु तथा विल्वं पक्वं शर्करया सह।
सन्धानाज्जायते मद्यं माध्वीकं शरतो रसं।।

[55] शतावरी टङ्कमूलं लक्षणं पद्ममेव च।
मधुना सह सन्धानात् टङ्कमाध्वीकमीरितं।।

[56] मालूरमूलं वदरी शर्करा च तथैव च।
एषामेकत्र सन्धानान् मैरेयं मद्यमीरितं।।

[57] दधि त्रैलोक्यविजया तथैव च करीकणा।
गुड़ेन सह सन्धानात् गौड़ीमद्यं प्रकीर्त्तितम्।।

[58] इन्द्रजिह्वा पक्वधात्री नारिकेलजलं तथा।
कदलीफलसन्धानात् मद्यं तन्नारिकेलजं।।

[59] शस्कुलीमर्द्धसिडान्नमुष्णोदकसमन्वितम्।
वह्नौ सन्तापयेत् किञ्चित् स्थापयित्वा दिनद्वयम्।।
शेषेऽहनि तु सम्प्राप्ते जीवनं तत्र निःक्षिपेत्।
शृंगवेरं मरीचञ्च मातुलङ्ंग तथैव च।।
एतेषामेव सन्धाानात् पैष्टीमद्यं प्रकीर्त्तितम्।।

prepared from the way above detailed, as will be seen in the sequel. All the other liquors noticed in Sanskrit works were, likewise, first fermented, and then distilled; none manufactured, as European wines are, by mere fermentation. In fact, they are all spirits differently flavoured with various kinds of spices, fruits, and herbs, to suit different tastes, and not wines; and the word wine has been used in this paper in its secondary sense of intoxicating liquor.

A liquor flavoured with aniseed has enjoyed considerable celebrity in India for a long time. It is said that a celebrated Tāntric *paṇḍit* of Nadiā, who bore the title of Āgamavāgīśa, or 'the Lord of the Science of Āgama', was particularly fond of it, and used to take a *loṭā* full of it every day. People, suspecting him of this weakness, watched him one evening when he was returning from his vesper prayers at the river side. He was seen to come out on the sly from a grog-shop with his water-pot filled with aniseed arrack, and taxed by a large crowd for conduct so disreputable in a brāhmaṇa of his learning and sanctity. He denied the charge, and placed the *loṭā,* before his accusers, when lo ! the pot appeared to contain milk. 'A miracle, a miracle', cried the crowd, and the *paṇḍit*, instead of being degraded, was canonized as the most favourite son of the Devī; the fact being, that the wily toper knew well that aniseed liquor mixed with a little water becomes milky, and had taken the precaution to doctor it so with a view to provide against possible contingencies.

Among the many omissions in Pulastya's list, the *ṭaṅka*, the *kolī*, and the *kādamvarī* appear the most prominent. The name of the first is met with largely in the Tantras. The second is of rare occurrence. The last was a favourite drink of Baladeva, and was at one time held in high repute. In medical works, various other kinds of liquor are also mentioned, mostly as aphrodisiacs, but some as medicinal. The following enjoys a high repute as an invigorating tonic. I quote a passage describing it as it is the only one in which an account is given (imperfect as it is) of the still used for distillation.

Take of fresh molasses 100 *palas,*[60] water 30 *palas*, and mix them in an earthen vessel. Take of *vāvarī* bark (*Cassia arabica?*) and jujube bark five *prasthas* each, (a *prastha* is equal to 128 *tolās*), a few betel-nuts, 32 *tolās* of *lodhra* (*Symplocos racemosa*), and two *palas* of ginger. Dilute the molasses mixture in water, add to it successively the ginger, the *vāvarī* bark, and the jujube bark, mix well, then cover the vessel, and lay it by for three days. Then add the betel-nuts and powdered *lodhra*, recover the vessel, tie down the cover, lute it, and lay it by for twenty days. Take the apparatus called *mayūra yantra,* a strong earthen vessel of the shape of a peacock, place it on a hearth over a slow fire, pour into it the fermented mixture, and add thereto half a *pala* each of powdered betel-nut, *sailabolaka*, *deodār* wood, cloves, *padmaka* (a drug), leaves of the *Andropogon muricatum* (a fragrant grass), sandal wood, *Anithum sowa, Ligusticuin ajwana*, black pepper, the white and the black cummin seed, carraway, *jaṭāmāṁsī*, nutmegs, *Cyprus rotundus* (*muthā*), *grinthi parṇī* (a drug), dried ginger, *methī* (a spice), and small cardamoms. Now cover the vessel with two upturned *chatties*, attach thereto two pipes, and carefully distil the liquor. This wine should be drunk daily. It promotes the secretion of the constituents of the body, and is invigorating.[61]

[60] A *pala*, according to some, is equal to 4 *tolās*; according to others, 8 *tolās*.

[61] नूतनं गुड़सङ्ग्राह्यं पलं तथा।
जलं त्रिंशत्पलं देयं स्थापयेन्मृदुभाजने।।
वावरीत्वचसङ्ग्राह्यं वदरीत्वचमेव च।
प्रस्थं प्रस्थं प्रदातव्यं पूगं देयं यथोचितं।।
लोध्रञ्च कुडवं दत्वा आर्द्रकञ्च पलद्वयं।
गुडं सङ्गोलकं दत्वा दापयेद्बुद्धिमान् भिषक्।।
प्रथमे चार्द्रकं देयं द्वितीये वावरीत्वचं।
तृतीये वदरीं दत्वा गोलयित्वा भिषग्वरः।।
मुखे शरावकं दत्वा स्थापयेद्दिवसत्रयं।
पूगञ्च लोध्रचूर्णाञ्च दापयेत्तदनन्तरं।।
मुखे शरावकं दत्वा यत्रं कृत्वा च बन्धने।
मुखसम्बन्धनं कृत्वा स्थापयेद्दिनविंशतिः।।
मृण्मये मोचिकापात्रे मयूराख्येऽपि यन्त्रके।
यथाविधि प्रकारेण मन्दमन्देन वह्निना।।

Although all the various Indian liquors are essentially the same, viz., rum, differing only in being differently flavoured, in the eye of the Hindu law, the liquors made from molasses, mowa, and rice are held to be more offensive than the others, and the punishment for drinking them, more severe.

The flavouring ingredients used in the preparation of these liquors, it is said, materially altered their virtues, and medical works prescribe different liquors for different complaints. For ordinary use the rum from molasses is described to be the most healthful in the dewy season (October and November), the arrack from paddy in the cold and rainy seasons; and the mowa liquor in spring, summer, and autumn. Connoisseurs were also formerly particular as to the age of their liquor, and the older the liquor, the better was it appreciated.

Nor were they, it would seem, content with their home manufactures, for it appears from Arrian's *Periplus of the Erythrian Sea* that large quantities of foreign wine were regularly imported two thousand years ago, and these met a ready sale in the country. The varieties mentioned are 1, Ααοδικηνος, or wine of Laodiceain Syria; 2, Ιταλικος or Italian wine, and 3, Αραβικος or Arabian

---

चुल्लीमध्ये निधातव्यं मृत्तिकाद्दढभाजने।
तदौषधञ्च तन्मध्ये उद्धरित्वा विनिक्षिपेत्।।
नालञ्च युगलं दत्वा कुम्भौ च गजकुम्भवत्।
कुम्भमध्ये निधातव्यं पूगञ्च शैलबालकं।।
दवदारु लवङ्गञ्च पद्मकोशीरचन्दनं।
शतपुष्पायमानी च मरिचं जीरकद्वयं।।
शठी मांसीत्वगेला च जातीफलसमुस्तकं।
ग्रन्थिपर्णी तथा शुण्ठी मेथी मेषी च चन्दनं।।
एषां चार्द्धपलान् भागान् कुट्टयित्वा विनिक्षिपेत्।
यथाविधिप्रकारेण चालनं दापयेत् सुधीः।।
बुद्धिमान् सौजनं ज्ञात्वा उद्धरेत् विधिवत् सुरां।
एतत्मद्यं पिवेन्नित्यं यथा धातुबलक्रमात्।।
इति शुक्राचार्यविनिर्मिता मृतसञ्जीवनी सुरा।।०।।

wine.[62] These, from the circumstance of their having been brought from distant countries, must have been much more costly than the spirituous liquors of India, and consequently none but the wealthy could afford to drink them.

The different liquors were always taken neat, and it was necessary, therefore, to take some saline, sub-acid, or sweet stuff, to remove the pungency or smarting caused in the mouth by the raw spirit. For this purpose fruits, roasted mince meat, and cakes were most approved by the higher classes, but the lower orders had to content themselves with parched or fried grains and pulses seasoned with salt and chilly. These wine biscuits were held in great requisition, and were known by various technical or slang names, such as *upadarśa, upadaṁśa, avadaṁśa, cakṣaṇa, madyapāsana, mudrā,* &c. I have noticed the word *nakula* also so used in the Bengali Caṇḍī and some of the Tantras, but I am not able to put my hand on the text of the latter just now. The word probably came from *nakulī* flesh-meat; but I learn from my friend Blochmann, that in Arabic the word is used in the same sense, and it is possible that some of the modern Tantras borrowed it from the Muhammadans. Anyhow the word has become generally current, and one of the names of Śiva is Nakuleśa or 'lord of wine biscuits', and no drinking party was formerly complete without a good supply of these tit-bits.

Looking to the nature of the climate, the character and temper of the people, and the anathemas which the Śāstras have, from time to time, hurled against the drunkard, it might be taken for granted that men of the higher castes, and good people generally, did set their faces against drinking, or, at least, did preserve an outward appearance of horror against those who openly outraged the mandates of the Smṛti; but it would seem that for all that cases of delirium tremens turned up pretty frequently, and several very expressive names were current in the country at one time to indicate the disease. One of them means 'wine

[62] Vincent's *Periplus II*, Appendix, p. 67.

horror' *madātaṅka,* another 'wine disease' *madātyaya,* a third 'wine complaint' *madavyādhi,* &c. The descriptions of the disease, as given in Sanskrit medical works, are detailed and precise, discriminating carefully between the illness caused by excess, and that by sudden abstinence after a protracted over-indulgence. These names and descriptions could not have come to existence, had there not been immoderate drinking in many instances to give rise to the complaint.

There is another indication in medical works which is worthy of note; it is the multiplicity of receipts for removing the odour of wine from the mouth. None but the rich or well-to-do could have required such prescriptions to guard against the accusation of having taken wine, and the existence of the recipes implies the existence of a class of men who were addicted to drinking, and yet wished to pass among their neighbours for teetotallers.

Of fermented beverages, which were drunk without previous distillation, four kinds are mentioned, viz., cocoa toddy, palm toddy, date toddy, and the soma nectar. The first was known only to those who inhabited the sea coasts, where alone the tree which yielded it, is met with. The acetous fermentation in its case was so rapid, that transmission of the liquor from one part of the country to another was out of the question, and none but those who lived in the neighbourhood of the tree could drink the juice in a vinous state. The date and the palm toddies suffered in the same way, and were unfit for transmission to distant places; but the trees which yielded them were common almost all over India, and so they were more easily accessible, and more widely known. But they never seem to have attained any great popularity. The *soma* nectar was likewise open to this objection; for it, too, had no keeping quality, and, for aught we know, was never manufactured for sale; but it was associated with the earliest history of the Aryans, even before they separated from the ancient Persians, and enjoyed the proud pre-eminence of a god as long as Vedic rites governed the conscience of the people. The *Ṛgveda Saṁhitā* is most lavish in its praise, and all the four Vedas furnish innumerable *mantras* for repetition at every stage of its manufacture, and from the moment a resolution was made to commence one of the rites at which it was to be used (and all the principal rites such as the Darśa, Paurṇamāsa, Jyotiṣṭōma, Ukthya, Śoḍaśimān, Vājapeya, Atirātra, Áptaryāma, &c., could not be celebrated without it), nothing could be done without appropriate *mantras*, and the ritual throughout was most complicated and tedious. It would be foreign to the object of this paper to describe in any detail the several steps in the manufacture of the beverage; suffice it to say that it was made with the expressed juice of a creeper (*Asclepias acida,* or *Sarcostema viminalis*), diluted with waiter, mixed with barley meal, clarified butter, and the meal of wild paddy (*nivāra*), and fermented in a jar for nine days.[63] The juice of the creeper is said to be of an acid taste, but I have not heard that it has any narcotic property; I am disposed to think, therefore, that the starch of the two kinds of meal supplied the material for the vinous fermentation, or, in other words, played the part of malt, and the *soma* juice served to promote vinous fermentation, flavour the beverage, and check acetous decomposition, in the same way that hop does in beer. Anyhow, it may be concluded that a beverage prepared by the vinous fermentation of barley meal, should have strong intoxicating effects, and it is not remarkable, therefore, that the Vedas should frequently refer to the exhilaration produced by its use in men and gods. The addresses to Indra, Agni, Mitra, and other gods in the *Ṛgveda* are full of allusions to exhilaration caused by the use of the *soma*. 'The sacred prayer, desiring your presence, offers to you both, INDRA and AGNI, for your exhilaration, the *soma* libation. Beholders of all things, seated at this sacrifice upon the sacred grass, be exhilarated by drinking of the effused libation' (I.7.XXVII.4-5). Other quotations on this subject may be

[63] Stevenson's *Sāmaveda*, p. 5. and Haug's *Aitareya Brāhmaṇa*, I, p. 6. Manning's *Ancient India*, I, p. 86. For the *mantras* used in the course of preparing the *soma* beverage vide, *Taittiriya Saṁhitā*, Kāṇḍa I, Prapāṭhākas II, III, IV, and Kāṇḍa VI, pt. I to IV. The Kalpasūtras and the *soma prayogas* supply the details.

easily multiplied, but they are not needed. Suffice it to say that the object of drinking the *soma* is expressly stated to be intoxication: *madāya arvenehi somakāmam tvāhe rayam sutastasya puā madāya;* and Indra drinks it in such large quantities, that his belly becomes enormously distended. *Uruvya cājaṭhara āvṛṣasva.* As regards men, its effects are described as equally exhilarating and inebriating. A story occurs in the *Black Yajurveda* in which a sage, Viśvarupa by name, son of Tvaṣṭu, while engaged at a *soma* sacrifice, is said to have indulged so inordinately in the exhilarating beverage as to have vomited on the animals brought before him for immolation. For this, however, no proof is wanted, for the effect of *soma* on the gods could have been only assumed by a knowledge of what it was on the worshippers.

The *soma* beer lasted for several days after its nine days' fermentation. In some of the rites it certainly lasted for twelve days, but how much longer I cannot ascertain. It is certain, however, that it could not be kept sound for any great length of time, without distillation, and in a distilled spirit the *soma* would be of no use. Accordingly, we find that no *soma* juice was used when arrack was distilled from fermented meal. The liquor, thus prepared, was, as already stated above, called *surā*, and it was used as an article of offering to the gods in two important rites, namely, the Sautrāmaṇi and the Vājapeya. The mode of preparing it is described in the canons of Baudhāyana and Kātyāyana. They recommend three articles, viz., sprouting paddy, the sprout brought on by steeping paddy in water very much in the same way as malt is produced, slightly parched barley steeped in curds and diluted butter milk, and coarse powder of tbe same steeped in whey. After proper fermentation, this was distilled in the usual way, and the liquor produced was poured in oblations on the sacred fire in lieu of the soma beer. The *Taittirīya Brāhmaṇa* supplies a number of *mantras* for the preparation of the liquor, but I can nowhere find any description of the still in which the distillation was effected. Kātyāyana recommends that the different articles required for the manufacture of the liquor should be obtained by barter, and not by purchase with coins. In the Sautrāmaṇi rite, the offering of the liquor should be preceded by the immolation of three animals, a bull being one of them. The worshippers were required to partake of the remnant of the offerings, as the ceremony would be incomplete without the repast.

CHAPTER 6

Soma/Haoma*

Rajesh Kochhar

Soma is a celebrated plant in the *Ṛgveda* as well as in the *Avesta*, where it is called Haoma, later shortened to Hom in Pahalvi. A drink of the same name was extracted from the plant by pressing or crushing its stalk, for offering to the gods and for drinking. (The name Soma comes from the root *su*, 'to squeeze'.) The Soma cult's significance is apparent from the fact that the *Ṛgveda* devotes a full *maṇḍala* to it. The longest hymn in the *Ṛgveda* (Ṛv 9.97) is addressed to it. In addition, there are numerous references to Soma in other hymns.[1] The Haoma plant figures in three hymns (9-11) in the Yasna.[2] Yasna 9 is called the Hom Yast, while Yasna (10.18) says, 'These are thy Gathas, holy Haoma'. The use of the term Gatha is significant because the Yasts believed to be composed by Zarathushtra himself are designated Gathas. Interestingly, the Zarathushtrian Gathas do not make any reference to Haoma.

While Haoma is offered to all the gods, Soma, also called Indu, is particularly associated with Indra who handsomely rewards his worshippers. The Ṛgvedic and Avestan mythologies associated

* Extracted from Rajesh Kochhar, *The Vedic People*, Orient Longman, New Delhi, 2000, pp. 98-104. Courtesy Orient BlackSwan.

[1] Hillebrandt 1927, 1: 129-51 provides a summary of the characteristics of the Soma plant is culled from the *Ṛgveda* and *Avesta*.

[2] *Sacred Books of the East*, 1887, 31: 230-47.

with Soma/Haoma run parallel. Some/Haoma is of celestial origin. In the *R̥gveda* (IV.27.3; IX.72.2), an eagle or falcon brings it to the earth against the wishes of the celestial guards like Kr̥śānu, who is known to the Avesta as Keresani (Yasna 9.24). In *R̥gveda* (VIII.12.16) Indra drinks Soma by Trita Āptya's side. Vālahilya (4.1) mentions Vivasvat's son Manu and Trita among the ancient sacrificers whose Soma had once pleased Indra. The Hom Yast lists the names of early Haoma-pressers, which in Sanskritized form are Vivasvat, the father of Yama; Āptya, the father of Traitana; and Trita whose two named sons are not known to the *R̥gveda*.

The *R̥gveda* makes a sharp distinction between those who press Soma and those who do not: 'You scattered the settlement of the non-pressers, maintaining your upper hand as the Soma drinker' (*R̥v* VIII.14.15); 'May we win in fights over those who do not press [Soma]' (*R̥v* I.110.7). There is rivalry among the Soma drinkers themselves, with different sacrificers aiming to enlist Indra's support. 'When you have mounted on your car, let your yoked Boy Steeds carry you past other men's libations' (*R̥v* VIII.33.14). Or, more simply, 'Let not other sacrificers hold you' (*R̥v* II.18.3). A specific instance of rivalry within the Soma club is provided by *R̥v* (VII.32.2): 'Indra preferred Vasiṣṭha's to the Soma pressed by Pāśadyumna Vāyata'.

Soma is the mascot of the Aryans. Whatever the Avestan and the R̥gvedic people needed or wished for at the individual and collective level, they asked Soma/Haoma to provide. Soma/Haoma is thus perceived as a giver of immortality, health and longevity, offspring, happiness, courage, strength, victory over enemies, wisdom, understanding and creativity. The attributes of Soma/Haoma fall into two categories. The culture-specific attributes tell us about the needs, fears, wishes, aspirations and accomplishments of the R̥gvedic and Avestan people. The role assigned to the Soma plant is incidental; these attributes could easily have been endowed on any other plant. In contrast, there are the object-specific details which tell us about the plant itself.

First, the culture-specific attributes. According to Yasna (9.23),

Haoma grants good husbands to maidens. In *R̥gveda* (VIII.80), a maiden, Apālā by name, plucks Soma twigs by the wayside and chews them with the purpose of becoming attractive to men. Haoma provides brilliant and righteous offspring to pregnant women (Yasna 9.22). Anyone who maltreats Haoma is cursed to remain childless (Yasna 11.3). As if aware of this, in *R̥gveda* (VIII.31.5), 'with constant draught of milk, husband and wife with one accord press out and wash the Soma juice', no doubt as a prelude to sexual intercourse. The Soma drink enables the poetic drinker to compose a hymn. Therefore, Soma is very frequently called a Kavi, 'poet'. Soma is 'the procreator of thoughts' (*R̥v* IX.95.5) and is *r̥ṣikr̥t*, 'the maker of seers' (IX.96.18). In *R̥gveda* (IX.107.18), 'the poet Soma procreates the thought'. The composer of *R̥gveda* (III.43.5) plainly asks: 'Will you not make me the protector of people, make me the king, O Soma-drinking lord, make me the *r̥ṣi* after I have drunk of Soma? Will you not give me of the excellent *amr̥ta*?'

In addition to these psychological attributes, we obtain some valuable object-specific physical characteristics. Soma prevents sleep; it keeps the drinker awake and alert.[3] 'The Gods seek him who presses out the Soma; they desire not sleep. They punish sloth unweariedly' (*R̥v* VIII.2.18). Indra is awake because he has drunk Soma (*R̥v* VIII.92.33). Soma is *jāgr̥vi*, 'awake' (*R̥v* IX.36.2; IX.44.3; IX.106.4).

It seems that some of the R̥gvedic poetry was composed at night after drinking Soma. As *R̥gveda* (V.44.14) puts it, 'The sacred hymns love him who wakes and watches; to him who watches come the *Sāman* verses. This Soma says to the man who watches, I rest and have my dwelling in thy friendship'. In *R̥gveda* (IX.97.37), Soma is awake and has become 'a singer most like Aṅgiras'. In the same creative spirit, the poet in *R̥gveda* (VIII.48.14) wishes that neither sleep nor idle talk should govern him after he has drunk Soma. Soma's ability to keep one awake was known outside the poetic

3 Falk 1989: 79.

circles also. To the gambler in *R̥gveda* (X.34.1), the die that never sleeps in dearer than the deep draught of Soma from Mūjavat.

Of all the Indo-Europeans, the Indo-Iranians are the only ones who took to composing (and preserving) hymns. One wonders whether this is due to Soma. Soma is called an ancient plant (*R̥v* IX.98.11). It was a matter of pride to have Soma drinkers among one's ancestors. 'With you, O Some Pavamana, our wise fathers conducted their affairs' (*R̥v* IX.96.11). Similarly, 'Our Soma-drinking fathers, the most excellent ones, who came for the Soma drink' (*R̥v* X.15.8). Does this mean that in the community there were members whose ancestors had been outside the Soma fold?

The Soma/Haoma tree was leafless. The juice was extracted from the shoots or stalks, never from the fruits or berries. A number of terms are used to denote the stalks: *aṁśu* (literally ray), *kṣip* (finger), *vakṣaṇa* (tube), *vāṇa* (cane). All these terms indicate that the shoots were long and thin. In the *Avesta*, the shoots are called *asu* (corresponding to *aṁśu*). The term frasparega is also used, where the word without the prefix *fra* corresponds to English sprig. The process of juice extraction is called milking in the *R̥gveda*, no doubt owing to the resemblance between the stalks and the cow's teats. The term *kṣip* is particularly apt, because the stalks, like the fingers, had joints called *parvan* or *parśu*.

The colour of the stalk was ruddy (*aruṇa*), brown (*babhru*), or golden (*hari*) corresponding to *zairi* in the *Avesta*. In the *Avesta*, the plant is called Haoma-zairi to distinguish it from three other Haomas, persons or deities.[4] A very important characteristic of the Soma plant was that it was sweet scented (Yasna 10.4; *R̥v* IX.97.19; IX.107.2).

The *R̥gveda* (but not the *Avesta*) uses the term *andhas* to denote the whole plant as well as the extracted juice.[5] The significant of the term lies in the fact that it is cognate with the Greek word *anthos*, meaning flower. Here then we have an old Indo-European word with a change in meaning.

4 Modi 1937: 283.

5 Hillebrandt 1927, 1: 145.

The *Ṛgveda* names a number of localities where Soma was consumed: Ārjīkā, Pastyāvant, Śaryaṇāvant, Suṣomā (a river), and others. Unfortunately, it is not possible to identify any of them.[6] An important piece of information is that Soma grew in the mountains. This fact is mentioned or alluded to in a number of places in the *Ṛgveda*. Thus Soma is called *parvatāvṛdh*, 'mountain grown' (*Ṛv* IX.46.1). (In the *Atharvaveda* [3.21.10] the mountains are called Somapṛṣṭha, 'carrying Soma on their back'.) *Ṛgveda* (X.34.1) uses the term *soma maujāvata*, 'the Soma from Mūjavat', which according to Yāska's *Nirukta* (9.8) was a mountain.[7]

Yasna (10.10) mentions Haraiti Bareza (also called Hara Barazaiti) as the Soma habitat. Haraiti is identified with Mount Elburz. 'But it must be borne in mind that the name Elburz not only denoted the present Mount Elburz, a peak in the Caucasus, but was applied to the whole range of mountains extending from the Hindu Kush in the East to the Caucasus in the West'.[8]

Yasna (10.17) quotes Zarathushtra as saying, 'I praise all the Haoma plants, as many as there are on the high plateaus of mountains, as many as there are in the depths of the valleys, as many as there are in the gorges, which are tied into the bundles of women'. Interestingly, while the *Avesta* shows familiarity with a much larger Soma-growing area than the *Ṛgveda*, the latter displays greater variety as regards the colour of the shoots.

The Soma ritual, though elaborate, comprised a number of simple steps: extraction of juice, its collection, purification, modification, libration and consumption. It is clear from the Ṛgvedic references that Soma pressing took place three times a day: in the morning, at noon, and in the evening. Yasna (10.2) refers to only two pressings a day.

There were two methods of extracting the juice from the Soma stalks. One could use a mortar (*ulukhala*) and pestle (*mantha*) for processing the plant. In *Ṛgveda* (I.28.3), a woman uses the mortar

[6] Hillebrandt 1927, 1: 175.

[7] Hillebrandt 1927, 1: 154-6.

[8] Modi 1937: 285.

in preparing the drink and refers (*Ṛv* I.28.5) to a similar practice in 'house after house'. To the extent it is permissible to generalize from a solitary hymn, mortar-and-pestle was the preferred (more convenient?) method of preparing the drink by the householders. Significantly, the Avestan practice was also to use a mortar, called *havana* (Vendidad 14.8).

A woman 'pushing [the pestle] backwards and forwards' had no place in the ritual. The ritualistic practice was to pound the stalks between two stones held by the hands. The stones, called *adri* or *gravan* (in singular) were held in high esteem. Three hymns (*Ṛv* X.76; X.94; X.175) are dedicated to them; in addition, these stones figure in many other hymns. The stones were pounded with a loud sound to scare away the evil spirits. At least in the later rituals, holes were bored to increase the sound. The stones were placed on cow-hide (*tvac*) which acted as a receptacle for the juice. Sometimes the stalks were soaked in water to increase the yield (*Ṛv* IX.75.9).

The next step was to purify the juice. This was done by passing the juice through a strainer made of sheep's wool. The most common designation for the Soma juice passing through the strainer is *pavamāna* or *punāna*, the action itself being denoted by the verb *pū*. (It is significant that in Punjabi the word for straining is *punanā* as against *chānanā* in Hindi.)

The juice was of the same colour as the stalks and of the same scent as the plant (*Ṛv* IX.97.9; IX.107.2). It could be taken either pure or mixed with other ingredients. The pure, unmixed Soma, called *śukra* or *śuci*, was offered to Vāyu and Indra. Vāyu is called *śucipa* (Ṛv VII.90.2, for instance) and *śukrapūtapā* (Ṛv VIII.46.26); both meaning 'pre-drinker'. Vāyu and Indra are jointly called *śucipa* in *Ṛgveda* (VII.91.4). A number of substances were available for addition to the pure Soma juice (described as *tīvra*, 'astringent'): milk, curd, water, barley, clarified butter (*ghee*), and perhaps honey. For later reference, we may note that poppy or cannabis was never added (chapter 8). It is noteworthy that in the whole procedure, there was no time for fermentation, nor was any fermented beverage (*surā*) ever added to Soma.

There is a striking similarity between the Vedic *agniṣṭoma* and the Zoroastrian Haoma ceremony, both of which must therefore have originated in the (common) Indo-Iranian period.[9] In the Brāhmaṇa period, the Soma plant ceased to be a commonplace. It became a prized item in the ritual, which was difficult to procure and so was first rationed and then substituted. In the *Baudhāyana Śrautasūtra* (6.14), the Adhvaryu asks the seller if the Soma came from Mūjavat, which obviously was still a source of supply. In the *Yajurveda* (*Maitrāyaṇī Saṁhitā* 1.160), the sacrificial offerings are hung from a tree with the words, 'This is your portion, O Rudra! With this food pass by beyond the Mūjavat'.[10] By now, Mūjavat is the civilizational outpost beyond which lies the unknown.

Kātyāyana Śrautasūtra (10.9.30) enjoins the priests not to give the genuine Soma to a Kṣatriya or a Vaiśya, even when it was available. They should instead be given the juice of the fruit of the *nyagrodha* tree (*Ficus indica*, the Indian fig).[11] *Śatapatha Brāhmaṇa* (4.5.10.2-6) lists the substitutes for use in the ritual when Soma is not available. In decreasing order of preference, they are the Phalguna plant with the red blossom; the *śyenahṛta* plant; the *ādāra* plant; the reddish *dūrvā* plant; or as the last resort, any of the golden coloured grasses.[12] The explicit mention of red and golden suggests that the substitutes were chosen to resemble the original Soma in one parameter, colour. Also, the cow to be given as the price for Soma should be red brown with red-brown eyes, no doubt because this was the Soma colour (*Śatapatha Brāhmaṇa* 3.3.1.14).[13]

The Soma substitutes are linked to the original through mythology. When Gāyatrī was bringing Soma, a shoot fell down

[9] Modi 1937: 282.
[10] Hillebrandt 1927, 1: 156.
[11] Hillebrandt 1927, 1: 158.
[12] O'Flaherty 1968: 96.
[13] Hillebrandt 1927, 1: 136.

and became the *śyenahṛta* plant. When the head of the sacrificial victim was cut-off, the *ādāra* took shape from the juice squirting forth from it. Therefore, *ādāra* can be used in place of Soma.[14]

The choice of the Soma substitute was not unique but depended on the school. *Tāṇḍya Mahābrāhmaṇa* (9.5.1-3) recommends the use of the *putika* creeper (*Guilandina bonduc* or *Basella cordifolia*). Or else the dark grass known as *arjunāni* could be used. Various other substitutes figure in the Brāhmaṇas: *śyāmaka* (cultivated millet), *muñja* grass, *kattṛṇa* (a fragrant grass) and *parṇa* (a sacred tree, *Butea frondosa*).[15]

The Brāhmaṇas reverentially reserve the name Soma for the original Ṛgvedic plant and talk of its substitutes. The reverence disappears in the later period, when the term Soma becomes free of all encumbrances and is applied – normally suffied with *latā* or *vallī* (meaning creeper) – to local plants. (These terms do not figure in the *Ṛgveda*.) There must still have been some memory of the original plant because like the Ṛgvedic Soma, all *somalatās* and *somavallīs* are leafless with fleshy stems.

At the same time, the original Soma became a mythical plant. The Vedic commentators and Sanskrit lexicographers freely speculated on Soma. Amara Siṁha, the earliest of the Indian lexicographers (*c.* AD 450), lists many synonyms of what he calls *somavallī* and also describes a plant *somarājī*. Śabarasvāmī in his commentary on the *Pūrvamīmāṁsasūtra* (2.2.17) calls Soma a creeper that yields milky juice. The milky attribute was probably based on the Ṛgvedic statements that Soma was mixed with milk.[16]

Even the medical texts give fanciful descriptions. *Suśruta Saṁhitā* (29) says that although originally there was created one *somavallī*, it was later divided into 24 varieties, one smelling like *ghee*, the other having leaves like those of garlic, still others looking like cast-off snake skins, and so on. *Suśruta Saṁhitā* (29.21-2) and *Caraka Saṁhitā* (1.4-6) both claim that Soma had 15 leaves

[14] Hillebrandt 1927, 1: 159.

[15] O'Flaherty 1968: 96-7.

[16] O'Flaherty 1968: 98.

which appeared one per day during the waxing moon (*śuklapakṣa*) and dropped off one by one during the waning moon (*kṛṣṇapakṣa*).[17]

To sum up thus far, the Ṛgvedic Soma (as well as the Avestan Haoma) is a scented leafless plant with thin and long-jointed juicy stalks, which grew in the mountainous region. The juice was extracted by pressing the stalks, and drunk unfermented. In effect, it was energizing, invigorating and anti-sleep. The Brāhmaṇa texts preserve the memory of the original Soma and prescribe various substitutes which, ranging as they do from grasses to trees, are unable to provide any clues to the master plant. In the later period, while on the one hand, the original Soma was mythified, on the other, the name Soma (often with a suffix) was given to a locally available field plant, usually a creeper.

IDENTITY OF ANCIENT SOMA

The question of the identity of the ancient Soma was taken up in the wake of ever-increasing European commercial and colonial interest in India and its neighbourhood. There is no gainsaying the fact that the Soma studies constitute the most disappointing part of the Indic scholarship. Instead of asking the question as to what the Ṛgvedic Soma/Avestan Haoma was, the studies were begun from the wrong chronological end. As part of the natural history survey that was progressively carried out in conjunction with the British territorial expansion, Latin names were assigned to Indian plants and juxtaposed with their native names, ascertained from local informers. This is how the various *somalatās*, *somavallīs* and *somarājīs* all over the country came to acquire their botanical names. Next, one or the other of these plants was boldly declared to be the plant of the ancient texts. In the absence of collation of diverse field data and of any worthwhile acquaintance with ancient texts, that could constrain free flights of fancy, Soma was reduced to a mere Sanskrit name that could be

[17] O'Flaherty 1968: 99.

tagged on to any of the superficially resembling plants. Somehow, an acquaintance with the Latin name of the plant gave the whole exercise a scholarly look.

In the whole debate lasting two centuries, not a single idea was rejected for good as being untenable nor was any accepted as constituting received wisdom on the subject. The debate remained open, superficial and repetitive, with the participants responding to each other rather than to the primary source material. Beating about the Soma bush became a badge of scholarship for a large number of European travellers and officers. Since the agenda was defined by dilettantes, even serious scholarship lost its moorings.

Historically, the European notice of Soma/Haoma began in 1771 with Du Perron's French translation of the *Avesta.* Du Perron quoted *Farhang Jahangiri* to say that Hom is a tree which grows in Persia in the mountains of Shirwan, Guillan, Mazendran and the neighbourhood of Yezd. It resembles sweet heather, its knots are very close to each other and the leaves are like those of jasmine. He went on to say that Hom did not grow in India and that 'the Dasturs of India are in the habit of sending at the end of a certain season two Parsees to Kerman to search for the branches of Hom'. The continuity in the Zoroastrian tradition provides a very valuable clue.[18] At that time, however, neither the Ṛgvedic Soma nor the Indo-Iranian connection was known. Du Perron's first-hand account therefore went unnoticed.

The first mention of Soma in English appeared in 1784 in Charles Wilkins' translation of the *Bhagavadgītā.* In a footnote, Wilkins added that Soma was a creeper whose juice was drunk at the conclusion of a sacrifice. The first attempt to identify Soma was made by William Jones in 1794 who proposed that Soma was a mountain rue.

Twenty years later, the exercise shifted from the library to the field. William Roxburgh, the first official superintendent of the East India Company's botanical garden in Calcutta during 1793-

[18] O'Flaherty 1968: 102.

1814, prepared a catalogue of its 3,500 plants. This catalogue called *Hortus Bengalensis* was published in 1814. (His magnum opus *Flora India* came out in 1832.) Roxburgh identified the plant locally known as *somalatā* with *Sarcostemma brevistigma* (*Asclepios acida*), 'a leafless bush of green succulent branches, growing upwards with flowers like those of an onion'. He also pointed out that a different plant, a rue called *Ruta graveolens*, was also called *somalatā*. More importantly, he observed that Hiamlayan plants do not grow in Bengal.[19] This point, of significance in the understanding of ancient texts, was ignored. The *Sarcostemma* saga had begun.

Sarcostemma juice, however, presented a problem. It was noted in 1832 that 'native travellers often suck the tender shoots to allay their thirst'.[20] It was pointed out in 1845 that 'Farmers use *S. brevistigma* to rid their fields of white ants'. Also, that the sap of the Asclepiads was bitter and acrid, and in the West Indies it was given to children in doses of a teaspoon to a tablespoon as a remedy for worms.[21]

These were hardly the attributes of a drink that was earlier enthusiastically imbibed three times a day. The contradiction perhaps had not been lost on the *Sarcostemma* using Vedic commentators who were as clueless to the identity of the original Soma as the later-day European enquirers. John Stevenson in his 1842 translation of the *Sāmaveda* says that Soma is *S. viminale* and that 'according to the commentator it is pressed and mixed with barley and allowed to stand for nine days'. Fermenation of the juice was probably a means of camouflaging its bitterness. Displaying an orientalist bent of mind, not uncommon those days, William Dwight Whitney could say patronizingly in 1853, 'The simple minded Arian [*sic*] people . . . had no sooner perceived that this liquid had power to . . . produce a temporary frenzy . . . than they found in it something divine.'[22]

[19] O'Flaherty 1968: 103.
[20] Watt 1890: 249.
[21] O'Flaherty 1968: 106.
[22] O'Flaherty 1968: 106-7.

In 1855, Max Müller dug up an old Ayurvedic verse[23] which described Soma as a black creeper, sour, leafless, yielding milk, having fleshy skin, dissolving (or producing?) phlegm, causing vomiting, and eaten by goats. Though the description fitted *Sarcostemma*, Max Müller asked a valid question: If this freely available plant was indeed the Soma, then why did the Brāhmaṇa-period priests have to use *putika* as a substitute? The passage was not taken up for discussion until thirty years later, when attention was drawn to its lateness and to the uncertainty whether the drug dissolved phlegm or produced phlegm.

Soon field data started becoming available from different parts of the country. In 1886, J. Forbes Watson described the 'Telugu' *somalatā* as *S. brevistigma*, and the 'Sanskrit' *somalatā* as *Ruta graveolens.*[24] In 1874, Arthur Coke Burnell pointed out that the Hindus on the Coromandel coast used *S. brevistigma* in their rites, while their counterparts on the Malabar coast used a different plant, *Ceropegia decaisneana* or *C. elegans.*[25]

In 1873, Rajendralal Mitra (1822[4?]-91), who later became the first president of the Asiatic Society, Calcutta, proposed a new hypothesis, doing away with the ancient texts as it were. The Soma juice, he said, was merely a figure of speech. The Soma plant did not provide a drink by itself. Rather, like hops, it was added to accelerate the fermentation of paddy and barley decoction to produce a kind of beer. It is a measure of the confused scholarship on the subject that this dubious hypothesis received wide support, including from Max Müller who concluded, to his satisfaction, that the original Soma was hop, later replaced by a *Sarcostemma*. He even suggested that the two words were etymologically related![26]

A hundred years after Du Perron, Haoma finally entered the debate. In 1878, Friedrich Spiegel reported afresh that the Indian

[23] The verse occurs in Dhūrtasvāmī's commentary on *Āpastamba Śrautasūtra* (O'Flaherty 1968: 100).

[24] O'Flaherty 1968: 108.

[25] O'Flaherty 1968: 110.

[26] O'Flaherty 1968: 109.

Parsees sent their priests to Kerman to bring Haoma.[27] In December 1884, the naturalist A. Houtum-Schindler wrote from Teheran that the plant used by the Zoroastrians in Kerman and Yezd agreed with the *Sarcostemma*.[28] In 1885, the botanist (Sir) George Watt wrote that Dr Dymock, surgeon-general at Bombay, had identified the Haoma plant used by Bombay Parsees as *Periploca aphylla*.[29] That these were misidentifications soon became obvious.

During 1884-6, the British sent a commission to Afghanistan to determine its boundaries in conjunction with a similar commission from Tsarist Russia. One of the members of the British commission was a professional botanist, James Edward Tierney Aitchison, who was asked to report on the Afghan flora and fauna. Earlier, Aitchison had supported the view that Soma was wine. The assignment made him change his opinion. While in Afghanistan, in 1885, he received from the Bombay-based Parsee scholar (Sir) Jivanji Jamshedji Modi samples of Hom for identification. Aitchison wrote back as follows:

> The specimens you sent me are the twigs of a species Ephedra. . . . A species grows all over this country – Baluchistan, Afghanistan, Kashmir and Western Thibet – which seems to be identical with the species received. This species is here, in all this country, called Hum (pronounced as the English word whom, also Huma). In Baluchistan, it, as well as totally a distinct plant, *Periploca aphylla* is called Hum. It grows equally on exposed hills and valleys, consisting of 'branches and sprigs', one mass of upright twig, if you notice, being made of joints like the joints of the fingers. When covered with male flowers, the bush (from 1 to 2 feet) is golden coloured, and the twigs are more or less so. . . . This plant has no leaves. It is all twigs and jointed. Among the Pathans of the Khyber pass and all over that country, the twigs are, with water, made into a decoction and employed very largely as a household remedy in sickness, and are considered as possessing health-giving and healing properties. Owing to a general likeness between the stiff rod-like growth, upright

27 O'Flaherty 1968: 110.
28 O'Flaherty 1968: 118.
29 Watt 1890: 248.

and erect, of the two plants, in Baluchistan the natives equally give both the same name. No one would mistake the jointed and true Hum for the non-jointed false Hum, *Periploca*.[30]

Aitchison concluded by saying, 'Before your letter and specimens came, I had made up my mind that the Ephedra was the nearest to the "Soma" plant that I got to, but as it was stated that the Parsees employed the twigs of *Periploca*, it rather put me out. Your specimens are all on my side.'[31]

On return to England, Aitchison published in 1887 a technical report on his findings. Further support came in 1893 when Joseph Bornmuller wrote (in German) about his encounter with a Zoroastrian priest in Yezd carrying Hum, which he at once recognized as *Ephedra distachya*. He added that large quantities of it were dried and sent to Bombay every year.[32]

In 1912 Macdonell and Keith, unable to cut through the maze of conflicting opinions, declared in their *Vedic Index* that 'it is very probable that the plant cannot now be identified'.[33] By sweeping the Soma problem under the carpet, a very important clue to the geography of the *R̥gveda* – which the *R̥gveda* itself furnishes – was ignored. Two years later, in 1914, archaeological evidence on the use of *Ephedra* in Central Asia about 2,000 years ago (but not necessarily as Soma/Haoma) was uncovered by Aurel Stein, who had been a student of the German Sanskritist Rudolf von Roth and was familiar with the official brief on Soma prepared for use by the Afghan Commission. An examination of widely distant cemeteries in the Lou-lan area of the Lop Desert in the western Chinese province of Xinjiang (Sinkiang) (chapter 8) revealed that in the case of six well-preserved graves in different cemeteries, small broken stalks of *Ephedra* had been tied up into little bunches on the edges of woollen shrouds. 'In most of the other graves at

30 Modi 1937: 285.
31 Modi 1937: 286.
32 O'Flaherty 1968: 122.
33 Macdonell and Keith 1912, 2: 475.

these cemeteries the bodies and their belongings were found in a badly decayed state not permitting of close examination of details. But it may be safely assumed that the provision of such small packets formed part of the regular practice among the indigenous people.'[34]

Stein recalled that the Chinese use an *Ephedra* called Mahuang to get an alkaloid drug (Ephedrine). He, however, naively concluded that *Ephedra* could not be Soma, because *Ephedra* was bitter, while Soma was sweet. If he had read his *R̥gveda* he would have realized that *Ephedra's* inherent bitterness was consistent with the fact mentioned earlier that the pure Soma juice was called astringent. Finally, in 1951, Karl Friedrich Geldner, in his posthumously published German translation of the Soma hymns, declared that the R̥gvedic Soma was indeed *Ephedra.*[35]

In reaction to the alcohol theory of Soma, there was proposed the hallucinogen theory which tried to equate Soma with hemp (*Cannabis sativa*), a mushroom (*Amanita muscaria*)[36] or the wild rue (*Peganum harmala*). In the *R̥gveda* and *Avesta*, there is no indication that the Soma/Haoma drinker loses his or her sense of reality. On the contrary, it is clearly indicated that s/he becomes more alert.

[34] Stein 1931: 503.

[35] Geldner 1951, 3: 2.

[36] The idea that Soma was a mushroom popularly known as fly-agaric or toadstool originated with R.G. Wasson in 1968 (Bender 1971), and was accepted by Needham (1974: 116). Wasson speculated: 'Did the priests initially have recourse to porters who travelled to the far north, to the forest belt of Eurasia, to assure their supplies of the divine plant? Two such porters could have carried loads of dried fly-agaric to last perhaps a whole year' (Bender 1971: 14). This runs counter to the R̥gvedic description of Soma being plucked from the wayside. 'If Soma was the fly-agaric, why was it abandoned?' Wasson asked, and proceeded to answer rather haughtily: 'If the Rigveda speaks in unmistakable terms about the fly-agaric as Soma . . . that settles the problem. I am concerned with the Vedic times. It is not incumbent on me to face the problem of post-Vedic history' (Bender 1971: 13). See Nyberg (1995) for a review of the pharmacological properties of the various candidate plants.

Also, mushroom is odourless, while the Soma plant is scented. The wild rue is burnt rather than pounded. All hallucinogenic substitutes can thus be ruled out.

While *Sarcostemma* may well have been the commonly used substitute for Soma in the later period, there is now a growing consensus among experts in the field that 'there is no need for a plant other than *Ephedra* for the original Soma. . . . *Ephedra* fits each and every detail of the texts.'[37]

The various varieties of *Ephedra* look like bushes of leafless, jointed twigs, some prostrate, but mostly standing erect, 1-6 ft high (Fig. 6.1). The plant has a pine-like aroma and a strong astringent taste. It owes its importance to the alkaloid Ephedrine ($C_{10}H_{15}ON$) extracted from its twigs. The alkaloidal content of the plant increases with age. Twigs are much richer in alkaloidal content than the woody stems, while the roots are bereft of it. The best plants are four years old and in blossom; the best time for harvesting the twigs is after the rains but before the winter frost.[38]

Ephedrine is soluble in water and can be taken orally. It stimulates the nervous system, increases the intake of oxygen, and acts as a restorative and a mild anaesthetic agent. Compared to adrenaline which must be injected, Ephedrine's effect is slower and less intense but more persistent. It dilates the pupil and contracts the uterus. Soma's role as an aphrodisiac can only be attributed to the general feeling of euphoria that Ephedrine causes. In excessive doses, Ephedrine causes nervousness, insomnia, headache, vertigo, palpitation, sweating, nausea and vomiting. When the R̥gvedic poet asks Soma to be 'sweet to our heart' (*R̥v* 8.68.7) and 'wound not our heart with dazzling flame' (*R̥v* 8.68.7), he is probably requesting for exemption from the effects of over indulgence.

Ephedra's utility as a geographical diagnostic comes from the fact that it does not grow everywhere and all its varieties do

[37] Falk 1989: 87.

[38] Sastri 1952: 177-8.

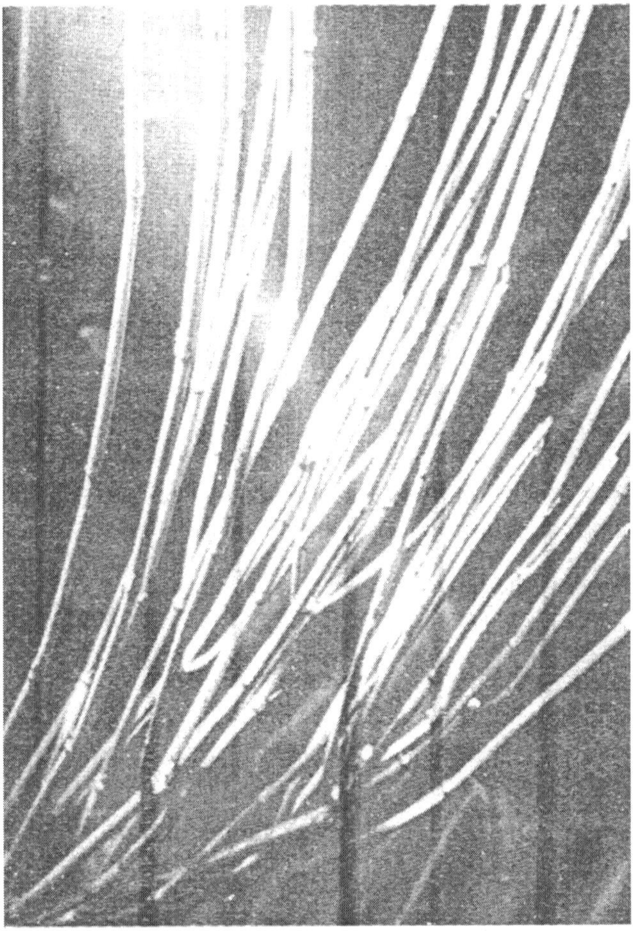

Fig. 6.1: Dried twigs of *Ephedra*

not contain Ephedrine. Four species of *Ephedra* are native to the mountaineous regions of north India, Afghanistan and Iran: *E. gerardiana* (*E. vulgaris*, *E. distachya*), *E. major* (*E. nebrodensis*), *E. intermedia* and *E. pachyclada*. They all contain Ephedrine. In addition, there is *E. foliata* which grows in the plains of south Punjab and Rajasthan. It does not contain any appreciable quantity of Ephedrine. The rest of India is not the natural habitat of any species of *Ephedra*. Local names of *Ephedra* were recorded a hundred years ago. Thus *E. gerardiana* is called *asmania, butshur, budshur* and *chewa* in Punjab; *phok* in the Satluj Valley; *tse, tsapatt* and *trano* in Ladhak; and *khanda* and *khama* in Kunawar [not identified].[39]

Since the R̥gvedic Aryans could pluck twigs from the wayside, they must have lived in the mountainous regions. Since the Avestans were also using Soma, the common residence can be narrowed down to the Hindu Kush and its western environs. The species native to Chitral, Baluchistan and Afghanistan, *E. pachyclada*, can then be singled out as the Soma of the *R̥gveda*. The name for the plant still survives in the region, as noted by Aitchison: Hum in the Heart Valley, as well as in Baluchi, Pashto and Brahui, and Som in Gilgit, Chitral and Kafiristan. The remarkable fact that the same name designates a plant in a vast area also points towards its great antiquity.

When we identify *Ephedra* as Soma and place the R̥gvedic people in the Ephedra-habitat Hindu Kush, all the diverse pieces of the puzzle fall into place. The vast Ephedra-growing area in Afghanistan and Iran was occupied by or was accessible to the Indo-Iranians who could develop a common Soma/Haoma cult. As the Indo-Aryans moved eastwards, their distance from Soma increased, first cutting down the supply and then stopping it altogether. Finally, in the plains, Soma's place in the rituals was given to the substitutes. In course of time, Soma became a mythical plant.

In its transition from an easily available herb that could be processed by husband and wife in their home to a myth even for the later-day medical celebrities, Soma records the distance that the Indo-Aryans traversed, figuratively and literally, from the Ṛgvedic times to the classical period.

[39] Watt 1890: 251-2.

BIBLIOGRAPHY

Falk, Harry, 'Soma I and II', *Bulletin of the School of Oriental Studies*, vol. 52 (1989).
Hillebrant, A., *Vedische Mythologie*, W. Kroebner, Breslau, 1927.
Modi, J.J., *The Religious Ceremonies and Customs of the Parsees*, Bombay, 1937.
O'Flaherty, Wendy, 'The Post-Vedic History of the Soma Plant', in R.G. Wasson, ed., *Soma: Divine Mushroom of Immortality*, New York, 1968.
Watt, G., *Dictionary of Economic Products of India*, Calcutta, 1890.

CHAPTER 7

The Soma-Haoma Problem*

Introductory Overview and Observations on the Discussion[1]

Jan E.M. Houben

Je suis ivre d'avoir bu tout l'univers . . .
Écoutez mes chants d'universelle ivrognerie.

Apollinaire 1913

[1] This Introduction is an elaboration of introductory remarks in my paper presented at the Leiden seminar on the Soma-Haoma issue (Leiden, 3-4 July 1999). For this seminar, support was received from the Research school CNWS – School of Asian, African, and Amerindian Studies (Leiden University). My own research in connection with the topic of the seminar was funded by the Royal Netherlands Academy of Arts and Sciences (KNAW), of which I was a research fellow from July 1999 till March 2003. I am grateful to the participants in the workshop for their contributions in the form of papers, remarks and discussions. Leonid Kulikov deserves special mention for his kindness to assist in occasional translations from Russian, and after the workshop to mediate between Leiden and Professor Sarianidi when the latter was staying in Moscow. Michiel de Vaan kindly helped me get hold of some of the publications I needed. I am indebted to Frits Staal, George Thompson for their critical reading of an earlier version of this introduction. I thank Michael Witzel for accepting to devote an issue of the *Electronic Journal of Vedic Studies* to the discussion on the Soma-Haoma problem.

*Reprinted from *Electronic Journal of Vedic Studies*, vol. 9, Issue 1 (May 2003).

It is no sign of scientific honesty to attempt
to claim for what is in reality a branch of
historical research, a character of
mathematical certainty.
. . . it is only the rawest recruit
who expects mathematical precision where,
from the nature of the case, we must
be satisfied with approximative aimings.

F. Max Müller 1888: xiv

INTRODUCTION

Practically since the beginning of Indology and Iranology, scholars have been trying to identify the plant that plays a central role in Vedic and Avestan hymns and that is called Soma in the Veda and Haoma in the Avesta. What is the plant of which the Vedic poet says (R̥V VIII.48.3):[2]

ápāma sómam am´r̥tā abhūma áganma jyótir ávidāma devā́n ।
kíṁ nūnám asmān kr̥ṇavad árātiḥ kím u dhūrtír amr̥ta mártyasya ॥

We just drank the Soma, we have become immortal, we have come to the light, we have found the gods. What can enmity do to us now, and what the mischief of a mortal, O immortal one?

And which plant is addressed by Zarathustra (Y 9.19-20) when he asks divine blessings such as 'long life of vitality' (*darë¤ô.jîtîm*

[2] In the email-version, the transcription of Sanskrit follows the conversion table for Old Indic/Sanskrit of TITUS (Thesaurus Indogermanischer Text-und Sprachmaterialien), http://titus.uni-frankfurt.de/software/fonts/titaind.htm, with the exception that names that do not appear in quotations or references to the Sanskrit word have their first letter capitalized. This creates occasional ambiguities which, however, disappear against the background of a general basic knowledge of Vedic/Sanskrit.

uõtānahe),[3, 4] 'the best world of the pious, shining and entirely glorious' (*vahiõtëm ahûm a÷šaonąm raocaÑhëm vîspô.xᵛārëϑëm*), and requests to become 'the vanquisher of hostility, the conqueror of the lie' (*t̰baê÷šô.tauruuā̊ drujëm.vanô*)?

EARLY IDEAS AND GUESSES ON SOMA AND HAOMA

Already Abraham Rogerius, the seventeenth century missionary from Holland, was familiar with the word *soma*, as he writes in his *Open Deure tot het Verborgen Heydendom* (*The Open Door to the Hidden Heathendom*, 1651) that it means 'moon' in the language which he calls 'Samscortam'.[5] But it seems that it was only in the second

[3] In the email-version, the transcription of Avestan follows the conversion table for Avestan of TITUS (Thesaurus Indogermanischer Text-und Sprachmaterialien), http://titus.uni-frankfurt.de/texte/avesta.htm .

[4] A regular epithet of Haoma, *dûraoõa*, has been interpreted as 'Todtwehrer' or the one who keeps 'destruction' or 'perdition' (*aoõa*) 'far away' (*dûra*) (cf. Bartholomae 1904 s.v.). Stuhrmann's suggestion (1985: 87 and 92 note 20) that the word derives from **dru-oṣa* 'holzbrennend' does not seem convincing in the context where it occurs; Flattery and Schwartz (1989: 130) want to understand it as 'keeping destruction far away' in connection with apotropaic powers of the Haoma-plant which it would especially have when it is burnt. However, if the association with burning is part of the term's synchronic semantics it would not suit contexts such as the beginning of Y 9 where there is no burning but a pressing and libation of Haoma. See for further references to the discussion Mayrhofer 1992: 733.

[5] Rogerius, *Open Deure tot het Verborgen Heydendom*, ed. Caland 1915: 3: in a discussion of the Somowansjam [*somavaṁśa*], the name of a royal dynasty, Rogerius writes 'inde gheseyde Tale beteyckent Somo de Maen'. Rogerius' work was translated into English, German and French and remained for more than a century an important source of knowledge on India and Indian religion.

A valuable discussion of early ideas, guesses and philological research on Soma is found in Doniger O'Flaherty 1969, where the reader will find references to a few additional contributions left out by me as they half of the eighteenth century that Europeans started to gather more detailed informations about Vedic rituals, including the use of Soma (in the meaning of the plant and the inebriating drink created from it). In an abridged text of the Jesuit Father Coeurdoux which remained unpublished but which was apparently the unacknowledged basis of J.A. Dubois' well-known work on the customs, institutions and ceremonies of the peoples of India (Abbé 1825), we read that Soma is the name of a certain liqueur of which the sacrificer and the Brahmins have to drink at the occasion of a sacrifice ('Soma est le nom d'une certaine liqueur dont lui [= celui qui préside à la cérémonie, J.H.] et les autres Brahmes doivent boire en cette occasion', Murr 1987: 126).

From Anquetil-Duperron (1771)[6] and Charles Wilkins (1785)[7] onward, the identity of the Avestan Haoma and of the Vedic Soma started to receive scholarly and scientific attention. In 1842, John Stevenson wrote in the preface to his translation of the *Sāmaveda* that in the preparation of a Soma ritual (*somayāga*) one should collect the 'moon-plant'. He identifies (p. IV) the plant as *Sarcostemma viminalis*. He moreover notes (p. X) that '[s]ince the English occupation of the Marátha country' the *somayāga* was performed three times (viz., in Nasik, Pune and Satara). In 1844, Eugène Burnouf observed in a study (p. 468) that the situation of the Avestan Haoma, the god whose name signifies both a plant

---

seemed less significant or influential. On the other hand, I mention here a few authors skipped or overlooked by Doniger O'Flaherty, or not available to her.

[6] Anquetil-Duperron 1771, vol. 2: 535. The classics are Anquetil-Duperron's frame of reference when he associates the Parsis' Hom (Haoma) with the *ámōmos* of the Greek and the *amomum* of the Romans.

[7] Wilkins 1785, in note 42 (p. 143) to the verse in 'Lecture IX' of the *Bhagavadgītā* in which reference is made to 'followers of the three Vēds, who drink of the juice of the Sōm' (*traividyā[ḥ] . . . somapāḥ*), observes that 'Sōm is the name of a creeper, the juice of which is commanded to be drank at the conclusion of a sacrifice, by the person for whom and at whose expense it is performed, and by the Brāhmăns who officiate at the altar.'

and the juice pressed from it, is exactly parallel with the Soma of Vedic sacrifice. Windischmann (1846) discussed ritual and linguistic parallels between the Soma- and Haoma-cult in more detail. He reports (1846: 129) that Soma is known to be *Sarcostemma viminalis*, or *Asclepias acida* (the latter nowadays also known as Sarcostemma acidum Voigt), to which he attributes a narcotic-intoxicating (*narkotisch-berauschende*) effect.

SOMA-HAOMA AND THE DEVELOPMENT OF MODERN BOTANY

The botanical identity of Soma and Haoma became problematized in the second half of the nineteenth century in a time when botany was trying to cope with the challenges of various exotic, newly-encountered floras. The use of the plant *Sarcostemma brevistigma* in recent Vedic sacrifices was acknowledged, but was this identical with the Soma which had inspired the ancient authors of the Vedic hymns? Max Müller expressed his doubts in an article published in 1855, in which he referred to a verse about Soma that appeared in a ritualistic commentary (Dhūrtasvāmī's commentary on the *Āpastamba Śrautasūtra*) and that was itself allegedly quoted from an Ayurvedic source. Adalbert Kuhn (1859), being primarily interested in Indo-European mythological parallels, accepts Windischmann's conclusions that the Soma-Haoma was already current among the proto-Indo-Iranians before they split into a Vedic and Iranian group. He leaves open the possibility that only the mythology and outward appearance of the Soma and Haoma are similar while the plants may be different. In 1881 Roth discussed in an article, 'Über den Soma', the nature of the plant that was used in modern times, the plant of olden times, the development in which the plant became rare and inaccessible to the Vedic people, and the admission and prescription of surrogates in later Vedic texts. He thinks it is likely that the ancient Soma was a *Sarcostemma* or a plant belonging, like the *Sarcostemma*, to the family of Asclepiadeae, but not the same kind as the one used in current sacrifices. Roth's article was the starting signal of a discussion by correspondence in an English weekly review of literature, art and science, *The Academy* of 1884-5; apart from Roth and Müller botanists such as J.G. Baker and W.T. Thiselton-Dyer participated. Julius Eggeling (1885: xxiv ff) gave a brief report of this discussion, which later on appeared again in Max Müller's *Biographies of Words and the Home of the Aryans* (1888: 222-42). From the title which Müller gives to the whole discussion, 'The Original Home of the Soma', it is clear which aspect of the problem interests him most: the possible indication that the plant's identity might give about 'the original home of the Aryans'. Eggeling notices that an official inquiry is undertaken by Dr. Aitchison, 'Botanist to the Afghan Boundary Commission' (Eggeling 1885: xxiv). A few decades later, Hillebrandt (1927: 194ff) gives a more detailed report of the same discussion and adds references to a few later contributions to the Soma-Haoma problem. As in the case of Eggeling, Hillebrandt cannot reach a final conclusion regarding the identity of the plant Soma and Haoma in the ancient period. Suggestions noted by Hillebrandt vary from wine (Watt and Aitchison) and beer (Rajendralal Mitra) to Cannabis (B.L. Mukherjee).[8] In a footnote, Hillebrandt writes about a 'Reisebrief aus Persien' by Bornmueller according to whom the 'Soma-twig (also called Homa and Huma)' in the hand of a Parsi priest in Yesd could be immediately recognized as Ephedra. A few years earlier, Jivanji Jamshedji Modi, in his work on the 'Religious Ceremonies and Customs of the Parsees' (1922: 303, fn. 1), reported that 'a few twigs of the Haoma plant used by the Indian Parsis in their

[8] When Hillebrandt (1927: 201) writes that Mukherjee rejects the identification of Soma and Cannabis (*Bhāng*), he seems to have misunderstood Mukherjee's rhetorical question (1921: 244) 'From what has been stated above, may we not conclude that the weight of evidence is in favor of the identification of Soma with Cannabis (Bhāng).' Mukherjee's view appears in more detail in a paper that appeared in 1922 (the 9-page booklet present in the Leiden University library is perhaps an offprint of the paper Mukherjee announces at the end of his 1921 article as appearing in the *Bulletin of the Indian Rationalistic Society of Calcutta*; the name of this journal is, however, nowhere mentioned in the paper).

ritual' were sent to Dr. Aitchison (spelled by Modi as Aitchinson) and identified by him as 'twigs of the species Ephedra (Nat. order Gnetaceae)'. Aitchison publishes his botanical descriptions of plants encountered at his trip through the 'Afghan boundary' area in 1888. In the valley of the Hari-rud River he notices (1888: 111-12) the presence of several varieties of Ephedra, including one which he and a colleague are the first to determine, as well as the *Ephedra pachyclada*, of which he reports as 'native names' Hum, Huma and Yehma.[9] Without committing himself to a candidate for the 'real Soma plant', Oldenberg (1894: 177 and 366ff) argued that the Vedic Soma plant was a replacement of an earlier, Indo-European substance inebriating men and gods: mead, an alcoholic drink derived from honey.

SOMA-HAOMA, THE BIOCHEMISTRY OF PLANTS, AND HUMAN PHYSIOLOGY

At the end of the nineteenth and the beginning of the twentieth century, another strand starts to be woven in the Soma-Haoma discussion. An active substance of the Ephedra plant, the alkaloid ephedrine, was found in the chinese herb Ma Huang (*Ephedra vulg.*) in 1885 by Yamanashi. In 1887 and 1892, it was isolated from the plant by Nagai, who gave it the name ephedrine.[10] In First World War, ephedrin and a number of other alkaloids (quinine, strychnine, yohimbine and harmaline), were tested on a group of soldiers; it was found that ephedrine worked most strongly on muscle strength as well as on the will to overcome fatigue.[11] In his 1938 *Lehrbuch der biologischen Heilmittel* (*Textbook*

[9] Aitchison (1888: 87) also discusses the *Periploca aphylla* (like the *Sarcostemma* belonging to the Asclepiadaceae) which he found in northern Baluchistan. He notices the native names 'Um, Uma; Punjabi Batta'. J.G. Baker suggested it as a candidate for Soma in a letter to the Academy in 1884.

[10] See Madaus 1938: 1261.

[11] Madaus 1938: 1264.

of Biological Remedies), Gerhard Madaus (1938: 1259-66) refers to a large number of studies on the effects, toxicity, etc., of ephedrine appearing in German and American scientific journals, and notes their employment in the treatment of asthma and low blood pressure. In the period between the two world wars, chemical substances (amphetamines) were explored which were close to ephedrine both in chemical structure and in physiological effects (Alles 1933, Fawcett and Busch 1998: 504). In Second World War it was the amphetamines that were widely used on both sides.

A GROWING PUBLIC FOR KNOWLEDGE AND EXPERIENCE OF PSYCHOACTIVE SUBSTANCES

A book that we may now call a textbook of psychoactive substances was published in 1924, with an enlarged edition in 1927: Louis Lewin's *Phantastica: Die betäubenden und erregenden Genussmittel für Ärzte and Nichtärzte* (*Phantastica: Narcotics and Stimulants, for Medical Doctors and Non-doctors*). Having researched several of the plants (the mexican 'mescal-button' cactus) and substances (e.g. cocaine) himself in the preceding decades, he gives detailed discussions of the uses and abuses of a wide range of narcotics, stimulants and popular remedies that were either available in Europe from all parts of the world or that had been studied abroad by ethnographers. He is aware (1927: 216) of the Soma-discussion, and of the main proposals, *Periploca aphylla*, *Sarcostemma brevistigma* and *Ephedra vulgaris*, which, however, he does not see as capable of 'producing the effects described with regard to the Soma' ('Keine von diesen Pflanzen kann Wirkungen veranlassen, wie sie von dem Soma geschildert werden'). He rather thinks that it may have been a 'strong alcoholic drink created by fermentation from a plant'.[12] An English translation of Lewin's

[12] Lewin thus passes over – is probably unaware of – the fact that neither the Vedic nor the Iranian ritual have any place for a process of distillation which would be required to achieve a drink deserving to be called 'strong alcoholic'.

book was read by Aldous Huxley in 1931, and it inspired him to write *Brave New World* (1932), the satirical fiction of a state where, with an inversion of Marx's statement, 'opium is the religion of the people'. The 'opium' in Huxley's novel is a chemical substance which he calls 'Soma' and which, dependent on the dose, can bring someone a happy feeling, ego-transcending ecstasy, or a deep sleep like a 'complete and absolute holiday'.[13] In a 1931 newspaper article in which he refers to his discovery of that 'ponderous book by a German pharmacologist' (i.e. Lewin's 1927 *Encyclopaedia of Drugs*), Huxley says that 'probably the ancient Hindus used alcohol to produce religious ecstasy' (in Huxley 1977: 4), a statement apparently deriving from Lewin's hasty and unconvincing suggestion for the identification of Soma with alcohol. The same book also informed him that 'the Mexicans procured the beatific vision by eating a poisonous cactus' and that 'a toadstool filled the Shamans of Siberia with enthusiasm and endowed them with the gift of tongues.' In 1958: 99, however, Huxley mentions another plant as the possibly real Vedic Soma: 'The original Soma, from which I took the name of this hypothetical drug, was an unknown plant (possibly *Asclepias acida*) used by the ancient Aryan invaders of India in one of the most solemn of their religious rites.' His novel *Island* of 1963 gives a description of a more positive Utopian world in the form of a community that uses a drug not called Soma but *mokṣa*, and made out of 'toadstools'. It provides 'the full-blown mystical experience'.[14]

[13] In his *Brave New World Revisited* (1959: 99-100) Huxley states in retrospect: 'The Soma of Brave New World had none of the drawbacks of its Indian original. In small doses it brought a sense of bliss, in larger doses it made you see visions and, if you took three tablets, you would sink in a few minutes into refreshing sleep.'

[14] Two papers appearing in a recent volume on Aldous Huxley (Barfoot 2001) are of considerable, direct importance for the Soma-problem: Albrecht Wezler's confrontation of Huxley's ideas on 'psychedelic' drugs in India with presently available data and theories on the use of drugs, especially Soma, and, from quite different contexts, *bhāng* (Cannabis), as

THE MAIN SOMA-HAOMA CANDIDATES UNTIL THE 1960s

In the meantime, indologists, ethnologists, botanists and pharmacologists had continued discussing and researching various candidates for the 'real Soma-Haoma'. The main plants discussed are *Ephedra*, *Sarcostemma brevistigma*, and *Rhubarb*. In the latter theory, defended, e.g. by Stein 1931, the reddish juice of the plant is thought to be the basis of an alcoholic drink. In the introduction to his translation of the ninth Maṇḍala of the *Ṛgveda* (Geldner 1951, vol. III), K.F. Geldner says that the Soma-plant 'can only have been a kind of Ephedra'. Geldner (1853-1929) worked on the translation of the ninth and tenth Maṇḍalas in the last years of his life. He justified his view by noting that a sample (apparently of a plant used in the Haoma-ceremony) given to him in Bombay by Parsi priests was identified as Ephedra by the renowned botanist O. Stapf; he also referred to a publication of Aitchison (*Notes on Products of Western Afghanistan and North Eastern Persia*, not available to me) and to Modi 1922: 303. In earlier publications such as the one on the Zoroastrian religion (1926) and his textbook on Vedism and Brahmanism (1928), Geldner had remained quite silent on the botanical identity of the Haoma-Soma, he only presented the two as identical. Geldner's German *Ṛgveda* translation became widely available only several years after Second World War, but then it became the scholarly standard translation for the next so many decades.

means to mystical experience; and Wilhelm Halbfass' profound analysis of philosophical problems related to drug-induced mystical experiences according to Huxley and in Indian philosophy. Relevant for, though not directly dealing with, the *interpretation* of the Soma-experience by Huxley is Johannes Bronkhorst's discussion of Huxley's theory of a *philosophia perennis* consisting of features which all or most religions would share.

THE FLY-AGARIC (*AMANITA MUSCARIA*): A NEW CANDIDATE PRESENTED, CRITICIZED AND DEFENDED

An altogether new theory was launched by R. Gordon Wasson in a book that appeared in 1969.[15] Wasson (1898-1986) was an English banker as well as ethnobotanist and mycologist.[16] Together with his wife, he earlier published a book on 'mushrooms in Russian history' in 1957. Wasson's 1969 book on a 'mushroom of immortality' as the original Soma presents an impressive array of circumstantial evidence in the form of ethnographic and botanic data on the use of the *Amanita muscaria* (fly-agaric) by isolated tribes in the far north-west of Siberia. In other words, what was literary fiction in Huxley's novel *Island* appears now as a scholarly hypothesis.[17] However, what should count as substantial

[15] The book is also often referred to as appearing in 1968. In the copy in the library of the Kern Institute I searched in vain for the publication date. In Richard Evans Schultes' Foreword in Wasson 1972a we read that 'Mr. R. Gordon Wasson' brought out his *SOMA Divine Mushroom of Immortality* on 15 April 1969. But in 1986 Wasson writes (p. 26): 'At the end of 1968 or the beginning of 1969 our *SOMA* finally apeared ... ' I will stick here to 1969 as its publicaton date.

[16] J. Brough (1971: 332 n. 1) notes that 'Mr. Wasson . . . was for 10 years a Research Fellow of the Botanical Museum of Harvard University, now Honorary Research Fellow; also Honorary Research Associate and former member of the Board of Managers of the New York Botanical Garden.'

[17] Huxley and Wasson knew each other quite well. Cf. Wasson in an autobiographical passage, 1969: 175: 'I do not recall when the Soma possibility first drew my attention. . . . From 1955 on I was in intermittent correspondence with Aldous Huxley, and often when he visited New York he would come down to Wall Street and have lunch with me.' And cf. Huxley, in a letter to a friend written in 1957 (in Huxley 1977: 132): 'While I was in New York, I lunched with Wasson [. . . .] [H]e has put an immense amount of work into his subject, and the material brought together in his vast tomes is very curious and suggestive. However, he does, as you say, like to think that his mushrooms are somehow unique and infinitely superior to everything else. I tried to disabuse him. But he likes to feel that he has got hold of the One and Only psychodelic –

evidence in Wasson's hypothesis remains utterly unconvincing. Wasson wants to take only the R̥gvedic hymns into account, from which he selects statements that would describe the Soma-plant. The hymns, however, are employed in the context of elaborate rituals and are generally directed to certain gods, e.g. Indra, Agni, Soma. The praises of the god contain references to mythological elements regarding his powers, feats and origination. To the extent that hymns to Soma contain references to concrete events – that is, to the extent they do not refer to cosmological themes or to microcosmic implications – these usually concern the ritual sphere. Wasson takes these references as detailed descriptions of the plant in its natural habitat, which is demonstrably incorrect. By isolating short phrases eclectically, Wasson does indeed succeed in collecting a number of statements which can be applied to the fly-agaric and its life cycle in nature. While the verses are apparently formulated so as to be suggestive of additional meanings (to allow interpretations concerning man and the cosmos), the immediate context of the isolated phrases usually make a link with the growing mushroom far-fetched while the suitablility for the ritual context remains. Even if occasionally mention is made of the mountains as the place where the Soma grows, the hymns of the ninth book of the *R̥gveda*, which forms the main source of evidence for Wasson, deal with the Soma in the process of purification (*pávamāna*). As Brough observed in 1973: 22: 'the Vedic priests were concentrating on the ritual situation, and on the plant, presumably in a dried state, at the time of the ritual pressing. It is thus improbable that the Vedic 'epithets and tropes' which Wasson believed reflected aspects of the striking beauty of the living plant were inspired in this way'.[18] A number of reviews

accept no substitutes, none genuine unless sold with the signature of the inventor.'

[18] Similarly, Kuiper 1970: 282: 'Generally speaking, his [Wasson's] interesting attempt to interpret the Vedic evidence in the light of his novel theory encounters difficulties when the separate passages are considered in the context of Vedic mythological and ritualistic thought.'

of Wasson's book appeared from the hand of anthropologists, botanists, writers, indologists, and historians of religion.[19] Those who were too hesitant in accepting Wasson's central thesis, Kuiper and Brough, received a rejoinder (Wasson 1970 and 1972a), where, however, we find repetitions of his earlier statements and more of the same but no indication that the problems pointed out by the reviewers were understood, let alone that these problems are convincingly addressed.[20]

Kuiper illustrates the point with Wasson's interpretation of *R̥gveda* IX.86.44c (Wasson 1969: 41) and of *R̥gveda* IX.97.9d (Wasson 1969, plate VIII a and b). Brough discusses Wasson's interpretations of IX.97.9d, IX.71.2d, IX.70.7d, IX.75.2 and of notions recurring in *R̥gveda*-translations such as 'the udder and Soma', 'Soma's 'head'', 'the single eye', 'mainstay of the sky', 'the filtres', and the Vedic *sah/asrabhr̥ṣṭi*.

[19] A list of 'principal reviews' of Wasson 1969 appears at the end of Wasson 1972a.

[20] Wasson goes so far as to indulge in near-abusive rhetorics on the reviewers who do not accept his hypothesis. Thus, in 1972a he writes: 'These two statements, Brough's and Kuiper's, reveal the absurd isolation in which some Vedic scholars live by choice.' Before embarking on his investigation of the points presented by Wasson, Brough (1971: 331) discusses the state of the art in the Soma-Haoma discussion before Wasson 1969 and observes '. . . and the opinion is widely held that the problem is insoluble'. In almost paranoiac fashion Wasson (1972a: 10) perceives here a conspiracy of 'Brough and other Vedic scholars' to be satisfied with the 'anonymity of Soma' as 'a built-in element in Vedic studies' and to want to keep it like that. As for the statement of Kuiper that enraged Wasson, it is: 'This means that the search for "the original Soma" might lead us far beyond the field of Indo-Iranian studies proper' (Kuiper 1970: 284). As linguist and as mythologist of the Indian area and of Indo-European cultures, Kuiper himself is habituated to 'go beyond the field of Indo-Iranian studies proper'. Immediately preceding this statement Kuiper is discussing aspects of Nordic myths relevant to the Soma-issue. The implication which Wasson connects with this statement is hence preposterous: '. . . as though such excursions were dangerous temptations to be avoided.' Apparently in a more balanced state of mind and with a strong sense of the importance of his own researches he writes elsewhere in a recapitulation of his argument for non-

Separate mention is to be made of Part Two of Wasson's book (pp. 93-147), which is written by indologist Wendy Doniger O'Flaherty and is entitled 'The Post-Vedic History of the Soma Plant'. This part is valuable for its discussion of researches on Soma and Haoma by Western scholars since the end of the eighteenth century to the time of her writing. The section on 'the Brāhmaṇas and the Śrautasūtras' (pp. 95-8), concerning a crucial episode in Soma's 'post-Vedic history' for which extensive material is available, is impressionistic and eclectic and hence defective,[21] but in spite of this both Doniger O'Flaherty and Wasson refer to it in their attempt to prove the absence of direct knowledge of Soma in this period.

Apart from its importance for the study of the use of the fly-agaric by tribes in distant north-east Siberia,[22] Wasson's book

---

indologists (1972b: 208): 'Professor F.B.J. Kuiper of Leiden is a thousand times right in saying that "the complexities of the problem should not . . . be underestimated."' He adds that the identification of Soma must take the seeker far beyond the confines of Indo-Iranian studies proper. This is where I have gone.' It is in any case ironic that Kuiper's review which infuriated Wasson in 1972a was read as an acceptance of Wasson's thesis as probable by Frits Staal in 1983, I: 106. Kuiper does conclude his discussion on a non-committal but quite positive tone when he writes: 'Wasson, with his unique knowledge of the use of hallucinogens in Eurasia, may be perfectly right in assuming that the original Soma plant was the *Amanita muscaria*, but to prove this the evidence of the Rigveda would seem to lack decisive force.'

[21] While Kashikar 1990 does more justice to the important and extensive branch of literature of this period, a comprehensive overview and study of relevant passages is still a desideratum.

[22] Wasson's enthusiastic presentation on the use of the fly-agaric with a view to identify them with the Vedic Soma may have to be amended in some respects. Cf. the conclusion of Nyberg 1995: 392-3 on *Amanita muscaria* as a candidate for Soma, especially his third point: 'In my opinion, *Amanita muscaria* is unsuitable for any identification with *soma/haoma* on the following grounds: 1. The mushroom produces visions, sleep and/or a peaceful state of intoxication; the duration of effects is short; 2. *soma/haoma* is prepared from stems or stalks, which

forms an undeniable landmark in the Soma-Haoma discussion. However, while initially he did receive more positive reactions to his central thesis from some indological reviewers (Bareau, Ingalls and Kramrisch), it hardly ever received full-fledged support from later Indologists writing on the subject. One important point is, however, widely accepted: the Soma might very well have been a hallucinogen. The line of reasoning underlying the argument presented in Wasson 1969 was: in the light of the utterances of the Vedic authors, Soma cannot have been alcoholic, it must have been a hallucinogen.[23] In his review of Wasson 1969, Brough (1971: 360f) made an important observation. Quoting from Wasson's evidence on the consumption of fly-agaric among tribes in North-East Siberia, Brough points out that there are repeated references to coma induced by the fly-agaric. Those who consume the mushroom attain 'an ecstatic stupor' or are transported into 'a state of unconsciousness'. Being 'in a stupor from three sun-dried agarics' the hero of one of Wasson's sources 'is unable to respond to the call to arms. But time passes and the urgency grows, and when the messengers press their appeal to throw off his stupor he finally calls for his arms'. Brough rightly observes: 'Here, it would seem, is a plant whose effects are totally unsuitable to stimulate

---

most probably should be regarded as fibrous (Brough 1971; Falk 1989) while the fleshy stems of *A. muscaria* contain only very small amounts of the pharmacologically active compounds, which are concentratred instead in the mushroom cap (these are the only parts of the mushroom used in northern Siberia); 3. culturally, the use of *A. muscaria* occurs only among the shamanistic peoples of northern Eurasia and it is neither a required part of any shamanistic rite, nor regarded as holy in them. On the contrary, only the "weak" shaman or a "recreational user" has to resort to the use of the mushroom (Eliade 1964: 210; Saar 1991); 4. the mushroom must have been rare in any of the proposed Indo-Iranian homelands. In contrast, when the use of *soma/haoma* began, the Aryans seem to have been inhabiting a region where the to-date unidentified plant was abundant.'

[23] See especially Wasson 1969, Part One, chapter IV: 'Soma Was Not Alcoholic'.

Indra and human warriors for battle.' In his answer to the problem indicated by Brough, Wasson sneers at Brough's self-admitted lack of specialist qualifications in chemistry and pharmacology and retorts (1972a: 15): 'Wine as one of the Elements in the Mass is analogous. From earliest times (indeed since Noah's days!) wine has been known to cause nausea, vomiting, and coma; yet its sacramental rôle stands unchallenged.'

The situation is, however, not the same. The 'ecstatic stupor' and 'state of unconsciousness' appear in Wasson's anecdotes of the use of fly-agaric as quite regular effects appearing quite soon after the consumption of doses that according to the descriptions are the normal ones (cf. also Nyberg 1995: 391). In the case of wine normal consumption seems rather accompanied by a whole range of effects from exhileration to drowsiness, while 'nausea, vomiting, and coma' befalls only those who consume it in great excess (or who drink bad wine). It is also striking that hallucinations and visions are reported in a considerable number of Wasson's *Amanita muscaria* anecdotes; they apparently occur quite soon after the consumption of the active substance of the mushrooms, and seem to be part of the experience actually sought by the consumer. Brough (1971: 361) draws attention to Ephedra, and to ephedrine isolated from *Ephedra sinica* (Ma Huang). Ephedrine, according to Brough, 'is a powerful stimulant, and would thus be a more plausible preparation for warriors about to go into battle than the fly-agaric, which is a depressant'.

In Wasson's presentation the choice was between alcohol and a hallucinogen. In Brough's formulation we have to choose between a hallucinogen and a stimulant, whereas an alcoholic drink is for him not a suitable candidate for the substance causing the Vedic people to attain exhilaration (*máda*). These seem to be the major options taken into consideration in the post-Wasson era of the Soma-Haoma discussion. In 1975 Frits Staal appended a discussion of the Soma-issue to his book on the exploration of mysticism. Staal is quite impressed by Wasson's argument (1975: 204: 'his identification stands in splendid isolation as the only, and therefore the best, theory'). But he shows that he is not entirely unaware of its methodological shortcomings (1975: 202):

> The only weakness that seems to be apparent for Wasson's theory is a certain unfalsifiability. A good theory should be liable to falsification. Theories which are true come what may and which can never be refuted by facts are uninformative, tautologous, or empty. In fact, apparent counterexamples to Wasson's theory can always be interpreted as consistent with the theory. When opponents point out, for example, that there are descriptions in the Veda which do not fit a mushroom, Wasson replies that the identity of the Soma was intentionally hidden by the Brahmans, or that these descriptions fit creepers or other substitutes.

Staal thus saw that Wasson takes the Veda at once as the document on the basis of which the Soma can be identified as a mushroom, and as a testimony of concerted attempts of Brahmins to mystify and hide this identity: a very flexible employment indeed of a source taken as crucial evidence.[24] Staal here distinguishes between only two options for Soma, alcohol and a hallucinogen, thus neglecting the relevance of psychoactive substances which have a primarily stimulant and ecstasy promoting effect (without excluding the occurrence of hallucinations or visions). In his book on the Agnicayana ritual (1983, I: 106), he formulates his position with reference to Wasson's thesis as follows: 'Wasson's thesis implies, but is not implied by, a weaker thesis, namely that the original Vedic Soma was a hallucinogenic plant [i.e. not necessarily a mushroom, J.H.]. I regard this as the most important part of

[24] In his 1969 book Wasson's strategy is to distinguish between the *R̥gveda* and later texts, and between a later part of the *R̥gveda* and an earlier one (the latter comprises the ninth or Soma-Maṇḍala). In his answers to Brough, however, he suggests (1972a: 14) that the crucial episode of the pressing of the Soma-plants with stones or stampers is adventitious, even if references to the pounding and the pressing stones and stampers occur dispersed throughout the different sections of the *R̥gveda*, including those which Wasson uses for his positive identifications.

Wasson's hypothesis. . . . 'The restriction of possible psychoactive candidates to substances known as hallucinogens, however, is unjustified.

A substitute for Soma mentioned in some of the ritual texts is *pūtī́ka*. The *pūtī́ka* is also one of the additives in the clay of the *pravargya* pot – an object that is central in an esoteric, priestly ritual, the *pravargya* (cf. van Buitenen 1968, Houben 1991 and 2000). In an article published in 1975 (later appearing as the third chapter in Wasson et al. 1986), Stella Kramrisch sought to prove that this *pūtī́ka* was a mushroom having psychotropic effects. According to her (1975: 230), 'Pûtika [*sic*], the foremost, and possibly the only direct surrogate for Soma, is a mushroom. When the fly-agaric no longer was available, another mushroom became its substitute. . . . The identification of Pūtika [*sic*], the Soma surrogate, supplies strong evidence that Soma indeed was a mushroom.' Kramrisch's identification goes via the mushroom called *putka* by the Santals in Eastern India. As Kuiper (1984) pointed out, the linguistic connection suggested by Kramrisch does not hold. As pointed out in Houben 1991: 110, the ritual texts prescribing the *pūtī́ka* as an additive to the clay of the *pravargya* pot present it as an *óṣadhi* (*Kaṭha Āraṇyaka* 2.11+) and as something providing a firm basis from which he can attack the demon Vṛ̥tra (*Taittirīya Āraṇyaka* 2.9-10). Like other additives such as the animal hairs and the material of an ant-hill, it was not exclusively symbolic as Kramrisch believes, but had no doubt a pragmatic basis in providing extra strength to the clay pot which is to withstand extremely high temperatures in the ritual of the heated milk offering. There is hence no basis to regard the *pūtī́ka* as a mushroom, which takes away the additional evidence that Soma were a mushroom.

Rainer Stuhrmann 1985 briefly reviews the Soma-discussion since Wasson 1969. He notes that critics of Wasson are right in maintaining that it is not possible to classify Soma, but that they went too far in entirely excluding a mushroom. He points out that even if the colour pictures which Wasson attaches to phrases from the *Ṛgveda* are seducingly suggestive, the questionable nature of Wasson's interpretation of the verses must be apparent to anyone who reads Geldner's or Renou's translation of the hymns in their entirety. According to him, there are nevertheless three points that can be considered settled:

1. From the Brāhmaṇas on, the original Soma was replaced by several other plants, and such substitution is already indicated in the tenth book of the *Ṛgveda.*
2. The original Soma cannot have been alcoholic, because there would not have been time for the fermentation of the sap after the pressing; moreover, both the *Ṛgveda* and the *Avesta* contrast the effects of Soma-Haoma with the alcoholic *súrā.*
3. The plant grows in the mountains.

Stuhrmann emphasizes that it is important to investigate the type of intoxication produced by Soma and to conclude on that basis what type of plant was used as Soma. He observes that several characteristics of the Soma-hymns, such as their 'formless tangle of images and mystic fantasies',[25] importance of optic qualities in epithets of Soma, can be well explained by hallucinogenic influence. Hence he concludes that in case Soma would not be the fly-agaric it must at least be a plant containing alkaloids.

Stuhrmann's argument is carefully phrased, but it is in several respects imprecise and contains a few crucial non-sequiturs. Stuhrmann states that from the Brāhmaṇas onwards the Soma was replaced by substitutes – a distorted representation of facts that goes back to Wasson and Doniger O'Flaherty: as we have seen, it is true that substitutes are mentioned, but there is also still an awareness of the real Soma and of the fetching of Soma from near by in case the 'top quality' Soma of mountain Mūjavat is stolen. The view that substitution would have started at the time of the composition of the tenth book of the *Ṛgveda* is also already found

[25] Stuhrmann 1985: 91 quotes here Oldenberg's expression (1894: 182) 'formloses Gewirr von Bildern und mystischen Phantasmen'.

with Wasson, and likewise, Wasson supports his statement with a reference to *R̥gveda* X.85.3

sómaṁ manyate papivā́n yát sampiṁṣanty óṣadhim ।
sómaṁ yáṁ brahmā́ṇo vidur ná tásyāśnāti káś caná ॥

One believes to have drunk the Soma when they press out the herb.
The Soma which the Brahmans know, no-one consumes of that one.

It is difficult to draw from this verse the conclusion that the Soma is not a herb, as Stuhrmann tries to do (1985: 91 n. 3), apart from being something more abstract in the knowledge of Brahmans. Since the word *óṣadhi* (herb) would otherwise contradict Wasson's mushroom theory, he was forced to see in the first two *pādas* of the verse a reference to a substitute, and in the last two *pādas* a reference to the real Soma held secret by the Brahmans. This in itself is already a quite contorted interpretation. In the larger context of the hymn it proves to be untenable. The first verse of this well-known hymn of the marriage of Sūryā́ (fem.) with Soma (masc.) says that Soma is placed in heaven, and hence makes it immediately clear that verse three presents a contrast between the pressing of the Soma-plant on the earth and the Soma as moon which latter cannot be consumed directly. There is no suggestion of a substitute, only of an additional insight of the Brahmans with regard to a plant (*óṣadhi*) which can be known and seen by all.

As for the exclusion of alcohol: the contrast with *súrā* is indeed there. Some process of fermentation or alteration of substances in the Soma plant can nevertheless not be entirely excluded in the period between their plucking and the employment in the ritual where the Soma-stalks are sprinkled on a number of consecutive days preceding the pressing. As for the mountains as the place of the Soma, it is clear that this applies to top-quality Soma. The *Avesta* (10.17) speaks of Soma occurring on mountains and in valleys (where the latter may, indeed, still be on high altitudes).

Next, Stuhrmann wants to infer the type of relevant plant-substance from the type of intoxication produced by Soma.

Stuhrmann refers here to *Ṛgveda* X.119 which is generally interpreted as the self-praise of Indra who became drunk from drinking Soma. The speaker in the poem makes statements such as: after having drunk the Soma, one of my wings is in heaven and the other is being dragged on the earth. While the whole hymn could be seen as poetic fiction, one may indeed see here a reference to a hallucination or distorted perception, and the Soma would have a place in the causal nexus leading to it. This does not mean that Soma must have been a hallucinogen in the strict, modern sense of the term, especially because references to Soma outside this exceptional hymn are not normally indicative of serious hallucinations on the part of the authors. The latter point was argued by Falk (1989), who, however, went too far in trying to completely exclude the possibility that *Ṛgveda* X.119 points to a hallucinatory experience. Even if we follow Stuhrmann for the moment in his acceptance of a hallucinogenic effect of Soma, his conclusion at the end that the Soma plant must have contained alkaloids is both too wide and too narrow. Even if alkaloids often have psychoactive properties, instead of being predominantly hallucinogen they also may have quite different properties such as CNS-stimulant, sleep-inducing, etc. On the other hand, hallucinations may have a basis in other substances than alkaloids: any substance that can interact with the biochemistry of the brain may induce distorted perceptions (among modern products petrol or gasoline would be an example; cf. already Lewin 1927: 268f). In addition, a lack of nutritients through fasting and thirsting may induce hallucinations as well. The same applies to the deprivation of sleep. Most importantly, whether a substance or the absence of substances does indeed produce a hallucination will usually depend to a large extent on the physiological and psychological condition of the subject, whereas the nature of the hallucination or vision will depend on his psychology and cultural background.

That the Soma was not a hallucinogen but a stimulant, probably from a species of Ephedra, was the view elaborated and defended by Harry Falk in 1987 at the World Sanskrit Conference in Leiden. In his paper (1989) he places previous theories in three categories:

(1) Soma is hallucinogenic; (2) Soma needs fermentation and is alcoholic; (3) Soma is a stimulant. Emphasizing the Vedic indications for a stimulant effect of Soma which contributes to staying awake all night,[26] he concludes that Soma-Haoma must again be identified with Ephedra. To establish his position he not only points out the properties of Ephedra and places in Vedic literature indicating wakefulness and aphrodisiac effect in connection with Soma, but also argues that the *R̥gveda* contains no references to hallucinations, not even in *R̥gveda* X.119 that is normally taken in that sense. (In the present issue George Thompson argues, convincingly I think, for a restoration of the 'hallucinatory' character of this hymn.)

A FRESH LOOK AT THE IRANIAN EVIDENCE AND A NEW HALLUCINOGENIC CANDIDATE

The same year 1989 saw the publication of the book *Haoma and Harmaline* by David Stophlet Flattery and Martin Schwartz. Here the authors base themselves mainly on Iranian evidence and provide an extensive and careful argument that the Haoma- and Soma-plant was in fact Harmel, which contains an alkaloid with hallucinogenic properties, harmaline (as well as harmine). The authors are aware (1989: 67-8) that for centuries Zoroastrians of central Iran have been using Ephedra – which they call *hom* – together with another plant – parts from a twig of the pomegranate tree – in their Haoma rituals. From the fact that in Nepal Ephedra is called *somalatā* (Soma creeper) they infer that Ephedra was the plant used as Soma before it was replaced by Sarcostemma which grows in tropical areas of India and which was in use by Brahmins encountered by the Europeans in nineteenth- century India (1989: 69). Yet, they think that Ephedra cannot have been the Haoma-Soma itself. For this, they have one main reason: we do

[26] Falk extends his argument too far when he says (1989: 82) not only that Soma creates wakefulness, but also that it originally must have been offered to Indra during the night.

not see that contemporaneous Zoroastrian priests using Ephedra become intoxicated. According to Flattery's and Schwartz's judgement,

> sauma must have been commonly known in ancient Iranian society as an intoxicating plant in order for the credibility of the sauma ceremonies, and the authority of Iranian priests claimed from them, to have been maintained. Despite being commonly designated *haoma* (and the like), Ephedra is without suitable psychoactive potential in fact (and is not regarded in traditional ethnobotany as having any psychoactive properties at all) and, therefore, it cannot have been believed to be the means to an experience from which the priests could claim religious authority or widely believed to be the essential ingredient of an *intoxicating* extract.

They conclude that (1989: 74)

> It is therefore neither likely that Ephedra was a substitute for sauma [Soma-Haoma] nor that it was sauma itself, yet, according to both Iranian and Indian traditions, Ephedra was essentially linked with the extract drunk during the ceremonies. The only way of reconciling this fact with the considerations of the preceding paragraphs is to view Ephedra as an archaic additive to the extract. Thus, Ephedra too would have been a soma-/haoma-'pressed out (plant)', though not the only (or fundamental) one.

The argument is carefully structured. However, it may be observed that their information regarding the properties of Ephedra and its alkaloids such as Ephedrine was apparently incomplete or outdated. It is true that Ephedrine and related alkaloids are best-known for their use in the case of asthma as well as low blood-pressure (hypotension), but it is since long known that it is also a general stimulant of the central nervous system. Hence its psychiatric use, e.g., in manic depressive disorder.[27] What the authors may not have been aware of in 1989

[27] Cf. Madaus 1938: 1263; on the modern use of stimulants in psychiatry with brief references to their history as well as to Ephedra: Fawcett and Busch 1998.

is that Ephedra would soon be marketed as the 'natural' (hence supposedly safe, and in any case less restricted and regulated) alternative for the popular designer drug Ecstasy (XTC).[28] It is not clear on which impressionistic basis they conclude that the priests are not 'intoxicated' nor what would qualify in their eyes as 'intoxication', i.e. the *maδa* of the Avestans and the *mada* of the Vedic Indians.[29]

THE EVIDENCE FROM BRAHMANIC TEXTS AND RITUAL

In 1990 the renowned specialist in Śrauta-literature C.G. Kashikar published his *Identification of Soma*, in which he argues for Ephedra as the original plant used in the Vedic and Zoroastrian rituals.[30] The main importance of this publication lies in the discussion of evidence of Vedic ritual texts which are chronologically immediately following the *Ṛgveda* (the latter forming the point of departure for Wasson's identification). Several Yajurvedic Saṁhitās, Brāhmaṇas and Śrautasūtras not only refer to the ceremonial purchase of Soma (where the seller is asked whether it comes from the Mūjavat mountain), but also to the contingency that the Soma is snatched away before the sacrifice starts. In that case new Soma is to be procured from the nearest spot. Only if Soma cannot be found the texts prescribe that substitutes are

[28] Cf. the discussion of 3,4-Methylenedioxymethamphetamine (MDMA) and its pharmacological properties by Shulgin and Nichols 1978. The authors are aware of its 'occasional and erratic appearance in the illicit street drug market', but apparently not yet familiar with its later popular name Ecstasy or XTC. Briefly on the relation between chemical structure and psychopharmacological effects of MDMA and related compounds: Fawcett and Busch 1998: 505-6.

[29] Cf. n. 36 below.

[30] Together with Asko Parpola, Kashikar published an overview of recent Śrauta traditions in India in vol. 2 of Staal's Agni, and remarked (Kashikar and Parpola 1983: 248) that for the original Soma '[t]he most likely candidate seems to be some species of Ephedra'.

to be resorted to.[31] It may be assumed that the Soma that is procured from nearby is of lower quality than the stolen Soma from mountain Mūjavat, otherwise it would have been employed in the first place. Several Śrautasūtras prescribe Soma-juice in the daily offering of the Agnihotra for those sacrificers who desire the lustre of Brahman. This points on the one hand to authors being settled near the northern part of the Indian subcontinent where Soma was still within reach; on the other hand it is clear that Soma is a plant that has a wider habitat than only a few mountains. The daily Soma of the Brahmins can hardly have been the precious top-quality Soma from mount Mūjavat required in the Agniṣṭoma. As for the botanical side of the issue, Kashikar relies mainly on research of Qazilbash and Mahdihassan (their publications, mainly appearing between 1960 and 1986, were unavailable to me at the moment of concluding this introduction).

In a review of Kashikar 1990, Thomas Oberlies 1995 makes some important remarks, apart from giving additional bibliographic references. Oberlies accepts with Kashikar that the Brāhmaṇas and Śrautasūtras are aware of *some* plant being the real Soma. However, there is insufficient evidence for a positive identification. Referring to Brough 1971, Kashikar had rejected Wasson's identification of Soma as the fly-agaric, a mushroom. He then simply takes the three main remaining plants that have been suggested by scholars as being the Soma, and by exclusion of the first two, *Sarcostemma brevistigma* and *Periploca aphylla*, he arrives at the conclusion that it must have been Ephedra. Even when the Brāhmaṇas and Śrautasūtras seem to suggest awareness of Soma plant as the unequivocally real Soma, Oberlies doubts whether it can be assumed that this was also the plant used in the *Ṛgveda*.

[31] Doniger O'Flaherty's brief section on the Brāhmaṇas and Śrautasūtras in her discussion of the post-Vedic history of the Soma-plant, was therefore misleading in that she presented these texts as only speaking of substitutes whereas it is clear that their authors presuppose those who employ the texts to be well aware of the distinction between the real Soma-plant and its substitutes.

This would only apply if there were an uninterrupted continuity between *Ṛgveda* and Yajurvedic texts. Oberlies mentions three problems with the identification of Soma with Ephedra:

1. The reddish-yellow (rot-gelb) colour is lacking (only the berries of Ephedra are red but the berries are not mentioned in the texts).
2. Juice pressed from Soma does not have a milky character, whereas the *Ṛgveda* speaks of 'milking the (Soma-)stalks' and of Soma as the cow's first milk after calving (*pīyū́ṣa* 'beestings').
3. Oberlies' most fundamental problem with the Ephedra-identification is that Ephedra does not have the required hallucinogenic effect that is attested in the Ṛgvedic hymns.

Oberlies concludes his discussion with the observation that it is the interpretation of the Soma-intoxication on the part of the Vedic poets in the context of their referential frame which should receive more interest and attention, rather than to lay excessive emphasis on the nature of the substance (cf. Oberlies 1998: 166). Similarly, Tatjana Elizarenkova (1996) has emphasized the importance of the style and structure of Ṛgvedic texts behind which there are insufficient traces of the direct impact of a psychoactive substance to make identification possible. Indeed, the importance of the cultural 'construction' of textual representations of personal, including mystical, experience should not be underestimated. And what applies to the study of mystical experience will apply equally to a large domain of experiences resulting from psychoactive substances. After earlier generations of authors with what may be called various 'essentialist' and 'perennialist' approaches to mystic experience (William James, Rudolph Otto, Mircea Eliade, Aldous Huxley), a constructivist paradigm found wide acceptance in academic scholarship in the latter half of the twentieth century; it has found committed and persistent expression in a series of collective volumes on mysticism directed by Steven T. Katz (1978, 1983, 1992, 2000).

In spite of his affinity with a constructivist approach when he argues for studying the Vedic poet first of all in his religious context, from Oberlies' third, most fundamental (*wesentlichste*) problem, it is clear that it is his unpronounced presupposition that indications for hallucinations in the *Ṛgveda* point directly to the use of a substance having hallucinogenic effects. As we have seen above, convincing indications for hallucinations, apart from the quite explicit *Ṛgveda* X.119, are rare, and even if these should not be explained away, they are to be weighed against other indications which point to an absence of hallucination, but rather to a powerful stimulant suitable to divine and human warriors who cannot afford to perceive things that have no basis in objective reality.

The second point is to be studied against the background of Ṛgvedic poetic usage, where among other things thoughts can be obtained from an udder (5.44.13), or where an inspired poem can be compared with a dairy cow (3.57.1), or where there is no problem in speaking of the 'udder of the father' (3.1.9). To satisfy the literalists who insist that, even with the extensive evidence that 'milking' is a central and flexible metaphor for 'deriving something precious from', *pīyū́ṣa* (beestings) (formerly also spelt 'biestings', medical name 'colostrum') must absolutely be taken as having not only relational but also physical characteristics of milk, it can be pointed out that the long sessions of beating the Soma-plant with the stampers or press-stones can be expected to give a pulpy-watery mixture in a first pressing which may have looked like the creamy fluid with special nutritious and protective ingredients that a cow produces for a new born calf. Such pulpy-watery mixture is what I saw come forth from the pounding of the Soma-substitute called *pūtīka* (probably *Sarcostemma brevistigma*) in Soma sacrifices in Maharashtra and New Delhi. Several ideas may hence underlie the use of the term *pīyū́ṣa*: the first juice appearing from the pressing is 'beestings' by virtue of its being the first fluid produced from the stalks; it is 'beestings' by virtue of its pulpy-watery, hence somewhat cream-like, character; it is 'beestings' on account of its nutritious and protective potency.

Finally, those invoking the Ṛgvedic references to beestings as an argument against Ephedra seem to have overlooked that the cow's first milk after calving is usually not white but may have all kinds of colours, from yellowish to greenish and purple, which does not constitute a contraindication for its quality. This applies at least to the cows common in Europe, as I understood from a well-informed relative.[32] The metaphoric flexibility of terms in the sphere of 'milking' in any case prevents *pīyū́ṣa* from being an argument against the Ephedra candidate. As for the problem of the reddish-yellow colour attributed to Soma: in Oberlies' brief statement, where he mixes up 'reddish-yellow (rot-gelb)' and 'red (rot)' or at least opaquely shifts from the one to the other, there is nothing that would invalidate Brough's 1971 extensive discussion of the colour-term in his criticism of Wasson.

A particularly problematic part in Oberlies' argument lies in his attempt to disconnect the evidence of Brāhmaṇas and Śrautasūtras from that of the *Ṛgveda*. Oberlies observes (1995: 236) that Kashikar presupposes that the plant used as Soma according to the Brāhmaṇas and Śrautasūtras is identical with that of the *Ṛgveda*. However, according to Oberlies this would apply only if there were an uninterrupted continuity from the *Ṛgveda* to the *Yajurveda* with regard to beliefs, rituals and cults. Since this cannot be accepted (Oberlies asks rhetorically: who could seriously believe this, with exclamation mark), statements in the Brāhmaṇas and Śrautasūtras would prove little for the *Ṛgveda* (with exclamation mark). A few paragraphs further (1995: 237), he acknowledges that Kashikar's conclusions provide new insights for the Brāhmaṇas. Here, the Soma may have been Ephedra. But, he adds, this was in all probability not the 'original' (with exclamation mark).

[32] A Maharashtrian sweet dish made out of beestings is reported to have a light yellowish colour (Madhav Deshpande, Indology Discussion Archive 11-02-2003, and, off-list, Vishal Agrawal 12-02-2003, in response to a question I asked on the Indology list – 11-02-2003 http://www.ucl.ac.uk/~ucgadkw/indology.html).

In spite of all the exclamation marks, Oberlies' line of reasoning is neither self-evident nor convincing. At first, he makes the *general statement* that we cannot assume there was an uninterrupted continuity from the *R̥gveda* to the *Yajurveda* with regard to beliefs, rituals and cults. On the next page, it is suddenly *most probable* that there is no continuity *in the specific case* of the knowledge of the Soma-plant. This is like observing first that one cannot be sure that traffic rules in Italy are the same as in France, and next that it is most probable that when the French drive on the right side of the road the Italians must drive left. It is well known that there are indeed important distinctions between the *R̥gveda* and the *Yajurveda* and subsequent sources, including distinctions with regard to the ritual. However, these distinctions appear only against the background of a massive flood of elementary and structural continuities, which in many cases extend even to proto-Indo-Iranian times. It is also well known that ritual in particular has a tendency to be conservative, even when interpretations and belief systems change. In the beginning days of Indology, scholars like Roth have emphasized the independence of the *R̥gveda* from the later ritual texts. Vedic hymns would be expressions of 'natural' lyrics which had little to do with the detailed liturgical practice as found in later texts. Close studies of scholars have in the meantime shown that there are numerous continuities and that the large majority of R̥gvedic hymns suit ritual contexts which are still part of the 'classical' ritual system as found in the Yajurvedic texts (cf. Gonda 1975: 83ff and 1978). In addition, in several specific cases such as the animal sacrifice (Bosch 1985) and the *pravargya* (Houben 2000), the basic continuities and structural changes have been demonstrated in detail. In the case of the Soma-ritual, pervading not only the ninth Maṇḍala but the entire *R̥gveda*, a comprehensive study and reconstruction of its R̥gvedic form is still a desideratum even if we have an important preliminary study in the form of Bergaigne's 'Recherches sur l'histoire de la liturgie védique' (1889; cf. also Renou 1962 and Witzel 1997: 288ff). In the light of this background of continuities, Oberlies' gratuitous assumption that there must be discontinuity in the case of the plant that is central in the most dominant Ṛgvedic Soma ritual is unsound. In the light of what we know of ritual in general and Vedic ritual and culture and in particular a much more reasonable starting point will be to assume that there is continuity unless there is an indication to the contrary. Such indications pointing to a rupture in the knowledge of a specific Soma-plant, as briefly indicated in Kashikar 1990, are not found in classical Yajurvedic texts which continue to refer the practising Brahman to an identifiable real Soma-plant even if he is occasionally allowed to sacrifice with a substitute.

A position somewhat parallel to the view of Oberlies was adopted by Frits Staal, who recently devoted an article to 'the case of Soma' (Staal 2001).[33] In his usual challenging and stimulating style, Staal argues that the elaborate Soma ritual as known from classical sources replaces an earlier phase where the 'real' Soma was known, and where ritualization was much less than later on. Hence the title of the article: How a psychoactive substance becomes a ritual. Again, in my view without sufficient basis two specific changes are assumed in the transition from Ṛgvedic ritual to the ritual of the Śrautasūtras: a loss in the knowledge of the original Soma and an increase in ritualization. He summarizes his main hypothesis in the form of a mathematical formula:

$$\text{ritualization} \times \text{psychoactivity} = S$$

where S is a constant. Unfortunately, no data are offered to substantiate this formula. The fact that the Śrautasūtras are later than the *Ṛgveda* neither means that ritual was absent in Ṛgvedic times nor that it was 'less' (in whichever way one may want to measure it) – even if there have been undeniable *transformations* as for instance in the transition from family-wise to school-wise organized ritual and religion, and the transition in the direction of a more *Yajurveda* dominated ritual. Even if there seems to have been more room for Ṛgvedic poetic creativity in earlier

[33] I thank the author for kindly sending me this paper on a subject about which we have discussed at a few occasions.

times, the activity of these poets followed strict ritual patterns and rules which are nowadays not known in detail but they are reflecting in regularities in the poetic productions. Since a substance may be 'psychoactive' in various dimensions, nothing can be said about its general relation with ritualization – if at all we would have sufficient data about the latter in different stages of its development, and if at all, with all those hypothetical data, the latter would be quantifiable. The terms ritualization and psychoactivity remain unquantified in Staal's article and are probably fundamentally unquantifiable the way they are used. Staal's formula may hence be understood in a 'metaphorically mathematical' sense, a bit like Bierstadt's proposal to take political and social power to be the product of 'men × resources × organization' (Bierstadt 1950 as referred to in Rappaport 1999: 473 n. 13). Even in such a 'metaphorically mathematical' sense, Staal's formula remains problematic – but can it perhaps be split into acceptable subformulas? One disturbing factor interfering with the phenomenon which Staal tries to catch in a formula is that ritual structure, including ritual utterances of linguistic forms, may itself be conducive to 'psychoactive' results.[34] More substantial problems arise on account of the fact that there are psychoactive substances which produce effects in a specific dimension such that its increase is correlated not with a decrease but with an *increase* of a subject's need for 'ritualistic' or 'compulsive' actions.[35] There are, moreover, wider theoretical

[34] In fact, this is a point in Staal's own argument twenty-six years earlier: Staal 1975, e.g. p. 195: 'So far, the following causes may be assumed to be conducive to mystical experiences: birth, meditation, asceticism, drugs, mantras, yantras, special devices like kaṣiṇa, *rituals*, devotion to a deity' (my emphasis, J.H.).

[35] Cf. already Lewin 1927: 180 on the effect of alkaloids in Belladonna and Datura: 'Ein Schneider, der unter den Einfluss von Belladonna und Datura gekommen war, zeigte die übliche Pupillenerweiterung neben Krämpfen. Nachdem diese nachgelassen hatten, setzte er sich im Bette so zurecht, als wäre er auf einem Schneidertisch, und manipulierte,

problems with the hypothesis and formula. Even when precise data generally become less and less if we go further back in time, there are theoretical reasons to assume that ritualization was more rather than less if we gradually approach the pre-human stage in the evolution of the human animal. Staal himself (1989: 110ff, 279ff) argued that ritual, which man shares with birds and other animals, precedes language as we know it with its lexical meanings, characteristic for humans. After having pointed out similarities between syntactic rules in language and ritual, he finds various reasons to believe that ritual is the cause: 'this suggests that the recursiveness which is the main characteristic of the syntax of human language has a ritual origin' (Staal 1989: 112). In language, syntax would be older than semantics (ibid.). Referring to the 'unenunciated chant' of the Sāmavedins and to meditation *mantras*, Staal observes: 'I am inclined to believe that what we witness here is not a curious collection of exotic facts, but a remnant or resurgence of a pre-linguistic stage of development, during which man or his ancestors used sound in a purely syntactic or ritual manner' (ibid.: 113). Staal also argued in detail that the similarity between Vedic *mantras* and bird songs are greater than that between *mantras* and ordinary meaning (ibid.: 279-93). The continuity with animal ritual has been argued for and demonstrated from quite a different angle by Walter Burkert, who took ancient Greek ritual as his starting point (cf. Burkert 1979 and 1996).

Against this theoretical background it is not convincing to let the Ṛgvedic Soma-ritual start in a romantic era in which man has direct religious experience through psychoactive substances and is not yet living a life replete with ritualizations.

---

als wenn er mit seiner Arbeit beschaftigt wäre, die Nadel oft einfädeln müsste usw. Dabei hörte und sah er nicht. Das Bewusstsein fehlte. Dieser Zustand hielt fünfzehn Stunden an.' Cf. also Fawcett and Busch 1998: 507: 'In humans, both cocaine and amphetamine produce behaviors characterized by repetitious arrangement of objects. Such behaviors may be analogous to stereotyped behaviours induced by amphetamines in animals' (K.S. Patrick et al. 1981).

An additional problematic point in Staal's article is the suggestion (Staal 2001: 771) that the descriptions found of Soma growing on high mountains would disqualify the 'ubiquitous' Ephedra (the latter, in fact, not being all that ubiquitous: it does not occur in mid- and south India, and has a preference for high altitudes). The argument would be tenable only if our sources presented the Soma as growing on high mountains *exclusively*, which is not the case. The ritualist's question to the Soma-seller 'is it from mount Mūjavat', as we have seen, asks for Soma-plants of top-quality, and it is presupposed that second-rate Soma-plants are more readily available.

PARAMETERS OF THE SOMA-HAOMA PROBLEM

In the present state of knowledge, any claim that the Soma has been identified is either rhetorical or it testifies to the methodological naivety of the author. In reviewing some of the more recent contributions from Wasson onwards I have not hidden my own direction of thinking. In spite of quite strong attempts to do away with Ephedra by those who are eager to see Soma as a hallucinogen, its status as a serious candidate for the Ṛgvedic Soma and Avestan Haoma still stands. For more than the serious candidacy of Ephedra (or more generally of a stimulant), however, there are at present no arguments; and alternative candidates cannot be excluded. The attention paid to the nature of the psycho-physiological state induced by the Soma, most dramatically emphasized by Wasson, is justified. The trap, however, in which Wasson and most scholars defending or attacking him have fallen is to assume that this psychophysiological state must be attributed directly to a psychoactive substance which brings about a similar state in modern, Western, well-fed, and possibly smoking and drinking subjects. It must be clear that this is a shortsighted, anachronistic presupposition.[36] It is generally forgotten that participants in a

[36] See also the criticism on Flattery and Schwartz uttered by Nyberg 1995: 399: 'To say that the effects of ephedras are "of insufficient

Vedic ritual have undergone preparations which include fasting, restraining speech, sleep deprivation, sensory deprivation by spending the day in a dark hut, etc. According to the Śrautasūtras, the sacrificer has to fast 'until he has become lean'. Less is known about the specific preparations of the priests for the sacrifice. I am not sure whether such preparations are simply not current among modern Brahmins performing in Vedic (Śrauta) rituals, or whether they have been mainly neglected by observers. (I do not find a reference to such a practice in Staal's overview of the preparations to the Agnicayana in Kerala, 1975, see Staal 1983, I: 193ff.) In any case, Stevenson, in the preface to his translation of the *Sāmaveda* (1842: VIIIff.), mentions references in a Brāhmaṇa of the *Sāmaveda* to extensive austerities (including living on restricted food for months and complete fasting for several days) to be undergone by the priest-singers of the *Sāmaveda* in preparation for a performance. It is well known that fasting alone is a suitable preparation for the physiology to receive visionary experiences. Of the North-American Indians of the Plains it is known that they undertake their vision quests without the help of specific psychoactive substances (except for some who recently adopted the use of substances used by Mexican Indians), but subject themselves to rigorous fasting and thirsting.[37]

---

intensity" or "too inconsistent in character' (in Flattery and Schwartz 1989: 72) seems to reflect a tendency to apply modern methods of clinical drug evaluation to an ancient culture having a very different psychological pattern and way of life when compared with modern Western culture.'

[37] Lowie 1954: 157: 'Woodland and Plains Indians deliberately went out to a lonely spot in order to obtain a revelation . . . the normal procedure was to go into solitude, fast and thirst for four days, and supplicate the spirits to take pity on the sufferer.' Blackfoot specialist L.M. Zuyderhout kindly drew my attention to the sections on visions and shamans in Lowie 1954, and informed me (email 27.01.2003) on the basis of her extensive fieldwork that also women may go on a vision quest and fast and thirst although there are hardly published sources on this. In addition, women had to fast in connection with the Blackfoot Sun Dance.

The human capacity for imagination, vision and hallucination seems to have been underestimated by Wasson and others. Merely because Apollinaire (1880-1918) published the 'visionary' poem 'Vendémiaire' in his collection *Alcools* we do not put the label 'hallucinogen' on alcohol. A frequently quoted phrase from William Blake (1757-1827), the poet who was influenced by Emanuel Swedenborg in his enlightened Christian views, is 'To see a world in a grain of sand, and a heaven in a wild flower, hold infinity in the palm of your hand, and eternity in an hour' – but there is no reason to assume that Blake's visions, reflected in his poetry and life anecdotes, were induced by a psychoactive substance.

Thus, with little R̥gvedic evidence for hallucinations in the strict sense of the word – i.e. perceptions without any objective basis – and with otherwise a wide spread of R̥gvedic statements pointing in the direction of a stimulant, the case for a substance which we label as a hallucinogen is far from compelling. Apart from X.119, most examples which should testify to hallucinatory experiences of the authors can be easily explained as expressions in a professional tradition of poetic imagery.[38] On the other hand, the case for a stimulant still stands,[39] even with the evidence

[38] Soma is connected with poetic inspiration and with dh/I or 'vision' (cf. Gonda 1963: 41, 51, 69, 73ff), but generally these cannot be regarded as 'hallucinations'; browsing through Geldner's Register to his *R̥gveda* translation, we find listed as the effects of Soma (Geldner 1957: 248-9) that it incites thought (I.129.6 *mánma réjati*, VI.47.3 *manīṣā́m . . . ajīgaḥ*), it is able to engender poetical thought (IX.95.1 *matī́r janayata*), is the progenitor of poetical thoughts (IX.96.5 *janitā́ matīnā́m*), opens the doors to the thoughts (I.46.5 *ādāró vāṁ matīnā́m*, IX.10.6 *ápa dvā́rā matīnā́m . . . r̥ṇvanti* [*sómāsaḥ*]).

[39] Cf. in Geldner's Register to his *R̥gveda* translation, among the effects of Soma (Geldner 1957: 248-9): Soma keeps awake (VIII.2.12 *jarante*, said of the Soma juices; III.37.8 *jā́gr̥vi* said of the Soma); it gives strength (IX.90.2 *vayodhā́*). Apart from this useful but quite incomplete thematic index cf. also statements such as IX.1.10ab *asyéd índro mádeṣv ā́ víśvā vr̥trā́ṇi jighnate* 'In the exhilarations of this (Soma), Indra destroys all

for occasional hallucinations and visions in the *R̥gveda*, because (a) hallucinations and visions may occur even on account of the absence of consumption of food or the deprivation of sleep rather than on account of the consumption of specific additives; (b) stimulants allow subjects to remain without food more easily (hence their use in weight-loss programmes), and by virtue of this they may be deemed to be able to contribute to hallucinations and visions; (c) in higher doses and under suitable circumstances (e.g. exposure to rhythms and music), stimulants such as cocaine and MDMA (XTC) are reported to lead to ecstasy and hallucinations.[40]

Apart from the distinction between stimulant and hallucinogen, a case can be made for a substance with more subtle psychoactivity than the sensational fly-agaric proposed by Wasson,[41] in

---

obstructions and obstructors'; IX.113.1 *śaryaṇā́vati sómam índraḥ pibatu vr̥trahā́ bálaṁ dádhāna ātmáni kariṣyán vīryaṁ mahád'* At the Śaryaṇā́vat (lake), Indra the Vr̥tra-killer must drink the Soma, putting strength in himself, about to perform a great heroic feat.'

[40] Cf. from Fischman's (1987: 1544) summary of the general effects of stimulants, in this case specifically cocaine and amphetamines – note their correlation with stereotyped behaviour (ritualization), my emphasis:

'Humans given single moderate doses of cocaine and amphetamine generally show a decrease in food intake and fatigue and an increase in activity, talkativeness, and reports of euphoria and general well-being. At higher doses *repetitive motor activity* (*stereotyped behaviour*) is often seen, and with further increases in dose, convulsions, hyperthermia, coma, and death ensue.

...

The effects of cocaine and amphetamine in most non-human species parallel those seen in humans. At lower doses, animals are active and alert, showing increases in responding maintained by other reinforcers but often decreasing food intake. Higher doses produce species-specific *stereotyped behavior patterns*, and further increases in dose are followed, as in humans, by convulsions, hyperthermia, coma, and death.'

[41] The case for a more subtle psychoactive substance as candidate for Soma and Haoma can be supported by contrasting the modern, 'secular' use of tobacco in recreational smoking, with its use among the

combination with an elaborate structure of beliefs, interpretations, and physiological preparations (fasting, silence) of subjects. Especially since Wasson, scholars interested in the identification of Soma have been overly focused on the single parameter of the psychoactive substance in the Soma-plant, and neglected the contributions of the ritual and the belief system to the construction of experiences reflected in R̥gvedic hymns. Others did emphasize the belief system and the construction of experience, e.g. Elizarenkova and to some extent Oberlies, and they declared the search for the identification of Soma to be more or less hopeless. No convincing attempt has so far been made to balance the available indications for all major dimensions of the issue.

'HUMMEL'S MIRACLE' AND OTHER DESIDERATA

In a posthumously published review of Wasson's book, Karl Hummel (1997: 90) once expressed the hope that perhaps some time, thanks to a miracle, a prehistorical find will give us pressing stones or wooden stampers with remains of the Soma-plant that can be investigated microscopically. As long as this does not happen, there are still useful fields of investigation to be explored in connection with Soma and Haoma. As for the 'circumstantial' ethnobiological evidence, at present the evidence of the use of

South-American Warao when communicating with the supernatural (Wilbert 1972). What is experienced as a light relaxing influence in modern society was associated with communication with a different world among the Warao. Wilbert 1972: 55: 'Even if it is not one of the "true" hallucinogens from the botanist's or pharmacologist's point of view, tobacco is often conceptually and functionally indistinguishable from them.' As for the Soma and the Soma ritual, with a more subtle psychoactive substance as candidate for Soma it will be easier to explain the gradual, noiseless disappearance of 'the real Soma' in the ceremony devoted to its celebration (imagine a marriage where no-one notices that the bridegroom has silently disappeared . . .), after an intermediate phase in which substitutes were occasionally permitted.

fly-agaric by tribes in distant north-east Siberia (according to Nyberg 1995 in the context of recreational use and by second rate shamans) may be regarded as cancelled by the evidence closer by of early and recent finds of mummies accompanied by bundles of Ephedra just across the Himalaya, as discussed, e.g. in Barber 1999 (esp. chapter 8) and Mallory and Mair 2000: 138, 152, 185-7. (For Soma and the life hereafter cf. *R̥V* IX.113.) A more critical evaluation of the evidence than the references by Mallory and Mair is needed with regard to the identification of Ephedra by various archeologists.[42] An investigation of the Vedic ritual and knowledge system, with much attention to the hymns on Soma, is one thing which has now received an important recent contribution from the point of view of religious studies by Oberlies (1998 and 1999). Caland and Henry's description of the Agniṣṭoma on the basis of Vedic texts (1906 and 1907) is still the basis for the study of the ritual context of the Soma; it would deserve elaboration and updating in the light of new developments, e.g. new texts that have become available. Kellens 1989 and Skjaervø 1997 give overviews of achievements and issues in the study and interpretation of Avestan texts. A detailed description of the Yasna ritual in which Hom is prepared and offered appeared from the hands of Kotwal and Boyd (1991). Apart from occasional and dispersed remarks on similarities in structure and detail of the Vedic and Zoroastrian rituals (e.g. Hillebrandt 1897: 11), little has

[42] On problems regarding Stein's finds in the 1930s cf. Flattery and Schwartz 1989: 73 n. 6; and on problems in connection with Ephedra in the Bactria-Margiana archeological complex cf. Bakels in the present issue. While the references by Mallory and Mair are frequent but marginal, Barber's discussion (1999, chapter 8) of the Ephedra found with the mummies is more elaborate, takes notice of the re-identification of some samples of mummy-Ephedra as Equisetum, and forms part of an argument for the ethnic identification of the mummies. Just as Mallory and Mair she takes Sarianidi's conclusions regarding the use of Ephedra in Margiana for granted – Bakels' contribution shows that such easy acceptance is unwarranted.

been done on the systematic comparison of the two. Next, the psycho-physiology of religious, and visionary or hallucinatory experiences, whatever their cause or occasion, is an important relevant field to be explored. The psycho-physiological effect of psychoactive substances and their possible role as catalysts for such experiences are to be investigated, taking into account the specific preparations undergone by the participants in the ritual. From the overview of the discussion it must have become clear that it has been suffering from a definite lack of terminological and conceptual precision, especially with regard to terms such as hallucination, vision, stimulant, and psychoactive. A noteworthy proposal with regard to psychoactive substances was made by classicist Carl A.P. Ruck and was accepted by Wasson in his later publication *Persephone's Quest*: it is better to speak of 'entheogen' rather than of 'hallucinogen', as the latter implies a judgemental falseness deriving from our modern outside perspective.[43] But it is not likely that terminological improvements alone are sufficient. Digging deeper, we stumble upon profound philosophical problems regarding the comparability of experiences, including mystical experiences, which can be understood as results of cultural and linguistic construction. Is there any experiential basis 'beyond language' left, once we find ourselves able to formulate

[43] Cf. Wasson in Wasson et al. 1986: 36-7: 'Some of us formed a committee under the Chairmanship of Carl Ruck to devise a new word for the potions that held Antiquity in awe. After trying out a number of words he came up with *entheogen*, "god generated within", which his committee unanimously adopted, not to replace the "Mystery" of the ancients, but to designate those plant substances that were and are at the very core of the Mysteries.' Unlike Wasson I see no reason to restrict the term to substances currently labelled as hallucinogens, but I would include psychostimulants, as well as alcohol and hashish which Wasson wants to exclude on account of their use as recreational drugs (he forgets that they have been and often still are used as instruments in mystical quests, cf. Wezler 2001, whereas, on the other hand, his fly-agaric is also in use as recreational drug, cf. Nyberg 1995: 392-3 quoted in n. 22), and tobacco (cf. previous note).

explanations of linguistic and cultural construction for diverse experiences related to the use of the same chemical substance in different cultural contexts?[44] In a comprehensive study of the Soma issue its implications for the theory of the 'entheogen' origin of all religions should also be evaluated. According to this theory for which Soma as understood by Wasson was a major example and support, man would originally have known the psychoactive properties of plants, and religions would be based on the visions produced by these substances (cf. Wasson 1986 and a considerable number of recent books in the category 'New Age'; only recently I found references to a publication, Spess (2000), where an argument is made for new candidates for Soma: the *Nelumbo nucifera* and members of the Nymphaea genus: cf. http:// www.innertraditions.com/titles/soma.htm). As we have seen, due to the 'constructed' nature of cognitive events even when incited by psychoactive substances, one cannot assume the connection

[44] With regard to K.C. Forman's question (1990: 5): 'Are there some experiences, or some specifiable aspects of human experience, that are not "constructed" by our language and belief?' the answer suggested by cross-cultural experience with psychoactive substances from tobacco and alcohol to CNS-stimulants and hallucinogens would seem to be that only very general aspects of the experience (e.g. euphoria, hallucination, synesthesia) have a stable correlation with specific substances, whereas the actual 'contents' of the experience are entirely constructed. An analysis of the category of 'experience' in the encounter between India and the West was given by Wilhelm Halbfass in 1988: 378-402. With regard to Huxley's interpretation of Indian traditions Halbfass points out (2001: 233) that '"Experience" is the common denominator in Huxley's fascination with drugs and his interest in Indian philosophy'; he observes that it is, however, only in Neo-Vedāntic thought that experience, rather than traditional authority, starts to play the decisive role accepted by Huxley. When Bronkhorst (2001) attempts to find shared features in the religions adduced by Huxley to establish his 'perennial philosophy' it is significant that it is precisely the category of 'experience' that he leaves out.

between substance and vision was as simple and straightforward as propounders of the theory have suggested.

An additional field to be explored is the history of research into the identity of Soma-Haoma, and the interaction of this research with the state of growing ethnobotanical and psychophysiological knowledge, as well as with popular experience with psychoactive substances – starting at the end of the eighteenth century, through the nineteenth century, the twentieth century before and after World War II, up to the present. An evaluative and bibliographic overview of the type Harry Falk (1993) wrote on the subject of the development of writing in ancient India would be most welcome and most useful to bring the discussion of the Soma-Haoma issue to a higher level (cf. Lehmann (2000) as an example of a recent publication characterized by a blissful neglect of textual evidence, positions held by various scholars and the arguments used to support them).[45] It is hoped that the present Introduction may serve as a small step in the direction of such an evaluative overview.

[45] According to Lehmann, the Soma of the *Ṛgveda* was pressed not from a green plant or from a mushroom but from honeycombs, especially from those of the Indian giant or rock bee. The significant difference with Oldenberg's honey-theory is that the latter saw evidence that already in proto-Indo-Iranian times the honey was replaced by a plant (to whose sap honey was added in the ritual!). Lehmann does not address the question why the knowledge of Soma as honeycomb and the techniques to press the honey out of them would have got lost over the centuries whereas honey itself remained a familiar product. As a bee from flower to flower, Lehmann (2000: 195: 'Mir fehlen Kentnisse des Sanskrit') jumps from the one to the other far-fetched text-interpretation that he deems 'possible', and happily concludes his paper with the statement that the Soma-problem is now solved. Still of interest is the attention he pays to the story of the monkeys in the Madhuvana (*Rāmāyaṇa* 5.59-61), and the state of *mada* they attain when consuming the available honey. It is possibly the earliest extensive literary description in the Sanskrit tradition of a *mada* in all its shades from happy exhileration to aggressive behaviour towards the guards of the 'honey grove'.

'HUMMEL'S MIRACLE' IN CENTRAL ASIA?

Under the circumstances sketched above, it was natural that something that almost seemed like the miracle hoped for by Hummel (1997) attracted wide attention. The relevant archeological find was not made in India but in Central Asia. The claim was that ancient ritual objects contained traces of plants, including some with well known psychoactive properties: poppy seeds and Ephedra stalks. This 'Hummel's miracle' was presented in publications of Victor I. Sarianidi (e.g. 1994, 1998), and his conclusions on the findings of Ephedra have been received positively, though not uncritically, e.g. by Parpola (1995) and Nyberg (1995). The latter had already investigated specimens provided by Sarianidi but could not confirm Sarianidi's claims. He concludes a long review of textual evidence and pharmacological and ethnobiological data with the conclusion that 'ephedras best meet both the textual and pharmacological requirements for the botanical identification of soma/haoma', but points to the need of 'further archeological discoveries' before conclusive evidence can be provided.

THE LEIDEN 1999 WORKSHOP ON SOMA-HAOMA

It was in order to subject these indications for a 'Hummel's miracle' in Central Asia to closer scrutiny that a workshop was organized in Leiden in 1999. Since Sarianidi's claims with regard to early Zoroastrian and Vedic religion focused on the presence of Ephedra, this candidate for the original Soma and Haoma was central in the workshop – which was a workshop in the real sense of the word: the contributors were not required to present a finished paper but were rather invited to share with others in the development of their thought on the subject. At the workshop (see the brief report below) Sarianidi presented his case, and he moreover generously offered to send some specimens of the material (a sediment in a pitcher) in which he claimed traces of Ephedra, papaver and hemp were present.

The specimens arrived a few weeks after the workshop, and C.C. Bakels, paleobotanist and specialist in papaver cultivation around the Mediterreanean and in ancient Europe, enthusiastically undertook their investigation in spite of her busy schedule. After a few months I received messages indicating that no proof could be found of any of the substances indicated by Sarianidi. Rather than hastily sticking to this conclusion, Bakels made efforts to show the specimens to other paleobotanists whom she met at international professional meetings. At the end of this lengthy procedure, no confirmation could be given of the presence of the mentioned plants in the material that was investigated. The traces of plant-substances rather pointed in the direction of a kind of millet. Since it was felt that proceeding with a publication on the basis of the presentations in the workshop was not useful as long as Bakels' research was in progress it was postponed till her results appeared, that is, untill 2002. In the meantime only a few contributors of the 1999 workshop were left who were intending to offer a paper for publication. On the other hand, we are happy that George Thompson, with a longstanding interest in the Soma-Haoma problem, was found willing to contribute a paper although he did not participate in the 1999 workshop.

The general report of the workshop, the research report of C.C. Bakels, and George Thompson's paper on 'Ecstasy in the *Ṛgveda*' are now published, together with the present introduction, in this first part of the EJVS Soma-Haoma issue. The second part of this issue is to contain a reworked version of the paper I presented in the 1999 workshop, as well as, hopefully, some other forthcoming papers and possible reactions to the present part.

SOME RELEVANT SITES AND LINKS

A. TITUS (http://titus.uni-frankfurt.de/indexe.htm) and GRETIL (http://www.sub.uni-goettingen.de/ebene_1/fiindolo/gretil.htm#Veda) for the *Ṛgveda* and other Vedic Texts.

B. Avesta.org (http://www.avesta.org/sitemap.htm) for Avestan texts with (often antiquated) translation.

C. Materials for the study of Vedic ritual (http://www.jyotistoma.nl/): introduction and overview of the Soma-ritual, example translation of first hymn of the Soma-book *R̥gveda* 9 (http://www.jyotistoma.nl/EN/First_hymn_of_the_ninth_book.html) and videoclip of Soma-pressing and of a Sāman sung at a Soma-ritual.

D. Amanita muscaria or Fly-agaric: http://www.mykoweb.com/CAF/species/Amanita_muscaria.html, http://www.zauberpilz.com/zauberpilzgallery/amanita_muscaria_index. htm.

E. Peganum harmala or Syrian rue, Photograph by Henriette Kress: http://www.ibiblio.org/herbmed/pictures/p10/pages/peganum-harmala.htm.

F. Flora of Asclepiadaceae, by Li Ping-tao, Michael G. Gilbert, W. Doublas Stevens (incl. information but no photos on Periploca, Sarcostemma): http://hua.huh.harvard.edu/china/mss/volume16/Asclepiadaceae.publis hed.pdf.

G. Soma-substitute 'Pûtîka' used in Soma-sacrifice in Barsi, Maharashtra, 2001, probably to be identified as Sarcostemma acidum (Roxburgh) Voigt (Asclepias acida Roxburgh, Sarcostemma brevistigma Wight & Arnott), photo (© J.E.M. Houben): http://www.jyotistoma.nl/EN/images/Putika.jpg.

H. Species of Ephedra: Photographs by Henriette Kress: http://www.ibiblio.org/herbmed/pictures/p05/index_3.htm, under Ephedra equisetina and Ephedra sinica; Christopher J. Earl's Gymnosperm Database hosted by Univ. of Bonn, Dep. of Botany: http://www.botanik.uni-bonn.de/conifers/ep/index.htm; a creeper of the family of Ephedra – of interest in the light of references in post-Vedic texts that Soma were a creeper – is known as Vine Ephedra (I don't have information on possible similar kinds of Ephedra creepers in Asia): http://aggie-horticulture.tamu.edu/ornamentals/nativeshrubs/ehpedrapeduncula.htm; healthnotes online on Ephedra: http://www.hollandandbarrett.com/Herb/Ephedra.htm.

BIBLIOGRAPHIC REFERENCES

Abbé, Jean Antoine. 1825. *Moeurs, institutions et cérémonies des peuples de l'Inde.* Paris.

Aitchison, J.E.T. 1888. *Transactions of the Linnean Society of London. 2nd Ser. Botany.* Vol. III, Part I: *The Botany of the Afghan Delimitation Commission.* London: The Linnean Society.

Anquetil-Duperron, Abraham-Hyacinthe. 1771. *Zend-Avesta, ouvrage de*

Zoroastre, contenant les idees theologiques, physiques & morales de ce legislateur, . . . Paris: Tilliard.

Apollinaire, Guillaume. 1913. *Alcools.* Lecture accompagnée par Henri Scepi. Paris: Gallimard, 1999.

Barber, Elizabeth J. Wayland. 1999. *The Mummies of Ürümchi.* New York: W.W. Norton and Company.

Bareau, André. 1969. 'Compte-rendu de Wasson'. *Journal Asiatique* 257: 173-6.

Barfoot, C.C. (ed.). 2001. *Aldous Huxley between East and West.* Amsterdam: Rodopi.

Bartholomae, Christian. 1904. *Altiranisches Wörterbuch.* Nachdruck: Berlin: Walter de Gruyter, 1961.

Bergaigne, Abel. 1889. 'Recherches sur l'histoire de la liturgie védique.' *Journal asiatique*, Janvier: 5-32, Février-Mars: 121-97.

van den Bosch, Lourens P. 1985. 'The Āprī hymns of the R̥gveda and their interpretation'. *Indo-Iranian Journal* 28: 95-122, 169-89.

Bronkhorst, Johannes. 2001. 'The Perennial Philosophy and the Law of Karma.' In: Barfoot 2001: 175-89.

Brough, John. 1971. 'Soma and Amanita muscaria'. *Bulletin of the School of Oriental and African Studies* 34.2: 331-62.

———. 1973. 'Problems of the «Soma-mushroom» theory'. *Indologica Taurinensia* 1: 21-32.

Burkert, Walter. 1979. *Structure and History in Greek Mythology and Ritual.* Berkeley: University of California Press.

———. 1996. *Creation of the Sacred: Tracks of Biology in Early Religions.* Cambridge, Mass.: Harvard University Press.

Burnouf, Eugène. 1844. 'Études sur la langue et les textes zends. IV: Le Dieu Homa'. *Journal Asiatique*, 8è série, no. 4, Décembre, pp. 449-505.

van Buitenen, J.A.B. 1968. *The Pravargya: An Ancient Indian Iconic Ritual, Described and Annotated.* Poona: Deccan College.

Caland, W. (ed.). 1915. *De Open-Deure tot het Verborgen Heydendom van Abraham Rogerius.* Uitgegeven door W. Caland. 's-Gravenhage: Martinus Nijhof. (Re-edition of Rogerius 1651.)

Caland, W. and V. Henry. 1906. *L'Agniṣṭoma: description complète de la forme normale du sacrifice de soma dans le culte vedique.* Tome premier. Paris: Ernest Leroux.

———. 1907. *L'Agniṣṭoma: description complète de la forme normale du sacrifice de soma dans le culte vedique.* Tome II. Paris: Ernest Leroux.

Doniger O'Flaherty, Wendy. 1969. 'The Post-Vedic History of the Soma Plant'. In: Wasson 1969: 93-147.

Eggeling, Julius. 1885. *Śatapatha-Brāhmaṇa according to the Text of the Mādhyandina School.* Part II: Books III and IV. Oxford: Clarendon Press.

Elizarenkova, Tatjana. 1996. 'The Problem of Soma in the Light of Language and Style of the Rgveda.' In: *Langue, style et structure dans le monde Indien. Colloque international pour le Centenaire de la Naissance de Louis Renou* (ed. par N. Balbir et G.-J. Pinault): 13-31. Paris: Unité de Recherche Associé 1058 'LACMI'.

Falk, Harry. 1989. 'Soma I and II'. *Bulletin of the School of Oriental and African Studies* 52: 77-90.

______. 1993. *Schrift im alten Indien. Ein Forschungsbericht mit Anmerkungen.* Tübingen: Gunter Narr Verlag.

Fawcett, Jan and Katie A. Busch. 1998. 'Stimulants in Psychiatry'. *Textbook of Psychopharmacology*, Second Edition (ed. A.F. Schatzberg and C.B. Nemeroff): 503-22. Washington D.C.: The American Psychiatric Press.

Fischman, Marian W. 1987. 'Cocaine and the Amphetamines'. In: *Psychopharmacology: The Third Generation of Progress* (ed. H.Y. Meltzer): 1543-53. New York: Raven Press.

Flattery, David Stophlet and Martin Schwartz. 1989. *Haoma and Harmaline. The Botanical Identity of the Indo-Iranian Sacred Hallucinogen 'Soma' and its Legacy in Religion, Language and Middle Eastern Folklore.* Berkeley: Univerity of California.

Forman, Robert K.C. (ed.). 1990. *The Problem of Pure Consciousness.* New York: Oxford University Press.

Furst, Peter T. (ed.). 1972. *Flesh of the Gods: The Ritual Use of Hallucinogens.* New York: Praeger Publ. Reissued with changes Waveland Press, Prospect Heights, Illinois, 1990.

Geldner, Karl F. 1926. *Die Zoroastrische Religion <Das Avestā>.* Tübingen: J.C.B. Mohr.

______. 1928. *Vedismus und Brahmanismus.* Religionsgeschichtliches Lesebuch, 9. Tübingen: Mohr.

______. 1951. *Der Rig-Veda: aus dem Sanskrit ins deutsche übersetzt und mit einem laufendem Kommentar versehen.* Teil I-III. Cambridge, Mass.: Harvard University Press.

______. 1957. *Der Rig-Veda: aus dem Sanskrit ins deutsche übersetzt und mit einem laufendem Kommentar versehen.* Vierter Teil: *Namen-und Sachregister zur Übersetzung dazu Nachträge und Verbesserungen.* Ed. Johannes Nobel. Cambridge, Mass.: Harvard University Press.

Gonda, Jan. 1963. *The Vision of the Vedic Poets.* The Hague: Mouton.

______. 1975. *Vedic Literature.* Wiesbaden: Harrassowitz.

______. 1978. *Hymns of the R̥gveda not Employed in the Solemn Ritual.* Amsterdam: North-Holland Publishing Company.

Halbfass, Wilhelm. 1988. *India and Europe: An Essay in Understanding.* Albany: SUNY Press.

______. 2001. 'Mescaline and Indian Philosophy: Aldous Huxley and the Mythology of Experience'. In: Barfoot 2001: 221-35.

Hillebrandt, Alfred. 1891. *Vedische Mythologie. I: Soma und verwandte Götter.* Breslau: Köbner.

______. 1927. *Vedische Mythologie.* Breslau: M. & H. Markus.

Houben, Jan E.M. 1991. *The Pravargya Brāhmaṇa of the Taittirīya Āraṇyaka: An Ancient Commentary on the Pravargya Ritual.* Delhi: Motilal Banarsidass.

______. 2000. 'The Ritual Pragmatics of a Vedic Hymn: The "Riddle Hymn" and the Pravargya Ritual'. *Journal of the American Oriental Society* 120.4: 499-536.

Hummel, Karl. 1997. 'Review of Wasson 1969'. *Studien zur Indologie und Iranistik* 21: 79-90.

Huxley, Aldous. 1932. *Brave New World.* London: Chatto and Windus.

______. 1959. *Brave New World Revisited.* London: Chatto and Windus.

______. 1977. *Moksha: Writings on Psychedelics and the Visionary Experience, 1931-1963* (ed. M. Horowitz and C. Palmer). London: Chatto and Windus.

Ingalls, Daniel H.H. 1971. 'Remarks on Mr. Wasson's Soma'. *Journal of the American Oriental Society* 91.2: 188-91.

Kashikar, C.G. 1990. *Identification of Soma.* Pune: Tilak Maharashtra Vidyapeeth.

Kashikar, C.G. and Asko Parpola. 1983. 'Śrauta Traditions in Recent Times'. In: Staal 1983, vol. II: 199-251.

Katz, Steven T. (ed.). 1978. *Mysticism and Philosophical Analysis.* London: Sheldon Press.

______. 1983. *Mysticism and Religious Traditions.* New York: Oxford University Press.

______. 1992. *Mysticism and Language.* New York: Oxford University Press.

______. 2000. *Mysticism and Sacred Scripture.* Oxford: Oxford University Press.

Kellens, Jean. 1989. 'Avesta'. In: *Encyclopaedia Iranica* (ed. Ehsan Yarshater), vol. III, pp. 35-44.

Kotwal, Dastur Firoze M. and James W. Boyd. 1991. *A Persian Offering: the Yasna: A Zoroastrian High Liturgy.* Paris: Association pour l'avancement des études iraniennes.

Kramrisch, Stella. 1972. 'Review of Wasson 1969'. *Artibus Asiae*, 34: 263-7.

———. 1975. 'The Mahāvīra Vessel and the Plant Pūtika [*sic*].' *Journal of the American Oriental Society* 95.2: 222-35. [Reprinted as chapter 3 in Wasson et al. 1986.]

Kuhn, Adalbert. 1859. *Die Herabkunft des Feuers und des Göttertranks.* Berlin: Ferd. Dümmler's Verlagsbuchhandlung.

Kuiper, F.B.J. 1970. 'Review of Wasson 1969'. *Indo-Iranian-Journal*, 12.4: 279-85.

———. 1984. 'Was the Pūtīka a Mushroom?.' In: *Amr̥tadhārā: Professor R.N. Dandekar Felicitation Volume* (ed. S.D. Joshi): 219-27. Delhi: Ajanta.

Lehmann, J. 2000. 'Die ursprüngliche rigvedische Somapflanze war weder gruene Pflanze noch Pilz: Gepresst wurden Bienenwaben. Sicht eines Entomologen.' In: *Indoarisch, Iranisch und die Indogermanistik: Arbeitstagung der Indogermanischen Gesellschaft vom 2. bis 5. Oktober 1997 in Erlangen* (herausg. v. B. Forssman und Robert Plath): 295-314. Wiesbaden: Reichert Verlag.

Lewin, L. 1927. *Phantastica: Die Betäubenden und erregenden Genussmittel – fuer Ärzte und Nichtärzte.* Berlin: Georg Stilke.

Lowie, Robert H. 1954. *Indians of the Plains.* New York: McGraw-Hill.

Mallory, J.P. and Victor H. Mair. 2000. *The Tarim Mummies: Ancient China and the Mystery of the Earliest Peoples from the West.* London: Thames & Hudson.

Mayrhofer, Manfred. 1992. *Etymologisches Wörterbuch des Altindoarischen.* Heidelberg: Carl Winter Universitätsverlag.

Modi, Jivanji Jamshedji. 1922. *The Religious Ceremonies and Customs of the Parsees.* Bombay. Reprint: New York, 1979.

Müller, Friedrich Max. 1855. 'Die Todtenbestattung bei den Brahmanen'. *Zeitschrift der Deutschen Morgenländischen Gesellschaft*, 9: I-LXXXII.

———. 1888. *Biographies of Words and the Home of the Aryans.* London: Longmans, Green & Co.

Mukherjee, Braja Lal. 1921. 'The Soma Plant'. *The Journal of the Royal Asiatic Society of Great Britain and Ireland for* 1921: 241-4.

———. 1922. 'The Soma Plant'. Calcutta: Weekly Notes Printing Press.

Murr, Sylvia (ed.). 1987. *L'Inde philosophique entre Bossuet et Voltaire – I: Moeurs et coutumes des indiens* (1777). Un inédit du Père G.-L. Cœurdoux s.j. dans la version de N.-J. Desvaulx. Paris: Ecole Française d'Extrème Orient.

Nyberg, Harri. 1995. 'The Problem of the Aryans and the Soma: The Botanical Evidence'. In: *The Indo-Aryans of Ancient South-Asia: Language, Material Culture and Ethnicity* (ed. George Erdosy): 382-406. Berlin: Walter de Gruyter.

Oberlies, Thomas. 1995. 'Review of Kashikar 1990'. *Wiener Zeitschrift für die Kunde Südasiens*, 39: 235-8.

______. 1998. *Die Religion des R̥gveda.* Erster Teil: *Das Religiöse System des R̥gveda.* Wien: Institut der Indologie der Universität Wien.

______. 1999. *Die Religion des R̥gveda.* Zweiter Teil: *Kompositionsanalyse der Soma-Hymnen des R̥gveda.* Wien: Institut der Indologie der Universität Wien.

Oldenberg, Herman. 1894. *Die Religion des Veda.* Berlin: Hertz (2nd revd. edn. 1917: Stuttgart, Cotta.)

Parpola, Asko. 1995. 'The Problem of the Aryans and the Soma: Textual-linguistic and Archaeological Evidence'. In: *The Indo-Aryans of Ancient South-Asia: Language, Material Culture and Ethnicity* (ed. George Erdosy): 353-81. Berlin: Walter de Gruyter.

Rappaport, Roy A. 1999. *Ritual and Religion in the Making of Humanity.* Cambridge: Cambridge University Press.

Renou, Louis. 1962. 'Recherches sur le rituel védique: la place du Rig-Veda dans l'ordonnance du culte'. *Journal asiatique* 250: 161-84.

Rogerius, Abraham. 1651. *De Open-Deure tot het Verborgen Heydendom Ofte Waerachtig vertoogh van het Leven ende Zeden, mitsgaders de Religie ende Godsdienst der Bramines op de Cust Chormandel, ende de Landen daar ontrent.* Leyden. 2nd edn.: Caland, 1915.

Sarianidi, Victor. 1994. 'New Discoveries at Ancient Gonur.' *Ancient Civilizations from Scythia to Siberia* 2.3: 289-310.

______. 1998. *Margiana and Proto-Zoroastrism.* Athens: Kapon Editions.

Shulgin, Alexander T. and David E. Nichols. 1978. 'Characterization of Three New Psychomimetics'. *The Psychopharmacology of Hallucinogens* (Proceedings of a two-day workshop held in Bethesda, Maryland, 21-2 December 1976) (ed. Richard C. Stillman and Robert E. Willette): 74-83. New York: Pergamon Press.

Skjaervø, Oktor P. 1997. 'The State of Old Avestan Scholarship'. *Journal of the American Oriental Society*, 117.1: 103-14.

Spess, David L. 2000. *Soma: The Divine Hallucinogen.* Rochester (Vermont): Inner Traditions. (Reference according to http://www.innertraditions.com/titles/soma.htm).

Staal, Frits. 1975. *Exploring Mysticism: A Methodological Essay.* Berkeley: University of California Press.

———. 1989. *Rules without Meaning: Ritual, Mantras and the Human Sciences.* New York: Peter Lang.

———. 2001. 'How a Psychoactive Substance becomes a Ritual: The Case of Soma'. *Social Research*, vol. 68.3: 745-78.

——— (ed.). 1983. *Agni: The Vedic Ritual of the Fire Altar.* Vols. I and II. Berkeley: Asian Humanities Press. [First Indian Edition: Delhi: Motilal Banarsidass, 2001.]

Stein, Aurel. 1931. 'On the ephedra, the Húm plant, and the Soma'. *Bulletin of the School for Oriental and African Studies* 6: 501-14.

Stevenson, John. 1842. *Translation of the Samhitá of the Sáma Veda.* London: Allen.

Stuhrmann, Rainer. 1985. 'Worum handelt es sich beim Soma?' *Indo-Iranian Journal* 28: 85-93.

Wasson, Valentina Pavlovna and Robert Gordon Wasson. 1957. *Mushrooms, Russia and History.* New York: Pantheon Books.

Wasson, R. Gordon. [1969.] *Soma: Divine Mushroom of Immortality.* New York: Harcourt, Brace, Jovanovich. [No publication date is indicated on the title or copyright page of the book available to me; in Wasson 1972a Wasson gives 1969 as the date of publication; we often also find the book mentioned as appearing in 1968.]

———. 1970. 'Soma: Comments Inspired by Professor Kuiper's Review'. *Indo-Iranian-Journal*, 12.4: 286-98.

———. 1972a. *Soma and the Fly-agaric. Mr. Wasson's Rejoinder to Professor Brough.* Cambridge, Mass.: Botanical Museum of Harvard University.

———. 1972b. 'What was the Soma of the Aryans?' In: Furst 1972: 201-13.

Wasson, R. Gordon et al. 1986. *Persephone's Quest: Entheogens and the Origins of Religion.* New Haven: Yale University Press.

Wezler, Albrecht. 2001. ''Psychedelic' Drugs as a Means to Mystical Experience: Aldous Huxley versus Indian Reality'. In: Barfoot 2001: 191-220.

Wilbert, Johannes. 1972. 'Tobacco and Shamanistic Ecstasy Among the Warao Indians of Venezuela'. In: Furst 1972: 55-83.

Wilkins, Charles. 1785. *Bhăgvăt-Gēētā or Dialogues of Krēēshnă and Ărjōōn in Eighteen Lectures with Notes, Translated from the Original, in the Sanskrēēt, or Ancient language of the Brāhmăns.* London: C. Nourse.

Windischmann, Fr. 1846. *Über den Somacultus der Arier. Abhandlungen der Philosoph.-philologischen Classe der Königlich Bayerischen Akademie der Wissenschaften.* IV.2: 125-42.

Witzel, Michael. 1997. 'The Development of the Vedic Canon and its Schools: The Social and Political Milieus'. In: *Inside the Texts - Beyond the Texts: New Approaches to the Study of the Vedas* (ed. Michael Witzel): 257-345. Cambridge, Mass.: Dept. of Sanskrit and Indian Studies, Harvard University.

CHAPTER 8

Madyam Apeyam

*Pentti Aalto**

Greek and Roman authors give us some information about the use of alcohol in India, but, as regrettably often, their tales are contradictory and obviously based on erroneous generalizations. Strabo (63 BC-AD 21), for instance, following his source Megasthenes says (§ 709) that in India wine was drunk only in sacrificial ceremonies and (§ 710) that it was permitted to kill a king who was drunk. On the other hand, Curtius Rufus (first century AD) tells us that in India the use of wine was common, and when a king was drunk, his harem-girls used to bear him to the bedroom invoking the gods of the night with traditional hymns. The story that the inhabitants of India were great drunkards, seems to go back to Khares of Mitylene, who belonged to the suite of Alexander the Great. He is the source of Athenaios' (X.49) and Ailianos' (var. hist. II 41) tales that Alexander arranged a drinking-competition for the Indians in honour of the Indian ascetic Kalanos (Kalyāṇa), who voluntarily ascended the pyre. The winner of the first prize (approx. £ 1000) drank about 24 pints, but died. Of the other competitors 35 died immediately, 8 a little later (cf. Lassen III pp. 50, 345).

* Extracted from Claus Vogel (ed.), *Jnanamuktavali*, Commemoration Volume in Honour of Johannes Nobel, International Academy of Indian Culture, New Delhi, 1963.

Chinese travellers who had visited India, are in general far more reliable sources. But among them, too, we meet such one-sided statements as that of Fa Hien (*c.* AD 400) that the Indians did not drink intoxicating liquors at all.

According to Greek myths, the god of wine, Dionysos or Bakkhos, grew up on Mount Nysa in India. There, too, he planted the first vine. According to Nearkhos and Aristobulos, who visited India as members of the suite of Alexander, the vine grew-only in the north-western parts, but the grapes did not ripen because of the rainy climate.[1] Indian sources (e.g. Kauṭilya) mention the vine, but do not tell that wine had been made from the grapes. Wine was, therefore, one of the most important items of merchandise bought from the Western countries. The *Periplus Maris Erythraei* (2nd half of the first century AD) speaks of Italian and Syrian wine-export to India. The commerce obviously passed through Arabia also, since 'Arabic wine' cannot refer to the land of origin (cf. Mitra, p. 416).

In India, wine was called *madhu* (MW 779) or *mārdvīka* (MW 813 < *mr̥dvīkā* MW 830).[2] *Madhu* and *mr̥dvīkāsāra* are mentioned as different drinks in Jaina sources (Jain, p. 125). Because of middlemen wine was also called *kāpiśāyana* and *hārahūra*,[3] though it was known that these sorts, too, originally came from the Greeks (*Yavana*). The strong wine *kairātika madhu* mentioned in *MBh* VII.124.14 derived its name from the north-western Kirāta people who transported the wine. When Megasthenes (*c.*300 BC) tells (quoted by Strabo § 709, § 988) that the Indians drank wine in sacrificial ceremonies, he probably means *soma*. Wine was obviously very expensive, and according to Kauṭilya (II.25.42) a 5 per cent duty had to be paid on wine and other imported drinks.

[1] Cf. Strabo § 694, Theophrastos IV 5, Solinus 52.

[2] It is possible that the names *mādhvi*, *mādhvīka*, and *mādhūka* (e.g. Manu XI.95, Viṣṇu XXII.38) may have also meant 'grape-wine'.

[3] Kauṭilya II.25.42 p. 187, and p. 717. *Kāpiśa*: the region of Kabul; *Hārahūra*: a people in Inner Asia, see Bailey in *Asiatica*, pp.16 ff.; according to Jaina sources, *kāpiśāyana*-wine was very rare (Jain, p. 125).

The Āryans used to offer *soma* (Old-Persian *haoma,* Parsi *hūm)* as a libation to their gods before they arrived on the Indian subcontinent. None of the principal rites could be celebrated without this drink. It was prepared from a certain plant whose scapes and sprouts were soaked in water. The juice was then expressed between two boards on a cow-hide and passed through a strainer into a wooden bucket. Warm milk and a decoction of grain (barley, *yava*) were added; paddy-meal (*nivara*) could also be added. The drink was then left to ferment 1-9 days. There are many suggestions as to the plant from which *soma* was pressed, e.g. *Asclepias acida, Periploca aphylla, Sarcostemma viminalis*, etc. According to *R̥gveda* commentaries, *soma* could be also produced from the herb *ādāra* or *pūtīka* (*Guilandina bonduc*?). The methods of preparation, too, seem to have varied.[4] It is, however, difficult to understand how *soma* caused that exhilarating intoxication which is so often praised in literature. The alcohol percentage cannot have been high. Perhaps the juice of the plant contained narcotic ingredients.

Liquor proper was called *madya* (since *Chāndogya Upaniṣad,* MW 779) and *surā* (MW 1235).[5] In mythology, liquor is the daughter of the god Varuṇa, born when the ocean was churned.[6] According, to *MBh* XIII.231.29, Brahma created *surā* from the essence of the dark element (*tamas)* of beings and threw it among men. *Surā* blinded the men, who up to that time had been wise, good, and magnanimous, making them foolish and sinful. For the sake of a drink, they are ready to perform the most menial tasks.[7]

[4] *Vedic Index* II, pp. 474 ff., Mitra, pp. 418 ff., Zimmer, pp. 276 ff., Eggeling SBE XXVI, pp. xxiv ff., MW 641.

[5] Manu XI.95, *Vedic Index* II, pp. 458 f., Ray, p. 122, Schmidt, p. 138, Zimmer, pp. 280 f.; Sanskrit *surā*, corresponds to Old-Persian *hura*, Lithuanian *sulà* 'birch sap'.

[6] *Vāruṇī* was also a certain kind of arrack made from juice of palm-date or *Terminalia bellerica* (Meyer *Kauṭilya*, p. 718, Vāgbhaṭa V I, 68; MW 944); *varavāruṇī* as the name of a drink occurs in Jaina texts (Jain, p. 125).

[7] Alcohol was thus the cause of the division of labour in the society

By the Vedic age already, *surā* was also the name of a special liquor, a spirit made originally from barley, later from rice.[8] Greek authors knew that the Indians made liquor from rice,[9] and the name *surā* is probably contained in *rhongkhosūra* mentioned by Kosmas Indikopleustes. According to Sanskrit sources,[10] *surā,* was prepared as follows: Malted rice (*śaṣpa*), malted barley (*tokma*), fried rice (*lājāḥ*), and various spices and ferments (*nagnahu*) were made ready. Rice and millet were mashed in two pots on a fire until they boiled over. The overflow was collected in two jars, 1/3 of the malt and 1/2 of the spice were added to each. This mixture (*māsara*) was dried and pounded, and 1/2 of the remaining malt was added to the two mashes, which were poured into a large vessel; the *māsara* was then mixed with the compound whilst pronouncing the formula: 'Thee, the sweet (I mix) with the sweet, the strong with the strong, the immortal with the immortal, the honeyed with the honeyed, thee I mix with *soma*'. Thus *surā* was made a form of *soma* (*ŚP* XII.7.3.5). The vessel was then kept fermenting for 3 days, while cow's milk and the remaining malt were added.

According to Ray, aboriginal tribes in far-off parts of India brew rice-beer by mixing a ferment called *bākhar* with boiled rice. The result, called *pāchavi,* is weak, but it can be strengthened by adding certain narcotic drugs to the ferment. The old medical works of Caraka (I.27) and Suśruta (I.45.10.10) mention a liquor *jagala,* which seems to have been rice-beer. How such beer then, probably since very early times, is distilled into rice-spirits is described in detail by Ray (pp. 130ff.): When the rice has been softened in moist steam,

---

and of the culture based on it. According to *Kāṭhaka* 14.6 and *Taittirīya Brāhmaṇa* 3.2.6, *surā*, was born from the sinful principle which the gods extracted from food.

[8] An unsettled question is since when the distillation of *surā* has been practised.

[9] Strabo § 709, Ailianos XIII.8, Aristarkhos hist. an. VIII.25.

[10] Kātyāyana XIX.1, 20 ff., Mahīdhara on *Vājasaneyi Saṁhitā* XIX.1.

it is thoroughly mixed with *bākhar*[11] in the ratio of 100:1. The temperature of the rice rises, and the mould-fungi contained in *bākhar* grow and entangle the rice in their filaments. After several operations, the mould becomes black and coats each grain of the rice. The rice-cakes are then put in large earthen vats, mixed with water, and left to ferment. As soon as the fermentation ends, the wort is distilled in an earthen still, two large jars connected by two straight pieces of bamboo as pipes. The whole process takes about 20 days. Though the technique is rather primitive, the result is relatively good. A Bihar peasant distillery working in a similar way and its terminology are described by Grierson, pp. 77 f.; cf. further *Hobson-Jobson*, p. 874.

Liquor prepared from rice or other malted grain was specifically called *paiṣṭī* or *paiṣṭikī* (< *piṣṭa* 'flour'). This term occurs already in the laws of Manu (XI.95, cf. Viṣṇu XXII.82), though it can hardly have meant the distilled liquor. Jaina sources know this name as *piṭṭhi* (Jain p. 126).[12]

Many other kinds of liquor were prepared from grains:

Medaka: 1 *droṇa* of water, 1/2 *āḍhaka* of rice, 3 *prasthas* of ferment (Kauṭilya II.25.42, p. 186; cf. *meraka* Jain, p. 125, identified by him with *goḍī* and *sīdhu*).

Prasannā: 12 *āḍhakas* of flour, 5 *prasthas* of ferment, nutmeg and rind of the *putraka* tree according to taste (Kauṭilya l. c., Jain, p. 125; the latter identifies *prasannā* with the fruit-liquor *phalasurā*).

[11] This is supplied by low castes living in mountains. It is a mixture of rice-flour with roots and barks of herbs and trees and has a slightly acid reaction. The enzymes contained in it can turn rice-starch into dextrine and maltose. It also contains spores like *Mucor racemosus*, *Aspergillus*, *Eurotium*, etc., which turn the rice into malt. Some of the herbal ingredients (hemp, etc.) have narcotic effects (Ray, pp. 134 ff.).

[12] Ray, pp. 129, 134, MW 649, Husain, p. 69, Schmidt, p. 139. According to Yaśodhara's commentary on the *Kāmasūtra* (Schmidt, p. 138), the ingredients were Cassia-bark, rice, and molasses; the *Matsyasūktatantra* quoted by Mitra, p. 413 lists half-boiled rice, barley, black pepper, lemon-juice, ginger, and hot water as ingredients of *surā*.

Kohala was according to Suśruta a drink prepared from barley, while the *Nighaṇṭuprakāśa* mentions *kohalī* as made from gourd (*kūṣmāṇḍasurā*).[13]

Parisrut, occurs in the oldest sourccs (*R̥V* 9.1.6) as an epithet of Soma; 'foaming, fermenting' (MW 604). In *Atharvaveda* and *Yajurveda*, however, it means a special liquor, 'neither *soma* nor *surā*' (*ŚP* V.1.2.14). According to Sāyaṇa, it differed from *surā* in that it was prepared from unripened rice; according to Mahīdhara, it was *puṣpebhyo niḥsr̥taṁ sāram* (Zimmer, p. 281). The origin of *parisrut* is also credited to mythology: When Indra had drunk too much *soma*, his energy flowed out from every limb: 'From his generative organ his essence flowed and became *parisrut*, from his hips his fire flowed and became *surā*, the essence of food' (*ŚP* XII.7.1.7). From the parallel in *ŚP* V.5.4.10: 'What flowed from the upper opening, that was the foaming spirit (*parisrut*)' as well as from other sources we can conclude that *parisrut* was incompletely fermented wort (cf. Zimmer, p. 281).

Beside cereals, sacchariferous saps and juices were used as the raw materials of liquors. Sugar cane (*śarkara*, Prākr̥t *sakkara* from which the European forms through Arabic) became known in the Western world very early through Megasthenes and Nearkhos as an important Indian product. It was even known that sugarcane was used for brewing liquor.[14]

[13] *Kohala* also means 'indistinct speech'. The origin of the name of the drink is unclear, and the explanations given are not convincing. Ray, p. 129 points to the similiarity with the word alcohol and supposes that the term had entered Arabic through the Indian physicians of the Caliphs of Baghdad. His explanation of the etymology of the Arabic word is not correct. Arabic *al kuḫl* 'paint for eyes' comes from Aramaic *kuḫla* and this again from Accadian *guḫlu*. As late as the sixteenth century alcohol still had the meaning 'colour from antimony' (cf. Lokotsch 1227).

[14] Strabo § 694, *Dioskorides* II.104, *Theophrastcos* IV.5, Ailianos var. hist. III.39, Plinius VI.16.1, XII.8.17, XIII.9.4, XIV.19.3, Seneca ep. 84, *Peripl. Mar.* Er. 14.1, Ktesias frg. 57, 29; Marco Polo tells that in Quilon wine was produced from palm-sugar (III.25).

Gauḍī was a rum-like drink produced from molasses (*guḍa*). Jaina texts know this liquor as *goḍī* (Jain, p. 126 identifies it with *meraka* and *sīdhu*). As *gouri* it is known also in modern times.[15]

Sīdhu was made either from sugar cane sap or from the flowers of *sīdhupuṣpa*. The *matsyaṇḍikā*-syrup was known as its 'antidote'.[16]

Āsava-liquor was prepared according to the following recipe: 1 *tulā* of fruits of the *kapittha*-tree (*Feronia elephantum*), 5 *tulās* of concentrated sugar cane sap, 1 *prastha* of honey.[17]

Maireya is a similar liquor prepared by mining molasses with a decoction of *meṣaśṛṅgi*-bark (*Odina pinnata*) and vegetable spices.[18]

Mādhūka-liquor was prepared from flowers of the *mādhūka*-tree (*Bassia, latifolia*). There are, however, three names, *mādhūka*, *mādhvīka*, *mādhvī*, used side by side, and it is unclear whether they mean the same or three different drinks (Manu XI.95, Viṣṇu XXII.82-3). According to Nandapaṇḍita, *mādhūka* was made from the above flowers, the others from honey. According to

[15] Manu XI.95, MW 369, Ray, p. 129, Husain, p. 69, Schmidt, p. 139.

[16] *Siddhāntakaumudī* 248, *Mṛcchakaṭikā* VI.29, *Mālavikāgnimitra* III.5-6, Husain, p. 67, MW 1218; Jaina sources mention *varasīdhu*, which Jain p. 126 identifies with *goḍī* and *meraka*.

[17] The name means 'distillate, decoction' MW 160; Mitra, p. 426 says it was 'pure rum'; cf. Kauṭilya II.25.42, p. 186, Yaśodhara on Vātsyāyana, p. 70, Schmidt, p. 138, Jain, p. 125; Viṣṇu XXII.83 calls a drink from the same materials *ṭāṅka* according to the other name of the *kapittha*-tree. Sugar cane rum is also called *aikṣava* (*ikṣu* 'sugar cane'); Jaina sources know *ikṣurasa* (Jain, p. 125); Mitra, p. 411 quotes *aikṣava* and *ṭāṅka* as flavoured with black pepper, plums, curds, and salt.

[18] *Piper longum*, *Piper nigrum* (*marica*, according to others *Strychnos potalorum*), nutmeg and areca-nuts, clove, 3 different fruits (either *Terminalia chebula*, *Terminalia bellerica*, *Phyllanthus emblica* or grape, pomegranate, date); Kauṭilya II.25.42, p. 186, Yaśodhara on Vātsyāyana (p. 70); according to Vācaspati quoted by Nandapaṇḍita, this liquor was prepared from the blossoms of *Grislea tomentosa* mixed with sugar, grains, and water. According to a commentary on Suśruta, *maireya* was a mixture of *surā* and *āsava*. Mitra, p. 412 identifies it with *gauḍī* and lists as its spices curds, hemp leaves, and a drug called *karīkanā*; on p. 426, he says it was rum seasoned with the blossoms of *Lythrum fruticosum*.

Kullūkabhaṭṭa, *mādhvī* meant the same flower. Hārīta, again, says that all three drinks were made either from flowers or from honey. Honey is mentioned as material also by Yaśodhara (Schmidt, p. 139) and Medhātithi (also Husain, p. 69), while Nārāyaṇa lists as ingredients flowers, honey, and grapes. The sources of Mitra (pp. 411 ff.) quote honey as material of *mādhūka,* the blossoms of *Bassia latifolia* as that of *mādhvīka* (cf. MW 779).[19]

Palm-toddy. A variety of arrack has been prepared since time immemorial from the fermented juice of the flower-spathes of various Indian palms. Such wine is mentioned by Ktesias (frg. 57, 29), Plinius, and Kosmas Indikopleustes (§ 336 *rhongkhosūra*), and later by Marco Polo (III.19, cf. III.25). A description of various kinds of palm-juice and their handling is given by Grierson, pp. 79 f. The Palmyra palm (*Borassus flabelliformis*) is called *āsava*-tree in old Sanskrit sources, and its toddy has been used in the production of spirits especially in Ceylon. In Sanskrit the tree is called *tāla,* and *tāla* or *tālaphala* accordingly was a drink made from its fruits, spiced with *Croton polyandrum* and leaves of the *kakubha*-plant (Mitra, pp. 411 f., Jain p. 126 fn. 44).[20]

Khārjūra was prepared from the juice of the Fenix palm (*Phoenix silvestris)* or of the wild date (Viṣṇu XXII.83, Schmidt, p. 140), and

[19] Meyer *Kauṭilya,* p. 718, Mitra, p. 411, Schmidt, p. 140. The *madhūka* tree is called *mahua* or *mowa* in present-day India. Its blossoms contain up to 58 per cent fermentable sugar. They have been used in producing liquor by a very primitive process. The ready liquor, therefore, contains a very high percentage of injurious by-products. According to Ray (p. 129), it is called *mādhvī.* The method of preparing it is also described by Grierson, p. 78. The name arrack is derived (Lokotsch, 92) from Arabic *'araq at-tamr* 'perspiration of dates'. It later spread into many Asiatic languages, e.g. Mongolian *arki,* Tungus *araka,* Korean *arang,* Japanese *sake*; in English the word is attested since 1516; see further *Hobson Jobson,* p. 36 and s.v. *fool's rack,* p. 356.

[20] From this are derived Hindi *tār* and *tāri,* the name of the wine; which has occurred in English since 1609 as *tarrie* and has later been distorted to *toddy* (Lokotsch 2035). The meaning 'a drink prepared from alcohol, hot water, and sugar' is attested in English since 1786 (see *Hobson-Jobson,* p. 927).

khārjūrasāra from dates is mentioned in Jaina sources (Jain, p. 125). According to the sources of Mitra (p. 412), it had ripe dates for its basis and was spiced with jack-fruit, ginger, and *soma.*

Pānasa had a basis of juice of the *jaka* or bread-fruit tree,[21] *nārikela* or *nālikera* or *nārikera* that of *Cocoa nucifera,*[22] *kaula*, again, that of the *jujuba*-tree (*Zizyphus jujuba;* Viṣṇu XXII.83; Schmidt, p. 140); *kaula* might be the same as *koli* in the *Viṣṇu Saṁhitā* quoted by Mitra, p. 411.

Drākṣa is met with in the Tāntric sources quoted by Mitra, pp. 410 ff. as made from distilled grape-juice fermented with curds, honey, and ghee and flavoured with *manjit* and *chiretta.*

Saira is found in some sources as being made from molasses and long pepper, while others, e.g. the Tāntristic (Mitra, p. 414), call it *ṭāṅka,* made from the roots of *Asparagus racemosus,* those of the wood-apple tree, a drug *lakṣman,* lotus-flowers, and honey.

Ariṣṭa (Mitra, p. 411) was made either from the soap-berry plant with molasses or from the root of *Aegle marmelos,* plums, and sugar.

Kādambarī, a favourite drink of Baladeva, was distilled from the ripe fruit of the *kadamba*-tree (*Nauclea kadamba*; Mitra, pp. 414, 426).

Kīlāla itself means simply 'a sweet beverage', but it also seems to be the name of one of the oldest kinds of liquor. In *Atharvaveda* 6.69.1, the singer hopes to obtain the glory of *surā* and the honey in *kīlāla* poured in his cup. The word often occurs as a name for heavenly nectar (*R̥V* X.91.14). According to Āpastamba, the *surākāra* distilled *kīlāla* from the *kīlālauṣadhi*-plant (MW 285, Zimmer, p. 281).

According to Jain (pp. 125 f.), several other liquors are mentioned in Jaina literature: *pūvasurā, odanasurā, kiṇṇapakkhittā,*

[21] MW 618, Manu XI.95, Visnu XXII.83; the *Matsyasūktatantra* quoted by Mitra, p. 411 lists as ingredients unripe jack, mango and plums, unboiled milk, fresh meat, hemp-leaves, and sweet-lime.

[22] Schmidt p. 140 has obviously mixed up the two English words cocoa since he translates *nāri-kela* with 'Kakaobohnenschnaps'. The above source of Mitra quotes narikela as made from milk of the cocoa-nut spiced with plantains, myrobalans, and the drug *indrajihvā.*

saubhāraśaṁyutta (*sammoha vinodinī*, p. 381), *candraprabhā*, *manisilākā*, *riṣṭabhā* or *jambuphalakalikā* (cf. above), *dugdhajālī*, *tallaka* (or *nellaka* or *mellaga*), *supakva*, *vaṁsī* (from bamboo-shoots), *sovīra*, *jāti* (from *jāti*-flowers, Vivāgasuya, p. 14); a very strong drink was *śatāu:* even though diluted a hundred times, it did not lose its true nature (Mitra, p. 416 states that Indian liquors were always taken undiluted). Grierson, p. 78 lists several modern peasant liquors.

Punch is also considered to be originally an Indian drink.[23]

Soma-liquor was libated to the gods, who liked it just because of its intoxicating effect. How the gods succeeded in eliminating its most dangerous effects is told in *AB* 6.1. The brahmans performing the sacrifice drank *soma*, too, and became drunk just like the gods. In literature, we meet innumerable praises of the sweetness of *soma*-intoxication. According to *R̥V* VIII.79.2, it veils that which is naked, heals that which is sick, through it the blind see, the lame walk. In *R̥V* VIII.48.3, Pragātha sings: 'We drank *soma,* we became immortal, we have come to the light, we have found the gods'. The drunkenness of the priests is described in the famous hymn *R̥V* VII.103, where they are compared with croaking frogs. The intoxication caused a 'hangover', too; in *ŚP* V.5.4.8, it is told that Indra drank too much of the pure *soma*, 'but it hurt him, it flowed in all directions from the openings of his vital airs', etc. The Sautrāmaṇi ceremony removed the ill effects of excessive *soma* drinking. (*ŚP* V.5.4.11 f.; Vāgbhaṭa IV.7.56. See further Stein BSOS VI, pp. 501 ff. and Muller in *Asiatica*, pp. 428 ff.)

Surā also was offered to the gods. Like *soma* it was considered to belong to Prajāpati. In libations, both had a symbolic meaning: *soma* was the symbol of truth, prosperity, light; *surā*, again, that of untruth, misery, darkness (but also of fame!). Ceremonies in which both these drinks played an important role, were the Sautrāmaṇī

[23] This name, attested in English since 1632, is generally derived from Hindi *pānch,* since the drink consists of five ingredients. From the point of view of the English language, however, this derivation is questionable. See further *Hobson-Jobson*, p. 737.

and the Vājapeya rites (ŚP V.1.2, 10 f.; 5.4.19 ff.; XII.7.3.12; several other rites with *surā* Mitra p. 419). When *parisrut* was used in the offerings, it was specially stipulated that it must be bought from a eunuch. In connection with wedding-ceremonies, *surā* according to Gobhila II.1.10 symbolized Kāma: A friend of the bride should besprinkle her with *surā* of first quality three times so that her whole body became wet, reciting the formula: 'Kāma, I know thy name, intoxication thou art by name', etc.

Liquor was abundantly drunk also by those attending religious festivities. *MBh* XIV.59.5 ff., for instance, describes how at the festival in honour of Raivataka Mountain the noise caused by the cheering drunk men and women reached to heaven. Meals as well as *surā* and *maireya* were distributed to the poor and needy. Great sacrificial feasts (e.g. *MBh* XIV.89.39 ff.) were celebrated in a similar way.

The obvious physical effects of alcohol caused it to be used to restore the health of the human body. Thus Vāgbhaṭa (I.5.62) states that it 'stimulates the digestion and the appetite, is strong and warming, gives joy and exuberance and colour, cures insomnia and sleepiness, etc.'. Various sorts of liquor are useful in various sicknesses, thus (ibid. 67) *surā* cures tumours in the lower part of the body, abscesses in the stomach, haemorrhoids, languishment, feeds up, and promotes the formation of fat, blood, milk, urine, slime, etc. During surgical and cauterizing operations, liquor helped the patient to endure the pains more easily (ibid. IV.7.73). Special drinks were even mixed for medical purposes, as is shown by the instance quoted by Mitra, pp. 414 f. The Jaina monks were allowed to drink liquor only in special circumstances, for instance, when they were sick, since alcohol was prescribed for good health (Jain, p. 125).

Alcohol was nutritious food: a Jaina work (*Āvaśyakacūrṇī* II, p. 171) tells how the queen Cellaṇā besmeared her hair with *śatāu*-liquor before visiting the king Seniya in the prison, where it served as food for him (Jain, p. 125 fn. 41).

The intoxicating qualities of the drinks could be strengthened, for instance, by adding *datura,* which is also said to be used to stupify people in order to rob them more easily (Tawney-Penzer, Kathās, I, p. 160 fn.).

The production and use of such liquors which served as pure intoxicants, also had very early its own well-established and regulated position in Indian society. A special supervisor (*surādhyakṣa*), whose duties are described in detail by Kauṭilya (II.25.42, p. 184), had to assign the distilling and sale of the liquors and their ferments in the capital, in the country, and in the encampment to persons who were competent to handle such things. It was further his duty to organize their purchase and marketing through a monopoly or through private licenced merchants. He had to fine such persons 600 *paṇas* who tried to prepare, sell, or buy intoxicating spirits without proper licences, and see to that no alcohol was carried out of villages or stocked up there to excess, since otherwise there would be a danger that those ordered to work would grow slovenly, and that the *āryas* would forget the requirements of decency and hot-tempered persons would easily lose self-control. Only persons of irreproachable conduct were entitled to take along restricted quanties (the greatest amount was less than 1 pint) from the taverns, the others had to drink on the premises.

The supervisor had further to keep a close eye on things which were offered to tavern-keepers as pledges or in payment, since they might be stolen. It was forbidden to spend too much money on liquor or to sell it below the controlled prices. Spoiled liquor always had to be sold elsewhere or given to slaves and workers or to riding-horses and pigs. Family fathers were granted permission to produce certain liquors for family celebrations and for medicinal purposes. During festivals, meetings, and processions, the supervisor had to grant a 4-day licence for drinking. A 5 per cent duty had to be paid for imported liquors, while the licence-fee for other drinks was 1/16 of the cubic measure sold.[24]

[24] The various craftsmen who prepared and distributed the liquors, as well as other conceptions combined with these activities had their

The laws provided, furthermore, that an alcoholic was not competent to act as a witness. Seduction of an intoxicated girl was regarded as the most base and sinful of the eight rites of wedding (Manu III.34). It was also prescribed that the heir of a party owing money was not obliged to pay off the debt if it had been incurred at play or was due for spirituous liquor.[25]

There were numerous local and seasonal differences in the way of preparing and drinking liquor. Lawgivers were in general opposed to the use of intoxicants, but in certain regions their use was permitted in practice or was quite a custom of the country. We are told, for example, that the customs peculiar to the north (viz. among the brahmans) were to deal in wool, to drink rum, to sell animals that have teeth in the upper and in the lower jaws, to follow the trade of arms, and to go to sea. In the north specifically, women were especially fond of liquor.[26] Commerce in wool and the drinking of rum are nowadays, too, mentioned as Cashmirian customs. The variety of local customs is described in a proverb (Böhtlingk 7562): 'It is no crime to drink rum in Magadha and arrack in Kaliṅga, to flirt with the wife of one's brother in Oḍra, to eat fish in Gauḍa'. According to Mitra (p. 416), various drinks were recommended in various seasons: rum was described as most healthful in autumn, rice-spirits in the cold and rainy seasons, *mādhūka*-liquor in spring, summer, and the rainy season. One should always drink only such spirits as suit the temperament (Vāgbhaṭa IV.7.96-100).

Parisrut was obviously used as a daily table-drink. In blessing a new house a pot of *parisrut* is given a special mention: 'To it the tender boy, to it the calf, with moving creatures, to it the jar

---

special designations: *surākāra, surājīva, rasavāṇijja* (in Jaina texts), *surālaya, surādhvaja, surāmūlya;* it is amusing that *surāpa* and *surāpāṇa* have the meaning 'drinker of *surā*' side by side with 'agreeable, wise' and 'a people in Eastern India' (Pāṇini VIII.4.9) respectively.

[25] Bṛhaspati VII.30, Manu VIII.159, Nārada I.90, Marco Polo III.20.3.

[26] Baudhāyana I.2.4, Bṛhaspati II.28, Marco Polo III.22, Meyer, p. 244.

of *parisrut,* with mugs of curd, have come' (*AV* 3.12.7). Zimmer (p. 282) quotes *Atharvaveda* 20.127.9, where *parisrut* is mentioned side by side with *dadhi* and *mantha* as a table-drink. Guests were of course entertained with better and stronger drinks: *surā, maireya,* etc. (Mitra, p. 396). According to the *Nāyādhammakahā* (16, p. 179 quoted by Jain, p. 125), the royal guests during the *svayamvara* of Dovaī were treated by the king Duvaya with surā, *majja* (*madya*), *sīdhu,* and *pasanna (prasannā).*

In cultured circles, alcohol was drunk according to certain urbane manners. The handbooks of erotics recommend that on propitious days gentlemen should arrange drinking-parties at their homes with artistical entertainment, music, dance, etc. Freely living cultured women (*gaṇikā*) should be also invited, though the *śāstras* condemned association with them, especially by women of the family (Vātsyāyana 52, Schmidt, p. 70, Mitra, p. 425). In such parties, the clinking of glasses was a general custom, and the male participants were especially eager to do so with the ladies of the company and to propose toasts to them. At the same time, various salt, sour, bitter, etc., palate-inciting titbits were eaten. Mitra (pp. 417, 425) lists among these *upadarśa, upadaṁśa, avadaṁśa, cakṣaṇa, madyopāśaṇa, mudrā,* etc.; he interprets the epithet of Śiva Nakuleśa as 'lord of wine biscuits'.

As the most convenient and healthy form of drinking Vāgbhaṭa (IV.7.76) recommends a banquet, which according to him should be arranged as follows: As soon as the participants have bathed, settled their home affairs, and paid their respects to the gods, the brahmans, and the most prominent persons, they gather in the antechamber of the dining-room. This must be sprinkled with perfumes and decorated with flowers. Lounging on comfortable divans, they, talk with friends and enjoy various performances of singers, dancers, musicians, etc. After having swallowed a dose of a refreshing and salubrious powder *(Pinus webbiana, Elettaria cardamomum,* etc.) and offered a libation to the gods, the guests drink well-cooled liquors perfumed with mango-juice, camphor, and moschus. They clink glasses with each other and propose toasts. It is necessary to drink quietly and with due consideration, remembering the precept 'not too little, not too much'. After having thus drunk off two glasses, the guests move into the dining-room and eat meat, pastry, fresh vegetable, ginger, etc., During the dinner, one may empty two or three glasses of the liquor which suits the constitution and health best. It is most useful to have a good physician among the guests. With the cakes served as dessert some liquor was drunk (Mitra, pp. 428 f.).

In palaces, there were apartments specially reserved as drinking-halls (Mitra, p. 401).

The intoxication given by alcohol was especially sought by those in love, and the proper use of spirits was therefore taught in the handbooks of erotic.[27] Vāgbhaṭa elucidates the rules a gentleman must follow when drinking together with his beloved so that excessive drinking would not overtire him or reduce his virility (IV.7.88 f.). Since eroticism was the main quality and task of the woman, alcohol as an erotic stimulant was specially advisable for her: it made her both beautiful and passionate. Women, therefore, were generally very fond of spirits, and Sītā, the paragon of Indian woman, was no exception in this respect any more than the nymph Urvaśī, the other ideal woman adored by the writers.[28] Vāgbhaṭa describes the erotically exciting power of alcohol (IV.7.59), stating that after having drunk it any lady of good family and consequently of respectable character is able to seduce even the most severe ascetic without any trouble.

To the life of a gentleman belonged also joyful picnics to beauty-spots and public parks, accompanied by beautiful women and supplied with palatable provision (Meyer, pp. 240 f., Vātsyāyana,

[27] Schmidt, pp. 138 ff., who quotes as instances *Kirātārjunīya* IX, *Śiśupālavadha* X, *Śrīkaṇṭhacarita* XIV, *Hammīramahākāvya* VII; further instances Mitra, pp. 400 ff.

[28] Further instances *MBh* I.81.1; III.45.46; 278.39; IV.14; VI.75, 34; 77.16; 100.19; X.9.37; XI.20.7; XII.167.38; *Rām.* III.47.45; IV.1.85; V.9; 10.30; 11.2; 18.10; Jain, pp. 124 f., Mitra, pp. 379, 399 ff.

p. 71). We meet numerous descriptions of such picnics in *Mahābhārata*. The heroes go on an outing with their families and thousands of courtesans and spend the day in bathing, feasting, drinking, singing, and dancing. In the picnic scene described in *Harivaṃśa* 146 f., translated by Mitra, pp. 340 ff., the princes were overcome with liquor and lifted in the air by *apsarases*. Baladeva's eyes and feet were unsteady under the influence of *kādambarī;* Balarāma, intoxicated, danced with his wife. By his divine power Kṛṣṇa conjured up urns full of various liquors. Excited by drink, the whole party began to frolic in the sea. Thereafter followed a banquet, richly supplied with drinks. Such persons as Uddhava Bhoja, however, who did not drink, are also mentioned as members of the party. Similar picnics are described in *MBh* I.81.1; I.222.14; etc.

Kathas. 28.113 shows that liquors were taken as provisions for journeys and drunk at halts.

It has been concluded from *R̥V* I.191.10 that the brewers and distillers of liquors were originally responsible for their retail sale. *R̥V* VII.86.6; *AV* 6.70.1; 14.1.35 show that *surā* was drunk in connection with gambling, and this combination often led to deplorable consequences (Mitra, p. 390, Zimmer, p. 287). Later, the taverns (*surālaya, surāgāra, surāgr̥ha,* etc.; in Jaina sources *pāṇāgara* and *kappasālā*, Jain, p. 124) sold smaller amounts of alcohol for consumption off the premises. The two highest castes were forbidden by Manu X 88 f. to sell *soma* and liquors. Numerous scenes in Indian dramas show how taverns were frequented by people. In general, *surā* and *sīdhu* were served, and besides drinking the guests used gnaw to radishes.[29]

Kauṭilya (II.25.42, pp. 185 f.) gives detailed instructions on how a tavern is to be organized. There should be several courtyards sufficiently equipped with beds and seats. In the drinking-halls incense should be burnt, and they must be provided with

[29] Husain, p. 69 and Mitra, p. 400 quote as instances *Abhiṣekha* II.4, *Mr̥cchakaṭika* IV.29 and VIII.3, *Śakuntalā* VI.

flowers and other seasonal decorations. The innkeeper must have attendants to watch the expenditure of his clients and to guard the jewellery of those fallen asleep. According to other sources, the tavern should be situated somewhat outside of the village. Drinking of intoxicants was permitted only there, in some cases only by night. The taverns were obviously often at the same time brothels (Śukra IV.4.89 f., Meyer, *Kauṭilya,* p. 717). According to the Veda literature and the epics, the prostitutes constituted part of the order of nature.[30] More highly esteemed were the cultured hetaerae (*gaṇikā*), considered by Vātsyāyana, for instance, as becoming company for a gentleman.

The intoxication caused by liquor was often praised in literature in the same way as that induced by *soma*: *surā* gives the great splendour of the Aśvins, the persuasive power of Sarasvatī, the valour of Indra, the might of Viṣṇu; when men have drunk *surā,* they are ready to risk their lives like a blade of grass; uneasiness, excitement, reluctance, pain have no effect; when someone has *surā* in his heart, he may consider Indra as a coward (Vāgbhaṭa IV.7.55 ff.). On the other hand, all sociability, every festival, every pleasure-garden without alcohol is totally devoid of charm (ibid. 64). But it was also established that the unfavourable effects of intoxication were dangerously close to the agreeable. In *AV* 6.30.2, the stages of intoxication are classified as follows:

1. *avakeśa*: in this the hair is loosened;
2. *vikeśa*: in this the hair is dishevelled;
3. *abhihasya*: this makes a man to be laughed at.

Intoxication also makes a man lose his judgement so that he might be ready to insult the gods. The inebriated unveils his true nature quite openly (*Pañcatantra* I.150). He might become totally

[30] There are also opposing attitudes to be noted. In *MBh* XII 125, 9, we meet a proverb: The wheel of an oil-presser is as bad a destroyer of living beings as 10 slaughter-houses, the sign-board of a tavern as bad as 10 oil-pressing wheels, a harlot as bad as 10 sign-boards, a king as bad as 10 harlots.

senseless, he can no longer recognize his nearest relatives and misunderstands everything in a ridiculous and miserable way. Totally demoralized, he loses his sense of the most elementary demands of life (Varāhamihira, *Yogayātrā* 2. 4 f.). According to Vāgbhaṭa (III.6.1 ff.), a man in the first stage of intoxication enters an abnormal mental state, in the second he loses his judgement, and in the third be starts to rave like an uncontrolled elephant. Regrettably often drinking seems to have resulted in indisposition and headache. In the *Black Yajurveda*, Viśvarūpa, celebrating a *soma* sacrifice, vomited on the animals brought before him for immolation (Mitra, p. 420). As remedies against 'hangover' Vāgbhaṭa (IV.7.106 ff.) recommends e.g. closing the mouth with a hand. In addition, it is good to lick roots and stalks of lotus, long pepper, *Terminalia chebula, Alhagi maura*, or *Cyperus rotundas* with honey, to drink cold water containing black pepper, kernels of *Zizyphus jujuba, Andropogon muricatus, Mesua ferrea,* etc. Excessive drinking caused a fever-like state combined with infirmity of the limbs. The drinker might finally fall to the ground and die if help was not forthcoming in time.[31]

A fatal coincidence of the unfavourable effects of alcohol might even provoke *delirium tremens.* This had several expressive names in Sanskrit: *madātāṅka, madātyaya, madavyādhi*, etc. (Mitra, p. 417). Among the causes of this state Vāgbhaṭa (IV.7.2) lists erroneous and ill-chosen or too abundant or even insufficient use of alcohol. Delirium leads to prompt death if the patient suffers a severe fit of ague, is emaciated, and has oily colour of face (ibid. II.5.79). The first and most important remedy for delirium is the proper and temperate use of liquor, in addition to which many sorts of herbal drugs are recommended. Part of the cure is also a well-built woman who is well versed in passionate embraces and massaging (IV.7.11 ff.).

The unfavourable consequences of intoxication and alcoholism gave Indian thinkers and lawgivers reason to warn people against

[31] *Pañcatantra* L.193; for the remedies see Vāgbhaṭa IV.7.101 ff., cf. III.6.

the dangers of liquor and even forbid its use. We often meet proverbial premonitions such as 'He who is afraid of doing what he ought not to do and of neglecting what he ought to do and of disclosing a secret, must not drink intoxicating liquors' (*MBh* V.1136). Especially dangerous was considered the drunkenness of ruling persons: 'Even a mighty prince does not accomplish anything if he becomes a drinker: the fire of hell cannot burn a single straw in the ocean.'[32] Manu (VII.47 and 50) warns a king against vices springing from love of pleasure such as drinking, gambling, excesses with women, and hunting (cf. *MBh* V.1078). Jaina sources tell us that too intense love of *kāyambarī-* (*kādambarī-*) liquor by the princes of the Bāravas caused the destruction of their capital (Jain, p. 125). This aversion results in a total prohibition of intoxicants by Manu (XI.94 f.): '*surā* indeed is the dirty refuse *(mala)* of grain, sin also is called dirt (*mala);* hence a Brāhmaṇa, a Kṣatriya, and a Vaiśya shall not drink *surā. Surā* one must know to be of three kinds, *gauḍī, paiṣṭikī,* and *mādhvī;* as the one named above so are all three sorts forbidden to the chief of the twice-born' (similarly Viṣṇu XXII.82). The commentators explain this as meaning that *paiṣṭikī surā* was forbidden to members of the Āryan castes, the two other sorts only to Brāhmaṇas. They seem to be right, since Hiuan Tsang who visited India in the seventh century, tells that the Vaiśyas were allowed to drink strong alcohol, the Kṣatriyas only grape-wine and sugar cane rum, while Brāhmaṇas and Buddhist monks could only drink syrup. Viṣṇu XXII.83 lists ten sorts of liquor which according to his next paragraph are permitted to Kṣatriyas and Vaiśyas but unclean for Brāhmaṇas (cf. Schmidt, p. 140, Meyer, *Kauṭilya*, p. 718). As a mythological argument for prohibition Manu (XI.96) states that *surā,* and other liquors are the food of the Yakṣas, Rākṣasas, and Piśācas, while according to *MBh* I.76 it was Śukrācārya, the high priest of the

[32] Śṛṅgadhara, *Rājanīti* 113. Further proverbs on alcohol Böhtlingk 17, 130, 265, 1246, 1486, 1539, 1582, 1618, 1674, 2238, 2724, 2991-4, 3899, 4043, 4045, 4492, 4493, 4495, 4617, 4673, 4753, 4778, 4932-3, 5726, 6283, 6490, 6828, 7562, 7576.

āsuras, who first prohibited the use of *surā* since he had swallowed the ashes of his pupil Kaca, a Brāhmaṇa, mixed with *surā* (Manu IX.235, XI.55, Viṣṇu XXXV.1, Mitra, pp. 391 ff.).[33] Several other grounds for prohibition are quoted by the lawgivers. Stupified by drunkenness, a Brāhmaṇa might fall on something impure or pronounce holy texts improperly. When the Brāhmaṇa or the Veda dwelling in his body is deluged with spirituous liquor even once, Brāhmaṇahood forsakes him and he becomes a Śūdra (Manu XI.97 f.). Just smelling at alcohol caused a Brāhmaṇa loss of caste (Manu XI.68, Viṣṇu XXXVIII.2); no wonder that medical works give several recipes for removing the odour of liquor from the mouth (cf. Mitra, p. 418). Brāhmaṇas were forbidden to sell liquor and to eat food served by a drunk (Manu X.89, IV.207), and they were not allowed to touch food containing herbs which were used in liquors. If a Brāhmaṇa happened to smell the odour exhaled by a drinker of *surā,* he thrice had to hold his breath in water and eat clarified butter; but if he swallowed anything that had touched *surā,* he had to be initiated again (Manu XI.150 f., Gautama XXIII.6, Viṣṇu LI.25). It was further provided that a Brāhmaṇa must avoid liquor during all stages of his life; the other castes were bound by prohibition only during their student time (Gautama II.20 and the commentary of Haradatta).

The women of the upper castes were also forbidden to drink *surā.* Manu (IX.13) says that drinking spirituous liquor is one of the six causes of ruin of women. According to Vasiṣṭha XXI.15, half the body of the husband falls if his wife drinks alcohol. Such a wife may therefore at any time be superseded by another (Manu IX.80). Against this, however, a wife must not show disrespect to her husband even if he is a drunkard (IX.78). Libations were not offered to women who had drunk spirituous liquor, the crime thus being regarded as equal to killing one's husband, etc. (ibid.

[33] Renou, p. 242. Ray p. 134 considers the cause of prohibition to be that liquors were prepared by low castes, but the lawgivers do not seem to support this opinion. Places of manufacture of spirituous liquors were ritually impure (Baudhāyana I.5.9.3).

V.90). Intercource with women who drank spirits, was punishable (Viṣṇu XXXVII.33, Vasiṣṭha XXI.5). The man who sees a woman of good family, drinking *surā,* must purify himself by looking at the sun, pronouncing the name of Viṣṇu, and bathing in the same clothes as he wore when he saw the woman (*Mahānirvāṇatantra* XI.163, Meyer, p. 244).

The punishments to be inflicted on those drinking spirits were generally very severe. A king must banish from his capital sellers of spirituous liquors (*śauṇḍika)* as well as, others that follow forbidden occupations (Manu IX.225).[34] This demand is in obvious conflict with Kauṭilya's description of the legal organization of the production and retail sale of liquor. It seems probable, therefore, that general prohibition was of a formal character only and that in practice this was sufficient to prevent the Brāhmaṇas from getting intoxicated. As for them, the drinking of liquor was reckoned among the mortal sins (*mahāpātaka*: Manu IX.235, XI.55; Mitra, pp. 393 f.). The first punishment was, of course, loss of caste (Manu IX.238 f., Gautama XXI.1); the guilty one was banished from his country, the flag of the sellers of liquor being branded on his forehead.[35]

The crime was visited with penalty not only in this life but after death and in the following rebirth. *Mārkaṇḍeya Purāṇa* XIV.92 places drinkers together with the murderers of Brāhmaṇas and other most heinons criminals headlong in a flaming hell (see Feer, *JA* 1893, 1, p. 139). In *MBh* VII.701 ff., they are found in similar company in the third hell, and according to the same work (ibid. 2957 ff.) they are also tortured in the 27th hell together with the higher-caste husbands of Śūdra women. The *Bhagavata Purāṇa* inflicts a punishment in hell only on Brāhmaṇas who were drunk

[34] Nandanācārya interprets 'drunkards', the other commentaries distillers' or 'sellers'.

[35] Baudhāyana I.9; 18.18; Manu IX.237; Āpastamba I.21; Meyer, *Kauṭilya*, p. 718; Viṣṇu V.3-5; Mitra, p. 394 states that such a flag is unknown; according to Jain, p. 125, flags of liquor- shops are mentioned in the *Bṛhatkalpabhāṣya* 2.3579.

while performing a religious ceremony. In the following rebirth, after having passed through dreadful hells for a large number of years, the Brāhmaṇa drinker enters the body of insects or of birds, feeding on ordure, and of destructive beasts.[36] According to Vasistha XXI,11, a Brāhmaṇa woman who had drunk liquor, was not allowed to be reborn in the same abode with her husband but as a leech or a pearl-oyster (Meyer, p. 224).

These punishments after death and in the following rebirth could be avoided only through horrible expiations. A twice-born who in delusion of mind had drunk *surā*, should drink that liquor or cow's urine, water, milk, clarified butter, or liquid cow-dung boiling hot till he died (Manu XI.9 1 ff.). Unintentional drinking could be expiated by a new initiation (Manu XI.147).[37] A considerable mitigation of the expiation to be endured is provided for in Manu XI.93: the guilty one must eat grains of rice or oil-cake during a year once a day at night, wearing clothes made of cow-hair and his own hair in braids and carrying a flag[38]. Much slighter contact with liquor or even with vessels where such had been preserved, also had to be expiated (Manu XI.148 ff., Viṣṇu LI.1 ff.).

A negative attitude towards alcohol was assumed even by religious reformers. Thus Buddha allowed his monks only the following right drinks: mango-syrup (from *Mangifera indica*), *jambu*-syrup (*Eugenia jambos*), plantain-syrup (*Musa paradisiaca*), *moca*-syrup (*Moringa pterygosperma* or *Musa sapientum*), honey, grape-juice, syrup from the root of the water-lily, and *parūṣaka*-syrup (*Grewia asiatica*). Juices of fruits, herbs, and flowers were allowed, except those used in spirituous liquors (*Mahāvagga* VI.35.6, *Pācittiya* LI, Renou, p. 243). *Cullavagga* XII.1.3 relates,

[36] According to Manu XI.49 and Viṣṇu XLV.4, he will have black teeth.

[37] Cf. the opinions of the various commentators quoted by Bühler SBE vol. XXV, p. 460 fn.; cf. further Mitra, pp. 393 f.

[38] Vasiṣṭha XX.19, Viṣṇu LI.1, Gautama XXII.1 f., Baudhāyana III.1.18 ff., Āpastamba I.9.25.3. The opinions of the commentators are divergent; see Bühler SBE vol. XXV, p. 449 fn., Meyer, *Kauṭilya*, p. 718; cf. Mitra, pp. 393 f., Schmidt, p. 140.

however, that there were both Brāhmaṇas and Samans (Buddhists) who drank liquor (cf. Mitra, p. 399). Since certain expressions of Buddha left room for interpretation, there were in the community those who taught that it was not forbidden to drink unfermented palm-wine. This heterodoxy was sharply condemned in the council of Vesāli (*Cullavagga* XII.1.10 and 2.8). In the Buddhist system of hells, there seems in the beginning to have been no special punishment for drinkers. Feer (*JA* 1892, VIII.20, p. 193) notes that according to Pāli sources intoxication causes other sins which are punished, and therefore it does not need any special penalty of its own. The later *Pañcaśikṣyānuśāṁsasūtra* (Otani Kanjur Catalogue No. 753), however, tells that drunkards are boiled in the 6th hell (*tāpana*, cf. Viṣṇu XLIII 10) for several thousand years (Feer l. c., p. 195). From there they pass to the 11th of the, smaller hell[39] where they are angled like fish. The Buddhists seem in any case to have been relatively faithful in observing prohibition of spirituous liquor. Fa Hien, for example, who visited India about the beginning of the fifth century AD, got the impression that the Indians, except *caṇḍālas,* did not drink alcohol at all.

The Jaina monks were not allowed to drink liquor or even dwell overnight in a room with liquor-jars (Jain, p. 125).

The Tāntric doctrines, however, which have largely coloured the later systems of Hinduism, give their votaries full liberty to indulge in alcohol, especially when this is done in the appropriate way, in mystic circles as an act of worship of the deity. Mitra, depicting the drinking-customs of the Tantrists (p. 405) quotes the description of the *Mahānirvāṇatantra* about the rites of the *kaulas*: 'They drink, drink and drink until they fall down on the ground in utter helplessness, then rising again they drink, in the hope of never having a second birth'. The *Mātṛkābhedatantra* describes spirits as leading directly to the deity: *suratvaṁ bhogamātreṇa surā*

[39] Feer ibid., p. 206 *vetaraṇī* (*chu bo rab med*); Viṣṇu XLIII.20 *dīpanadī* is explained by Nandapaṇḍita to mean *vaitaraṇī*. Jolly, *SBE*, vol. VII, p. 141 fn. 20 refers to the description given in the *Garuḍa Purāṇa.*

tena prakīrtitā (Mitra, p. 409). Late Tāntristic sects of Buddhism have indulged in similar usages.

The attitude of the lawgivers towards the use of liquor among the lower castes was more liberal than for the Brāhmaṇas. Even Manu V.56 says that 'there is no sin in eating meat, in drinking spirituous liquor, and in carnal intercourse, for that is the natural way of created beings, but abstention brings great rewards'. According to medical works, too, drinking is completely harmless if done in moderation. Drunk thus, spirits become nectar and promote the well-being of the man. This instruction, however, can be observed only by the rich (Vāgbhaṭa III.6.1-41; IV.5.74-6, IV.7.90-3).[40]

On the whole, as we have seen above, the principle presented in the Smr̥ti *madyam apeyam adeyaṁ agrāhyam,* quoted in our title, remained pure theory.

[40] Dube p. 176 tells that also in present-day India the Brāhmaṇas are not allowed to drink intoxicating liquor. In most of the lower castes, however, it is permitted even for women.

SOURCES AND ABBREVIATIONS

Asiatica, Festschrift Friedrich Weller. Leipzig, 1954.
Böhtlingk, O., *Indische Sprüche*, I-III. St. Petersburg, 1870-3.
BSOS: *Bulletin of the School of Oriental Studies.* London.
Dube, Sh. Ch., *Indian Village.* London, 1955.
Grierson, G.A., *Bihar Peasant Life.* Calcutta, 1885.
Hobson-Jobson: Yule, H., and A.C. Burnell, *Hobson-Jobson.* London, 1903.
Husain, A., *La societe dans le drame sanskrit.* Paris, 1939.
'India', in Pauly-Wissowa, Realencyclopadie der olassischen Alteriumswissenschaft), vol. IX, col. 1264-1325. Stuttgart, 1916.
JA: *Journal Asiatique.* Paris.
Jain, J. Ch., *Life in Ancient India as Depicted in the Jain Canons.* Bombay, 1947.
Kauṭilya: Das altindische Buch vom Welt- und Staatsleben, das Arthaçāstra des Kauṭilya, übers. von, J. J. Meyer. Hannover, 1925-6.
Lassen, Chr., *Indische Alterthumskunde*, I-III. Bonn 1847-61.

Lokotsch, K., *Etymologisches Worterbuch der europaischen Worter orientalischen Ursprungs*. Heidelberg, 1927.
Meyer, J. J., *DasWeib im altindischen Epos*. Leipzig, 1915.
MW: Monier-Williams, M., *A Sanskrit-English Dictionary*. Oxford, 1899.
Mitra, Rajendralala, *Indo-Āryans*, I-II. Calcutta, 1881.
Ray, J.C., 'On the Hindu Method of Manufacturing Spirit from Rice, and its Scientific Explanation'. *Journal and Proceedings of the Asiatic Society of Bengal*, New Ser. vol. II, pp. 129-42. Calcutta, 1907.
Renou, L., *La civilisation de l'lnde ancienne apres les textes sanskrits*. Paris, 1950.
SBE: Sacred Books of the East.
Schmidts, R., *Beitrage zur indischen Erotik*. Berlin, 1911.
Vātsyāyana: Das Kāmasūtram des Vātsyāyana nebst dem vollständigen Kommentare des Yaśodhara, ubers. u. hrsg. von Richard Schmidt. Berlin, 1907.
Vedic Index of Names and Subjects by A.A. Macdonell and Arthur B. Keith I-II. London, 1912.
Zimmer, H., *Altindisches Leben*. Berlin, 1879.

CHAPTER 9

Dionysiac Aspects of Kuṣāṇa Art

*Martha L. Carter**

> Nous y reconnaisons au passage la plupart des figurants habituels du cortège de Bacchus, tout comme s'il les avait oubliés derrière lui, à son retour de l'Inde, dans la lointaine vallée ou la tradition plaçait la fameuse Nysa et qui est encore célèbre aujourd'hui pour ses raisins magnifiques.[1]

This observation by the great Alfred Foucher recalls most eloquently a striking and often overlooked aspect of Kuṣāṇa sculptural imagery. In using the term 'dionysiac', I must explain at the outset that it should be understood not simply as that which may be associated with any specific theme from the classical repertoire but rather in a freely improvised generic sense appropriate within the context of the Kuṣāṇa world. This would include all the varied and curiously bacchanalian scenes of wine drinking, drunken and amorous carousal, harvesting, and pressing of grapes, in addition to the symbols of the grapevine, grape cluster, and wine vessel. Since a purely Western interpretation of the origin and significance of such motives does not seem adequate to justify their basic *raison d'être*, we must, of necessity,

[1] A. Foucher, *L'art gréco-bouddhique du Gandhâra*, Paris, 1907, vol. I, p. 246.

*Reprinted from *Ars Orientalis*, vol. 7 (1968).

search for it primarily within the diverse elements from which the traditions of Kuṣāṇa art were created.[2]

The most spectacular sculptural forms of this imagery occur on Mathurān double-sided relief blocks, of which the so-called Stacy Silenus and Pālikhēṛā block are the best known examples. Both are so familiar, in fact, that it may seem redundant to describe in detail the features which lend them their markedly dionysiac character; yet, despite all that has been written about these extraordinary works, the essential problem of their usage and inherent meaning remains unresolved.

The Stacy Silenus was brought to light in 1836 by Colonel L.R. Stacy who suggested that it might have been the base of an offering vessel or περιρραντηριον used for wine oblations outside a Greek temple.[3] The top of the block displays a hemispherical

[2] Benjamin Rowland has recently taken to task those scholars who have tended to dismiss the suggestion of classical content or style in the Bacchanalian Groups of Mathurā, and he is undoubtedly correct in pointing to strong elements of Western influence (foreword to J. Rosenfield's *Dynastic Arts of the Kushāns*, Berkeley, 1967, p. x.). Although classical prototypes may be found for Kuṣāṇa dionysiac imagery in some instances, in others none exist. Seen as a whole, it presents a stylistic and iconographic amalgam, not a patent borrowing; and even when this does occur we may assume that some transformation of meaning has taken place. The most pertinent iconographic problem is thus not what motives were borrowed from classical sources, but rather why they were selected and for what purposes. Perhaps the best illustration of this selective process of assimilation in late antiquity may be found in the transmutation of pagan into Christian themes. Here the old Life Symbols of the *kantharos* and vine of Dionysos took on new significance to become the Eucharistic chalice and the Vine of Christ. Cf. G.W. Elderkin, Kantharos, Princeton, 1928, *The Continuity of Pagan and Christian Eucharistic Symbolism*, pp. 41-7.

[3] L.R. Stacy, 'Note on the Discovery of a Relic of Grecian Sculpture in Upper India', *Journal of the Asiatic Society of Bengal*, vol. 5, 1836, pp. 567-70, pl. XXXI. See also F. S. Growse, 'A Supposed Greek Sculpture from Mathurā', *JASB*, vol. 44, pls. XII-XIII; J. Burgess, *Ancient Monuments, Temples, and Sculpture of India*, London, 1897, p.4, pls. 60-61; V.A. Smith, *A*

cavity, approximately 16 inches wide and 8 inches deep, giving the obvious impression that it was meant to be a socket of some sort. The relief on its obverse face Stacy observed to be a drunken Silenus supported by a male and female bacchant, and, although it is much damaged and the heads of the figures all but obliterated, the main protagonist of the scene is indeed a corpulent male with an enormous paunch, seated precariously on a rock or mound with one leg tucked under him and the other hanging down. On either side stands a naked infant in an attitude of playful familiarity and directly above each one an attendant supporting one of the inebriate's outstretched arms. The Silenus wears a drape over his thighs covering his right leg and a chaplet of vine leaves in his hair. Whereas the male attendant on his left wears only a mantle fastened at the neck by a clasp, the female is fully clothed in a long skirt and sleeved tunic reaching to mid-thigh, a form of attire often depicted in Gandhāra sculpture.[4]

On the reverse stand four alternately male and female figures, perhaps more appropriately seen as two couples, against a background of flowering *aśoka* trees. Both women wear the same costume as that on the opposite side of the relief, with the addition of a drape across the legs and left arm and jewellery consisting of heavy anklets, bracelets, necklaces, and earrings. The male on the left side of the scene turns on unsteadily crossed legs toward his companion, his left arm around her and his right lifted toward her, as if to offer something which is now unfortunately lost. He wears a loincloth and mantle tied at the neck. The couple to his

---

History of Fine Art in India and Ceylon, Oxford, 1911, p. 136, pl. 3 I; R. Chanda, *The Mathura School of Sculpture*, Archaeological Survey of India, Annual Reports, 1922-23, p. 167, pl. 37; J.Ph. Vogel, 'La sculpture de Mathurā', *Ars Asiatica*, vol. 15, Paris, 1930, pp. 54-5, p. 118, pl. LVII, a (Indian Museum, Calcutta, no. M 1. ht. 3' 8").

[4] For comparable styles, see H. Ingholt, *Gandhāran Art in Pakistan*, New York, 1957, nos. 7, 41, 136, 310, 361; also M. Chandra, 'The History of Indian Costume from the 1st century AD to the beginning of the 4th century', *Journal of the Indian Society of Oriental Art*, vol. 8, 1940, pp. 203-5.

right appear to be merely spectators, but the male is distinctive in that he is dressed in a short-sleeved tunic covering the knees over a pair of tightfitting trousers. Two covered vessels are shown on the ground on either side of the second lady.

The Pālikhēṛā block was discovered in 1875 by F.S. Growse, who noted its close relationship in form and dimensions to the Stacy block but preferred to believe that both works were intended as pillar bases at the entrance to a shrine, and that their reliefs represented either Balarāma and his family or some unknown Buddhist legend.[5] The obverse face of this block is essentially the same composition as that of the Stacy block, the only difference being that here the seat of the central personage is clearly a rusticated mound or mountain form. On the reverse (Fig. 9.1), however, another portly Silenus is seated on the left side holding in his right hand a peculiarly shaped tankard with a handle joined at the lip and foot of the vessel.[6] To his right appear a naked infant at his knee and a male wearing a mantle who looks over his shoulder. Beside them stands a lady, in a costume much like

[5] Growse, *JASB*, vol. 44, p. 214; F. S. Growse, *Mathurā, a District Memoir*, Allahabad, 1883, p. 124, p. 166; A. Cunningham, *Mathurā*, Archaeological Survey of India, Reports, vol. I, 1861-2, p. 242. See also J.Ph. Vogel, *Catalogue of the Archaeological Museum at Mathurā*, Allahabad, 1910, p. 83, pl. 13; Smith, p. 136, fig. 80; Foucher, vol. 2, p. 149, 604, fig. 492; Rosenfield, p. 248, fig. 47; V.S. Agrawala, 'A Catalogue of Images of Brahmā, Vishṇu, and Śiva in Mathurā Art', *Journal of the United Provinces Historical Society*, vol. 22, 1949, pp. 194-6. (Mathurā Museum no. C 2, ht. 5' 1/2".)

[6] The tankard seems to be an unusual goblet-form to which a handle has been added. The decoration consists of schematized rosettes on the body, and a band of lotus ornament around the juncture of the body and the foot. The closest pottery shape to this is a footed vessel with a loop handle found at Taxila and called a censer (J. Marshall, *Taxila*, Cambridge, 1951, vol. I, p. 286, vol. 2, p. 421, nos. 133-4, vol. 3, pl. 125, nos. 133-4). The decoration recalls that of a schist goblet from Taxila (ibid., vol. 2, p. 492, nos. 60-1, vol. 3, pl. 141, j and pl. 143, o). Marshall calls this a *ciborium*. It has a heavy stemmed foot but no handle. The decoration consists of lotus-leaves in a band springing upward from the stem, and quatrefoil rosettes between dogtooth borders on the body.

Fig. 9.1a: Right Side of Pālikhēṛā Bacchanalian Group. Mathurā Museum. Photo courtesy of John Rosenfield.

Fig. 9.1b: Left Side of Pālikhēṛā Bacchanalian Group.

those described above, whose hair, hanging in loose curls over her shoulders, is bound with a wreath. She holds another vessel, almost identical to the first, as if to offer a fresh cup to her master; and a similarly clothed female behind her holds a large grape cluster. On the opposite side of the relief, behind the drinker's elbow, stands a male dressed in a long-sleeved coat, trousers, and boots, cluthing the stem of another bunch of grapes. By his costume and placement in the scene, he appears to be an Indo-Scythian devotee of the type commonly associated with Kuṣāṇa Buddhist sculpture.[7]

Even a cursory study of Mathurān imagery of the Kuṣāṇa era will provide plentiful evidence that the Sileni of the Stacy and Pālikhēṛā blocks correspond to pot-bellied and often bibulous Yakṣa figures, with a cup or goblet attribute, who were intended to represent the Yakṣa King Kubera or an intimately related Yakṣa type.[8] Whether we may see the classicizing influence of a Silenus,

[7] See Rosenfield, p. 248, fig. 47, a.

[8] There are, in the Mathurā Museum, numerous images of the Kubera-type, either singly or attended by one or more females. Almost all hold a cup or goblet, while the other attributes vary. See Agrawala, *JUPHS*, vol. 22, chap. XIX, 'Kubera and Yakṣas': no. C 4 (seated Kubera-type holding cup in right hand, sack or mongoose in left, with a female on either side, one of whom holds a pitcher). The group is surmounted by a solid projection and may have been a bowl support, according to Agrawala; no. C 5 (seated Kubera-type holding a sack in left hand and a cup in right into which a female pours liquid from a pitcher); no. C 6, badly broken Kubera-type image which originally held grapes in one hand and a cup in the other (cf. Vogel, *Catalogue*, p. 87); also nos. C 8, C9, C10, C11, C24, C25, C26, C27, C28, C29, KT55, 138, 240, 242, 244, KT246, 499, 594, et al. The use of the cup attribute persisted well into Gupta times, if not longer. These images were probably not all specifically Kubera but any of a constellation of royal Yakṣa-types, similar in form and function. One such was published by K.D. Bajpai (A New Inscribed Image of a Yakṣa, in *India Antiqua*, Leiden, 1947, pp. 7-8). It bears an inscription rendered by the author: 'The Mahārāja, Graha Yakṣa, called Dharmanitya, makes it known that in his hand is the *prasāda* of the god.' The image (Mat. Mus. no. 3232) is that of a seated pot-bellied Yakṣa, nimbate and holding a cup

Bacchus, or Heracles as stylistic prototype, the fact remains that, in the Mathurān sculptural idiom, the deity most obviously resembling the royal personage of the block reliefs is Kubera, disporting in bacchanalian fashion with his Yakṣa entourage on Mt. Kailāśa (represented by his mountain-shaped throne).[9]

It is probable that some of the single Yakṣa images of the Kubera type were originally intended to be atlantes used as bowl supports, as Vogel first suggested. These usually show an obese squatting or seated dwarf-like figure with raised arms, although in almost every instance the arms are gone and their pose must be reconstructed from the position of the shoulders.[10] To substantiate his theory, Vogel pointed to representations of bowl-bearing dwarf Yakṣas shown on either side of the *toraṇas* of *āyāgapaṭṭas* at Amarāvatī.[11] More recently, Mme. J.E. van Lohuizen-de Leeuw has found two relief panels from Mathurā which show the same form.[12] The use of dwarf Yakṣas as decorative architectural supports is,

---

and a fruit. From its inscription it is not Kubera, but a Graha (Guhya?) Yakṣa named Dharmanitya. If he is a Guhya he would be an attendant of Kubera, lord of the Guhyas (*guhyapati*). Since the fruit and vessel ostensibly belong to Kubera, he appears to hold them on his behalf.

[9] Cf. Smith, p. 137.

[10] Vogel, *Sculpture de Mathurā*, pp. 54-5. Vogel points to an armless Yakṣa figure of the Kubera-type (pl. XLIX, b. Mat. Mus. no. C 3) and another of similar pose (Mat. Mus. no. C 7). We may also add to this class no. C4 (vide, note 8), and possibly some others.

[11] Vogel, loc. cit.; see J. Fergusson, *Tree and Serpent Worship*, 2nd edn., London, 1873, pls. LXXV-LXXXI; J. Burgess, *The Buddhist Stūpas of Amarāvatī and Jaggayyapeṭa*, London, 1887.

[12] J. E. van Lohuizen-de Leeuw, 'Two Notes on Mathurā Sculpture', in *India Antiqua*, 1947, pp. 234 5, pl. XVII, d (Mat. Mus. no. J 13), and pl. XVII, e (Mat. Mus. no. J 17). Both are on the central panels of *stambhas* and show scenes of a figure depositing flowers in a bowl borne by a dwarf atlantid base. Another armless Yakṣa image which could easily have served this purpose was found at Ahichchattra and is now in the National Museum, New Delhi. (*Ancient Sculpture of India*, Govt. of India exhibition in U.S.A., 1964-5, catalogue, Cleveland, 1964, fig. 63.)

of course, common at Bhārhut and Sāñcī, but we now have actual evidence that such figures were used, prior to the Kuṣāṇa era, as bowl supports within early Buddhist establishments. A well-documented example of a Yakṣa image of this type was uncovered several years ago in the forecourt of Cave III at Pītalkhorā (datable by its inscription and surroundings to the second century BC).[13] It may be that this grinning gnomelike bearer with raised arms is Saṅkārin, who, according to the *Mahāmāyūrī*, was the tutelary Yakṣa of Pītaṅgalya (ancient Pītalkhorā).[14]

To return to the Mathurān relief blocks, it seems reasonable to concur with Vogel's theory that these, too, were used to support large vessels.[15] A massive stone bowl was found at Pālikhēṛā and would have required a base at least as large as the Pālikhēṛā block, although Vogel was forced to admit that the two would not have fitted together. Whether stone bowls of this size were made for sculptured supports or simply placed on pediments, as van Lohuizen believes,[16] their carved decoration has much in common with the bacchanalian blocks. The Pālikhēṛā bowl is cylindrical and flat-bottomed, displaying a band of ornament containing a running vine motive of *aśoka* flowers, grapes, and other fruit above a design of schematized lotus petals.[17] The vine issues from the mouth of a squatting Yakṣa, encircles the bowl, and returns to be held by the same figure. A second Mathurān stone vase of unknown provenance is rounded in contour and

[13] M.N. Deshpande, Rock-cut caves of Pitalkhorā, *Ancient India*, vol. 15, 1959, pp. 81-2, pl. LVI. Cave III belongs to the second century BC. The inscription is rendered: 'made by Kaṇhadāsa, a goldsmith'.

[14] Ibid., p. 82; S. Levi, 'Le catalogue des Yaksa dans la Mahāmāyūri', *Journal Asiatique*, II ser., vol. 5, 1915, p. 93, no. 42. This is possibly the Petirgala of Ptolemy (*Geography* vii.1.8 3).

[15] Vogel, *Sculpture de Mathurā*, pp. 54-6.

[16] van Lohuizen-de Leeuw, *India Antiqua*, p. 235. The central panel of a *stambha* (pl. VII, f., Mat. Mus. no. J 60) shows two laymen depositing a garland in a large bowl on a pediment. It is impossible to tell whether the bowl has any prominent decorative features.

[17] Vogel, *Sculpture de Mathurā*, p. 54, 76, pl. XLVIII, b.

displays a similar lotus petal design below a band of running grape-and-leaf pattern.[18]

There can be little doubt that most if not all the works described above were, like the Pitalkhorā Yakṣa, intended for some use in or around a Buddhist shrine. The Pālikhēṛā bowl bears a dedicatory inscription to the Mahāsāṁghika sect,[19] and the head of a Yakṣa pedestal figure from Jamna Bagh was donated by one Ayala, son of Indrasama for the Suvaṇakāravihāra, according to its inscription.[20] Vogel maintained that these bowl-and-pedestal forms were meant for pious offerings of the faithful, and that the stone vessels represented the *piṇḍa-pātra* of the Buddha.[21] Coomaraswamy, however, noted that the stone vases are unlike the Buddha's alms bowl in shape, and that the ornamentation of a *piṇḍa-pātra* was explicitly prohibited by Vinaya rule. He, in turn, suggested that since the Yakṣa pedestal figures are connected with the idea of liquid, either water or intoxicating liquor, that they should be interpreted as ablution bowls (*ācamana-kumbhī* or *ācāma-kumbhī*), '. . . regularly placed at the entrances to Buddhist shrines to hold water for washing the hands and feet of the visiting worshipper.'[22] We know from their representation on Mathurān relief panels that some of the single bowl-bearing Yakṣas were used to contain flower offerings, but we cannot assume that all related forms were intended as such.[23] The theories of both Vogel and Coomaraswamy are plausible and may be accepted in many instances; yet they do not satisfactorily explain one essential iconographic problem. If the Stacy and Pālikhēṛā blocks were used as bases for offering bowls or ablution vessels, why do they specifically allude to a

[18] Ibid., pl. XLVIII, a.

[19] See H. Lüders, *Mathurā Inscriptions*, Göttingen, 1961, p. 165 (143 d), insc. no. 125.

[20] Ibid., p. 122 (97 a), incs. no. 89.

[21] Vogel, *Sculpture de Mathurā*, pp. 55-6.

[22] A. Coomaraswamy, *Yakṣas*, Washington, D.C., 1928, 1931, pt. II, p. 65.

[23] See van Lohuizen-de Leeuw, *India Antiqua*, pp. 234-5. She has proved this by her illustrations of flower offerings in bowls (pl. XVII, d, e, f).

Yakṣa bacchanale and to wine as the vehicle of their intoxication?

A uniquely Mathurān variation on the theme of drunken Yakṣas may be found on a second series of pedestal blocks displaying the motive of an unsteady female supported by a male and a child. This group includes three works, from Narolī, Maholī, and Tusaran Bihār respectively, which follow the models of the Pālikhēṛā and Stacy blocks, but are more indigenously Indian in style and subject.[24] The best preserved, from Maholi (Fig. 9.2), shows a female of Yakṣī or Devatā type seemingly on the verge of collapse with her left knee resting on the ground. Her right arm is held by a male companion and her left is draped limply over the shoulder of a young girl who carries a footed goblet. An older personage of indeterminate sex stands to one side with the left hand on the chest and the right pointing to the mouth in what seems to be a gesture of surprise.[25] The opposite side of the block shows a female with an umbrella who turns toward a dancing lady on her left. The dancer appears to be holding something in her left hand which may be the end of a scarf or a tree branch. A male onlooker is represented on the right side of the scene, and another male, now headless, stands behind the first with hands on his shoulder and right arm, and seems to be whispering something to him in confidence.[26]

In all the pedestal blocks described above, the common motive is that of a drunken reveler whose balance is precariously maintained by a pair of attendants. This same theme also occurs

[24] For the Narōlī block, see R. Chanda, *ASIAR*, 1922-3, p. 167, pl. 38, b. For the fragmentary block from Tusaran Bihār, see A. Cunningham, *ASIR*, vol. II, 1875-8, pp. 64-6, pl. XX. For the Maholī block see V.S. Agrawala, 'A new Bodhisattva and a bacchanalian group from Mathurā', *JISOA*, vol. 6, 1938, pp. 70-2, pls. XXI-XXII.

[25] Agrawala, *JISOA*, 1938, pp. 70-1. Agrawala calls the figure a hermaphrodite harem-attendant, and the gesture, the *vismaya* attitude. I cannot see a family group here or, as Codrington supposes, some scene involving the birth of the Buddha (see *Art of India and Pakistan*, ed. L. Ashton, London, 1947, p. 25) (Mathurā Museum, no. 2800, ht. 3'4").

[26] Agrawala, loc. cit., pl. XXII.

Fig. 9.2: Maholī Bacchanalian Group. Mathurā Museum.

in relief scene on two stone toilet trays from Gandhāra. One, from an unknown site in Swat, depicts a nude standing male with his arms draped over two robed females, one of whom holds a cup (Fig. 9.3).[27] The other, found in the Parthian stratum at Sirkap, represents a bearded male in a short robe either striding or dancing while supported by a female on either side.[28] Both of these appear to be of pre-Kuṣāṇa date, and the first in particular recalls the classical theme of the drunken Dionysos or Silenus; yet it would be hasty to conclude that it was intended as such by its creator.

Fig. 9.3: Stone Tray from Swat. Photo courtesy Archaeological Survey of India. Taken from MASI, no. C4, *Excavations in Swat and Explorations in the Oxus Territories of Afghanistan*, pl. VIII, no. 4 (no. 21)

[27] E. Barger and P. Wright, *Excavations in Swat and Explorations in the Oxus Territories of Afghanistan, Memoirs of the Archaeological Survey of India*, no. 64, 1941, pl. VIII, 4, no. 21.

[28] Marshall, *Taxila*, vol. I, p. 168, vol. 2, p. 495, no. 66, vol. 3, pl. 144, no. 66. This may not actually represent a dance but may be a clumsy attempt to show movement.

A similar theme may even be found at Sāñcī, although it is usually given a much different interpretation. A panel from the west pillar of the South Gateway of Stūpa I displays a scene designated by Marshall and Foucher as the grief stricken Aśoka mourning the death of the Buddha's sacred tree.[29] Here we may see a royal figure supported by two of a group of solicitous court ladies who surround him. One of the group holds an umbrella over him, and another carries a pitcher with an overturned cup as a lid. Garlands hanging on pegs are represented on the right side of the group.[30] Whatever the identity of the royal personage may be, his unsteady posture, together with the festive atmosphere of the scene, could easily evoke the idea of a courtly drinking party.

Even more numerous depictions of dionysiac activities are found in the relief sculpture of Kuṣāṇa Gandhāra. One such relief (Fig. 9.4) now in the Lahore Museum shows four scenes separated by vinestocks with overhanging branches and leaves.[31] In the centre a naked Silenus rides a lion while holding a cup in his right hand, and to his immediate right, a lady in long robes offers his mount an object, probably a bowl to drink from, as seen in

Fig. 9.4: Dionysiac Scene. Lahore Museum. Courtesy Islay Lyons and Harold Ingholt. Taken from *Gandhāran Art in Pakistan*, no. 397.

[29] J. Marshall and A. Foucher, *Monuments of Sāñcī*, Calcutta, 1940, vol. I, p. 212; vol. 2, pl. 18b2. See also vol. 3, pl. 79, 27b, for a similar relief from Stūpa II.

[30] Ibid., vol. 2, pl. 18. Between scenes a3 and b3 the border decoration is a running grapevine which issues from an elephant's mouth. This clearly shows the presence of this motive in India before the appearance of the Kuṣāṇa vine scroll.

[31] Foucher, vol. 1, p. 246, fig. 129; Burgess, p. 39, pl. 144; Ingholt, p. 157, no. 397; cf. Foucher, vol. 1, p. 251, fig. 128 (Lahore Mus., no. 1493).

representations of Gandhāran *amorini* and their vehicles.[32] On their left a vintager tramps grapes in a rectangular vat with a spout, and a second vintager carries in a basket of grapes to be added to the vat. On the opposite side appears an embracing couple, and to the far right a naked *amorino* playfully pulls the mane of the lion he is riding, while a second places a krater of wine before the animal.

A more thorough representation of the manufacture and consumption of wine occurs on a relief in the Peshawar Museum (Fig. 9.5), beginning in the center where two vintagers tramp grapes in a vat with a lionheaded spout from which the juices flow into a shallow vessel, while a third vintager supplies more grapes.[33] To his right, two more workers supervise the filtration of the liquid through a bag suspended on a tripod. In the last scene on the right side of the panel the process reaches its logical conclusion as two revelers pour wine from a large vase into the mouth of a third

Fig. 9.5: Winemaking Scene. Peshawar Museum. Photo courtesy of Islay Lyons and Harold Ingholt. Taken from *Gandharan Art in Pakistan*, no. 175.

[32] See Ingholt, pp. 156-7, no. 296 (a fragmentary relief in the Peshawar Museum of a cup-bearing *amorino* riding a dragon while another offers the monster a drink from a cup); ibid., p. 177, no. 453 (another work in the Peshawar Museum of an *amorino* between the forepaws of a seated lion and offering the beast a drink from his cup); also A. Coomaraswamy, *Catalogue of the Indian Collection in the Museum of Fine Arts*, Boston, 1923, no. 07.488; and Marshall, *Taxila*, vol. 2, p. 496, no. 72, vol. 3, pl. 144, no. 72.

[33] Ingholt, pp. 183-4, no. 175.

who lies beneath them. The scene on the far left side, although badly abraded, shows a royal personage wearing a wreath, seated on a throne equipped with a canopy suspended on poles.[34] In his left hand he holds a spear, the end of which rests against his right foot. His right hand is raised, either in gesture or to hold an object which is now missing. Standing male attendants on either side of the throne turn toward their master, one gesturing with his right hand and the other holding what may have been a vessel of some type.

In a discussion of this limited length it would be impossible to include more than a few of the better known examples of the drinking or cup-bearing dionysiac figures of Gandhāra sculpture. Perhaps the most remarkable of these is contained in a scene carved between the lion-legs of a statue base in the Lahore Museum (Fig. 9.6).[35] On the left side of the block a bare-chested

Fig. 9.6: Bacchanalian scene on statue base. Lahore Museum.

[34] Cf. Marshall, *Taxila*, vol. 2, pp. 112-13, no. 93; vol. 3, p. 217, no. 93. This is a relief scene from the Dharmarājikā Stūpa showing the instigation of the *bodhisattva* by the gods. The future Buddha is enthroned under a canopy with slender shafts which rise from acanthus capitals of Indo-Corinthian columns, and is obviously a royal *baldachin*.

[35] See J. Burgess, 'Gandhāra Sculpture', *Journal of Indian Art and Industry*, vol. 8, 1900, p. 40, pl. 22,7; Foucher, vol. I, pp. 246 and 248, fig. 130; Ingholt, p. 157, no. 398. For a relief with a similar couple, see A. von Le Coq, *Die Buddhistische Spätantike*, Berlin, 1922, vol. 1, *Die Plastik*, pl. 16.

beardless young man sits holding on his knee a woman whose undraped back is adorned with crossed bands.[36] To their right sits a similarly posed couple: the female in the same obviously classicizing back-view and the male, a more mature bearded fellow, who wears vine-leaves in his hair and offers his mistress a drink from his goblet.

In addition to the purely human figures who drink together in Gandhāran reliefs, even tritons and ichthyocentaurs occasionally do likewise.[37] One such representation on a triangular panel in the Lahore Museum (Fig. 9.7) shows a male and female ichthyocentaur with tails intertwined holding cups. The male turns toward his mate and tenderly offers her a drink from his vessel, much in the manner of the statue base relief scene.

Fig. 9.7: Triangular relief with ichthyocentaur couple. Lahore Museum. Photo courtesy of John Rosenfield

[36] The crossed bands are of Western Asiatic origin seen on Aphrodite-Atargatis types. See Du Mesnil du Boisson, *Le sautoir d'Atargatis et la chaine des amulettes*, Leiden, 1947; cf. Marshall, *Taxila*, vol. 2, p. 701, nos. 3-4; vol. 3, pl. 211, nos. 3-41.

[37] See Ingholt, pp. 155-6, no. 390 (a triton drinking from a tankard); ibid., p. 155, no. 389 (a male and female ichthyocentaur holding cups).

Although in many instances motives such as these evoke the retinue of Bacchus, together with the accessory piscine monsters of sarcophagus reliefs, one should not be misled by too direct a comparison. The strong influence of Hellenism was obviously at work in Kuṣāṇa Gandhāra, but the basic theme of festal drinking, and especially of amorous drinking couples, cannot be said to have been introduced to India as late as the Kuṣāṇa era.

One of the most frequent motives of the toilet trays from the Śaka-Indo-Parthian period at Sirkap is that of a loving-couple sharing the contents of a cup.[38] No obvious counterpart for this occurs in the classical repertoire, but there can be no doubt that it was known in Indian art prior to the Kuṣāṇa era. One notable example, dated to the second century BC, may be found on a railing pillar from Amīn (Fig. 9.8), in a traditional depiction of a *mithuna* pair. Each stands with one arm around the other's shoulder, and the male holds a cup as if to offer his companion a drink.[39] A number of other drinking couples may be seen among the accessory figures at Sāñcī,[40] especially in two elaborate landscape panels from the Northern and Western gateways of

[38] Marshall, *Taxila*, vol. 1, p. 194; vol. 2, p. 495, no. 67; vol. 3, pl. 144, no. 67 (upper compartment of a tray showing half-figures of a male and female holding cups); ibid., vol. 1, p. 194; vol. 2, p. 496, no. 69; vol. 3, pl. 144, no. 69; ibid., vol. 1, p. 182; vol. 2, pp. 495-6, no. 68; vol. 3, pl. 144, no. 68 (a tray with nine compartments and a drinking couple in the centre square); ibid., vol. 1, p. 181; vol. 2, p. 496, no. 71; vol. 3, pl. 144, no. 71 (a tray with six radiating compartments and a standing couple with a cup in each segment); ibid., vol. I, p. 190; vol. 2, p. 496, no. 70; vol. 3, pl. 144, no. 70 (a more Indianizing version of the same motive); also Ingholt, p. 177, no. 486.

[39] Coomaraswamy, *Yakṣas*, pt. I, p. 39 and pl. 7, b; G. Combaz, *L'Inde et l'orient classique*, Paris, 1937, vol. 1, p. 179; vol. 2, pl. 123.

[40] See *Sāñcī*, vol. 3, pl. 74 Ib (ground balustrade of Stūpa II showing a *mithuna* pair with a vessel); and, pl. 88, b (central panels shows a male with a sword and a female with a cup); also Deshpande, *Ancient India*, 1959, pl. LXI, b; A. Coomaraswamy, *La sculpture de Bodhgayā*, Paris, 1935, pp. 50-1, pls. LIV and XXXIII, 64.

Fig. 9.8: Relief of *mithuna* couple from Amin. Courtesy Archaeological Survey of India. Photo from A. Coomaraswamy, *Yakṣas*, pt. I, pl. 7

Stūpa I. The Northern Gateway relief shows two amorous pairs seated on either side of a waterfall on a rocky hillside.[41] The male of the couple on the right side holds a cup for his lady, who sits on his knee with her arm around his neck (a pose reminiscent of that on the Lahore statue base). Below, in the foreground, two more sets of lovers cavort in a pool with a pair of elephants who have large lotuses in their trunks. In the panel from the Western Gateway, the setting is a paradisical garden with rich vegetation, scarf and jewelled-ornament producing trees, and a lotus-filled pond.[42] One of the males appears to be picking a jewelled necklace or girdle from a tree for his mistress. Of the five pairs of lovers in the landscape, two display the identical gesture of the offering of the cup to the coy female.

It is not surprising that this same essentially indigenous theme continued relatively unchanged in the Kuṣāṇa Mathurā school, where it may be seen among the half-figures of couples on balconies above the elegant Yakshīs of the Bhūteṣar railing pillars.[43] Another similar motive occurs on a Mathurān relief in the Museum of Ethnology in Munich, which shows a *mithuna* pair, each of whom holds a heavy stemmed goblet in a lovers' toast.[44] Likewise in Āndhra sculpture, the male of a regally attired couple, carved on the right side of a *bodhisattva* group at Kārlī, holds a vertically fluted stemmed goblet,[45] and at Nāgārjunakoṇḍa goblet-bearing couples occur with relative frequency.[46]

The idyllic scenes of the Sāñcī gateways portray an Elysium

[41] *Sāñcī*, vol. 2, pl. 34b v (lower panel on front face of east pillar of Northern Gateway).

[42] Ibid., vol. 2, pl. 64 C I (front face of north pillar of Western Gateway).

[43] Vogel, *Sculpture de Mathurā*, pp. 30-1 and 100-1, pl. XVIII, b and d, pl. XIX, b and c.

[44] L. Bachhofer, *Early Indian Sculpture*, New York, 1929, vol. 2, pl. 100 (left panel).

[45] Ibid., vol. 2, pl. 167.

[46] See A.H. Longhurst, 'The Buddhist Antiquities of Nāgariunakoṇḍa', MASI, no. 54, 1938, pl. XXXII, c, pl. XXXIII, b, pl. XXXIII, c, pl. XXXVI, a, pl. XXXVIII, a, pl. XXXVIII, b. R. Rao notes that the proferred cup of wine

as seductive as any from Roman Bacchic sarcophagi, but a thoroughly Indian one, replete with lotus-filled pools, jewel producing trees, and playful lovers belonging to the *mithuna* tradition. V.S. Agrawala has suggested that such paradisical motives may illustrate the fabulous Uttarakuru of Indian legend, described in the *Mahābhārata* as a land of jewel, ornament, and even garment producing trees, where its inhabitants, perfect in dress and appearance, draw sustenance from the nectar of trees.[47] At Bhārhut and Sāñcī, however, the whole repertoire of jewel and ornament producing vegetation, particularly the lotus-vine, is most closely related to Yakṣas or Yakṣa vehicles, from whose mouths or navels they often emanate.[48] Yakṣas themselves were also considered to dwell in the paradise of Ālaka, the happy abode of Kubera and his hosts on Mt. Kailāsa. In Kālidāsa's *Meghadūta* (II.3), a Yakṣa exile wistfully recalls its delightful groves of jewelled trees, wherein Yakṣas of Kubera's court drink (with lovely women) the wine of the *kalpavr̥kśa* tree to engender passion.

In view of the prominence of Yakṣa imagery in early Indian art, it seems probable that the motive of the lovers' toast, or of the offering of the cup to the female among *mithuna* types, should be seen as a theme belonging to the Yakṣas. It appears again at Kuṣāṇa Mathurā in relatively unchanged form, but in Gandhāra the influence of Hellenism has transformed the cup-bearing *mithuna* couples into seeming bacchants of the *thiasos* of Dionysos.

The whole panoply of Gandhāran *amorini*, *sileni*, vintagers, inebriates, and lovers appear to have been intended to be seen as Yakṣas. Although the classicizing proclivities of the Gandhāran sculptor eschewed the depiction of a Yakṣa producing vegetation from mouth or navel, he seems to have come as close as possible

---

is common among the Nāgārjunakoṇḍa *mithunas* (*The Art of Nāgarjuna-koṇḍa*, Madras, 1956, p. 82).

47 V.S. Agrawala, in introduction to A. Cunningham's, *The Stūpa of Bhārhut*, 2nd edn., Varanasi, 1962, p. viii (*Mahābhārata* vi.6.208 ff.).

48 See *Sāñcī*, vol. 2, pl. 2 (Southern Gateway lintel, Stūpa I); Coomaraswamy, *Yakṣas*, pt. II, pp. 58-60, pl. 12, 1, pl. 13, 1, pl. 29, 5, pl. 30, 2, pl. 34, 1, pl. 34, 2.

to it in a jamb relief from the Peshawar Museum which shows a figure, in a short tunic, who holds the ends of a large vinestock rising above him.[49] Moreover, the dionysiac Yakṣa vintagers, *sileni*, and *mithuna* couples are frequently seen within the Gandhāran inhabited double-vine scroll in a relationship essentially similar to that of earlier Indian Yakṣas and the lotus-vine.[50] Even the tritons and ichthyocentaurs of Gandhāra are obvious Yakṣa variants, much like their fish-tailed predecessors on the rail coping at Bodh Gayā who have the same gnome-like faces and big ears as the human-bodied Yakṣas, and function in the same ways.[51]

Together with the Yakṣas, the Nāgas must also be included in Kuṣāṇa dionysiac imagery. Mathurān Nāgarāja images often display the goblet or *kalaśa* as an attribute,[52] and in Gandhāra, a

[49] J. Marshall, *The Buddhist Art of Gandhāra*, Cambridge, 1960, pp. 58-9, pl. 54, fig. 78.

[50] See B. Rowland, 'The Vine Scroll in Gandhāra', *Artibus Asiae*, vol. 19, 1956, pp. 353-61 and fig. 1. Rowland discusses the very fine Gandhāran inhabited double-vine on a door jamb, now in the Museum of Fine Arts, Boston (no. 39.36). Within the medallions are consecutively a *silenus* drinking from a rhyton, an amorous couple, a vintager with a basket of grapes, another treading grapes with a child on his shoulder, and an archer. Rowland's stylistic comparison with the medallion vines of the Severid School at Leptis Magna is most appropriate, but we cannot assume that, in the case of the Gandhāran inhabited vine, the figures were introduced haphazardly, as from a copybook. The *silenus* may be equated with a Kubera-type of Yakṣa, the vintagers with lesser Yakṣas of Gandhāra who tend the vines and produce wine much as their Indian counterparts at Sāñcī literally produce and inhabit the lotus-vine. Rowland sees the loving-couple as a possible nymph and satyr, but in Gandhāra they are more appropriately a *mithuna*. See also Foucher, vol. I, p. 155, fig. 127 (a similar medallion vine frieze from Nutthu); B. Dagans, M. le Berre, D. Schlumberger, *Monuments pré-islamiques d'Afghanistan, Memoires de la délégation archéologique française en Afghanistan*, vol. 19, 1964, p. 31, nos. 81-3, pl. XX (a frieze in the Kabul Museum).

[51] Coomaraswamy, *Yakṣas*, pt. II, pp. 49-50, pl. 50.

[52] See Vogel, *Sculpture de Mathurā*, pp. 48-9, p. 14, pl. XLI, a-b (a Nāga

Fig. 9.9: Relief of Bacchanalian Nāgas. Photo courtesy British Museum.

relief panel from Kāfir-Kot, now in the British Museum (Fig. 9.9) shows a Nāgarāja and his queen seated on a wide throne drinking from cups.[53] On their left stand three Nāgīs holding vessels, one of which is a rhyton. Three more figures on the opposite side include a Nāgī with a goblet, a wineskin bearer pouring wine into a large krater, and a female holding flowers or fruit. Combaz has pointed out a possible precedent for this scene in a balustrade relief from Stūpa I at Sāñcī which shows the adoration of the Bodhi Tree above a seated Nāgarāja surrounded on either side by Nāgīs who entertain him with music and share the contents of a shallow bowl.[54]

If the Gandhāran Yakṣas are frequently associated with dionysiac activities, their chief, Pāñcika, *alter-ego* of the usually benign Mathurān Kubera, is no less so. A typical Pāñcika image, now in the British Museum (Fig. 9.10), portrays the truculent Yakṣa *senāpati* seated between two tiny attendants on a high-backed throne with a spear held diagonally in his left hand.[55] Above the

image from Chargaon appears to have held a goblet), pl. XLI, c (a Nāga image from Kukargam holding a goblet), pl. XLI, d (a Nāga image of unknown provenance holding a *kalaśa*). See also Agrawala, *JUPHS*, 1949, chap. XXII, *Nāga Images*, nos. C 14, 21, 439, 966, 1314, 1610, 2665.

[53] Foucher, vol. I, p. 256, fig. 133b; Marshall, *Buddhist Art*, p. 60, pl. 56, fig. 82. See also the companion panel to this one, showing the Nāgaraja alone on the throne entertained by Nāgī musicians (Foucher, vol. I, p. 256, fig. 133, a; Marshall, *Buddhist Art*, p. 60, pl. 56, fig. 83).

[54] Combaz, vol. I, p. 179; vol. 2, pl. 123; *Sāñchī*, vol. 2, pl. 65 a2.

[55] Foucher, vol. 2, p. 113, fig. 370; Rosenfield, p. 245, fig. 75.

Fig. 9.10: Relief of Seated Gandhāra Pāñcika.
Photo courtesy British Museum

throne back appear two more small figures. A relief panel on the base shows a reveler in tunic and trousers, possibly nimbate, seated on a recumbent lion while brandishing a cup in his right hand. He is attended by an *amorino* on his left and by a kneeling male and female devotee. The male appears to offer a large spirally wound object which Rosenfield suggests might be a wine jar.[56] The

56 Rosenfield, p. 245.

general posture and spear attribute of this Pāñcika image, and a number of others, immediately recalls the enthroned royal figure of the Peshawar dionysiac panel. Ingholt is perhaps justified in noting that this royal figure under a canopy was probably intended to be Pāñcika.[57] The base of the well-known Pāñcika and Hāritī group from Sahrī-Bahlol displays no less than fourteen playful *amorini*-Yakṣas and two *sileni*, one of whom rides a donkey.[58] Between the royal couple is a small cup-bearing attendant of a type often repeated in other images of the Gandhāran Tutelary Pair.[59] The persistent inclusion of this figure holding a drinking vessel suggests that this attribute had a significance similar to the vessel held by the Mathurān Kubera.

In other Gandhāran representations, the Tutelary Couple are actually shown equipped with drinking vessels. One such relief, now in the British Museum (Fig. 9.11), shows them seated together on their usual wide throne with a small adorant and the ubiquitous *genius* between them. Both Pāñcika and Hāritī appear to be drinking from the cups which they hold. Another version of the Tutelary Couple, from Takht-i-Bāhi, is of a distinctly different type (Fig. 9.12).[60] Here, the male, a less corpulent and more youthful beardless figure, wears a short tunic, greaves, and a fillet in his curly hair. The female is attired in a double chiton, with the remains of what probably was a *polos* on her head. She holds in her left hand a cornucopia with an animal-headed finial and her consort turns toward her holding up a large *kylix* in his right hand. The motives of the small child clinging to the woman's knee, the demonic figures pouring out the contents of large vases beneath the feet of the couple, and the small bearded *genius* who peers over the back of the throne with a full money-bag in his hand may all be related to the general scheme of the imagery of Pāñcika and

[57] Ingholt, p. 104.
[58] Ibid., p. 147, no. 342.
[59] See Foucher, vol. 2, p. 137, fig. 379, p. 145, fig. 382, p. 149, fig. 383.
[60] Rosenfield, p. 247, fig. 78.

Fig. 9.11: Pāñcika and Hāritī. British Museum.
Photo courtesy British Museum

Fig. 9.12: Tutelary Couple. British Museum.
Photo courtesy British Museum

Hāritī.[61] Bachhofer has observed, however, that the clothing and attributes of pairs such as these are derived from the images of PHARRO and ARDOXSHO on Kuṣāṇa coins; but he has perhaps gone too far in asserting that these deities were meant to be an Iranian replacement for the more familiar Indo-Kuṣāṇa Tutelary Couple.[62] It seems apparent from the many characteristics that they shared with Pāñcika and Hāritī that they were identical in the functions of bestowing wealth and progeny to their Gandhāran devotees.

It is evident from the wealth and variety of the imagery of the Tutelary Couple that their following was a large one in the lands to the south of the Hindu Kush in the era of Kuṣāṇa domination. Since this region included a mixed population with the elements of Indian, Iranian, and even Greek cultural inheritance, it would not seem too unusual to find the Tutelary Couple in a number of differing guises, depending on the time and/or place they were created. If a Graeco-Iranian, or perhaps more precisely Dynastic Kuṣāṇa influence, is to be held responsible for transforming the

[61] Hāritī, in the more usual version of the Tutelary Couple, is frequently shown with numerous infants. The Shāhjī-ki-Ḍherī group in the Peshawar Museum has the identical motive of the child clinging to her right knee (Ingholt, p. 147, no. 344). The theme of the half-figures pouring out the contents of vases is more complex. In a version of the Tutelary Couple from Jamalgarhi, in the Peshawar Museum, these vessels are money bags streaming coins (ibid., p. 147, no. 343). But, in another representation from Sahrī-Balhol, of the PHARRO and ARDOXSHO type, the motive has become a stylized pattern of two vases lying on their sides, exuding a design that is more vegetal than coin-shaped (ibid., pp. 147-8, no. 345).

[62] See L. Bachhofer, *Pāñcika und Hāritī: Pharo und Ardoxsho, Ostasiatische Zeitschrift*, n. f. 13, 1937, pp. 6-15. Bachhofer believes PHARRO and ARDOXSHO to be an Iranian reaction against Indian influence, but this does not seem probable. There is too much syncretism of imagery, and both share too many attributes to be entirely separate entities. Rosenfield notes the appearance of a figure resembling PHARRO in the place of Kubera-Vaiśravaṇa as chief of the Four Guardian Kings, in a scene of the donation of the four bowls to the Buddha (p. 247, fig. 83).

usual Pāñcika and Hāritī into the equivalent of PHARRO and ARDOXSHO, something of the same hybridization must have produced the extraordinary representation on the medallion of a silver bowl found near Tank in the Punjab (Fig. 9.13). Here, surrounded by an undulating vine motive, a pot-bellied, mustachioed, nude male sits drinking from a rhyton with an animal-headed spout.[63] He wears vine-leaves in his hair, a thin

Fig. 9.13: Silver Bowl from Tank. British Museum.
Photo courtesy British Museum

[63] O.M. Dalton, *Treasure of the Oxus*, British Museum, 2nd edn., 1926, pp. 58-9, no. 204, and pl. XXXIII. Dalton first suggested an identification of the main figure as Kubera cf. ibid., pp. 51-2, no. 198, and pl. XXVIII. This is a silver roundel showing a seated goddess on a high-backed throne decorated with a running vine motive. She holds a bunch of grapes in her right hand to a small adorant with a bowl. The goddess is most likely an Hāritī-ARDOXSHO type. ARDOXSHO is commonly seen seated on a high-backed throne on later Kuṣāṇa coinage (see V. Smith, *Catalogue of the Coins in the Indian Museum, Calcutta*, Oxford, 1906, vol. 1, pl. XIII, no. 11, pl. XIV nos. 2, 5, and 6; Foucher, vol. 2, pl. V, no. 20; A. Cunningham, Later Indo-Scythians, *Numismatic Chronicle*, 1893, pl. IX). The grape cluster held by the goddess may be related to that of the Shāhjī-ki-Ḍherī Hāritī (Ingholt, p. 25, Pl. II, 3).

drape over his thighs, and boots with turned-up toes. In his left hand he clutches the neck of a full wineskin. A smaller seated female on his right is dressed in a long skirt, a shawl fastened with a brooch at the neck, and a diaphanous upper garment. She carries a footed goblet in her right hand and a wreath or diadem in her left. This wreath is very close to one held by a royal personage in a festal scene engraved on a silver plate of Sasanian type in the Walters Art Gallery;[64] and the undulating channels which radiate from the edge of the medallion to the rim of the bowl are almost identical to those found on another Sasanian silver dish in a private collection in Teheran.[65] Although we cannot believe that the Tank bowl was the product of a Sasanian atelier, it does bear the mark of a tradition contemporary with cultures within the Sasanian orbit which display elements of a dionysiac symbolism in silverwork decoration in many ways parallel to that found in Gandhāra.

The portly vine-wreathed wine drinker of the Tank Bowl belongs most obviously to the Kuṣāṇa dionysiac Yakṣa tradition and corresponds most closely with Kubera. It is a work which appears to have been created out of a series of iconographic and stylistic amalgamations that preceded it and thus to have been produced in a very late era of Kuṣāṇa influence. One significant piece of evidence that seems to corroborate this view is a large

[64] F. Sarre, *Die kunst des alten Persien*, Berlin, 1922, p. 65, pl. 3; K. Erdmann, *Die kunst Irans zur zeit der Sasaniden*, Berlin, 1943, p. 98, fig. 69. This plate, unlike those of the more usual applied-relief or repoussé techniques of Sasanian silverwork, is engraved. Its date is as problematic as its provenance, which could be from Central Asia rather than Iran. Some of the Chionite coin types from the group to the north of the Hindu Kush show royal profiles having a crown with a peculiar lobe-shaped *korymbos*-device, similar to that on the crown of the royal figure on the Walters Art Gallery plate (cf. R. Ghirshman, *Les Chionites-Hephtalites*, MDAFA, vol. 13, 1948, pp. 9-10, figs. 5-6).

[65] *Sept mille ans d'art en Iran*, exhibition catalogue, Paris, 1961, no. 821. The central medallion has a monogram in the form of a trident. The bowl was supposedly found in Deilaman.

square clay tablet seal modelled on both faces, from Taxila.[66] The obverse shows a *garuḍa*, or possibly a cock with a lotus stalk in its beak, trampling a snake, represented above a Brāhmī inscription of Gupta character, belonging, according to Marshall, to the fifth century AD. On the reverse (Fig. 9.14), is a seated figure with legs spread apart, wearing a fillet with long tails and a thin drape over the thighs, and holding aloft in his right hand a horn-shaped object. This led Marshall to identify him as a wind god blowing a horn. Some sort of foliage and a small attendant bearing indistinguishable objects appear on his left, and on the opposite side are two dwarf-like figures, one of whom holds a long-necked vase. Comparisons between the so-called 'wind god' and the deity of the Tank bowl are unavoidable; both are seated in the same

Fig. 9.14: Clay seal from Taxila. Photo taken from J. Marshall, *Taxila*, vol. 3, pl. 208-59b.

[66] Marshall, *Taxila*, vol. 2, p. 682, no. 38; vol. 3, pl. 208, no. 59 a, b. Marshall renders the inscription: 'of Harischanda'.

manner, with a drape across the thighs, and both hold a horn-shaped object, which on the Tank bowl is obviously a rhyton. Since the 'horn' does not appear to touch the lips of the figure on the seal, it seems likely that it is not a musical instrument at all but a horn-shaped rhyton from which he drinks in proper Iranian fashion.

A similar motive occurs on a moulded relief roundel on a large unglazed amphora of Sasanian type from Khotan, again displaying a portly figure, here bearded and nimbate, seated with an animal-headed rhyton in his right hand and a vessel or sack in his left.[67] Another of the roundels shows a female attendant with a tall ewer.

Of the three examples of the Kubera-with-rhyton motive described above, the third is surprisingly far removed from its original Kuṣāṇa habitat. This migration of imagery, however, may be explained in large part by the wave of Buddhist Indian civilization, emanating from Kuṣāṇa controlled area of north India, which swept along the trade routes of Central Asia to China beginning in the second century AD Kubera (Vaiśravaṇa) appears to have been brought to this region through the medium of Kuṣāṇa Buddhist influence where his cult became extremely popular, particularly in his function as treasure guardian. Hsiuan-tsang mentions an image of the King of the Spirits at a Buddhist monastery in Kāpiśa which protected a treasure beneath its right foot. When a petty king tried to dig it up, the parrot on the figure's headdress flapped its wings and the earth shook causing the terrified ruler to flee.[68] In a similar report by Hsüan-tsang, we are told of a spear-bearing image of Vaiśravaṇa at Balkh placed in front of a monastery which was the repository of a vast treasure. A Turkish prince who had intended to raid the place dreamed

[67] A. von Le Coq, *Die vierte deutsche Turfan-expedition*, Turan, 1918, pp. 338-43, pl.V; R. Ettinghausen, Parthian and Sasanian Pottery, *Survey of Persian Art*, ed. A.U. Pope, rev. edn., London, 1964, vol. 1, p. 672; vol. 7, pl. 186, b.

[68] Hsüan-tsang, *Si-yu-ki*, trans. S. Beal in *Buddhist Records of the Western World*, London, 1884, vol. 1, p. 59.

he was pierced by Vaiśravaṇa's lance and subsequently died.[69] According to the *Annals of Li-yul*, a Tibetan history of Khotan, Vaiśravaṇa was not only a tutelary deity of the country but also the divine parent of its first king.[70]

It may also be of some significance that the *Candragarbha-sūtra*, written in the second half of the sixth century AD, refers to Kubera and Hāritī as tutelary deities of Persia.[71] This is obviously not Iran as a geographical entity but probably an area of Sasanian control in Central Asia. Sung-yun (*c.* 520) speaks of Persia as a wild and backward region in the western foothills of the Pamir (T'sung-ling) mountains.[72] Sung-yun's report comes, of course, from an era prior to that of the Sasanian Khosro I and the reappearance of Iran as a formidable power in Central Asia in the second half of the sixth century. If the *Candragarbha-sūtra* is a product of the era following the destruction of the Hephthalite Empire, as it seems to be, then 'Persia' may mean a large area under Sasanian control up to the Oxus.

To return to India and an earlier period, yet another and even more unlikely image of a deity holding a rhyton may be found on a pillar relief from the palace site of Vijayapurī at Nāgārjunakoṇḍa (Fig. 9.15).[73] Here the personage is represented standing and semi-nude, with a drape across his thighs. He is bearded and holds aloft in his left hand a rhyton-shaped vessel which, if it is such, has been completely misunderstood since the figure appears to be about to drink from the wrong end. Longhurst has called this image 'Dionysus', noting that it was probably an

[69] Ibid., vol. I, p. 45.

[70] F.W. Thomas, *Tibetan Literary Texts and Documents concerning Chinese Turkestan*, London, 1935, vol. 1, pp. 98-9 and 303-9. Hsüan-tsang has a different version of this story in which the founder of the dynasty, Kustana, miraculously appeared as an infant from the head of an image of Vaiśravaṇa (Beal, vol. 2, pp. 310-11).

[71] S. Levi, *Notes chinoises sur l'Inde*, Bulletin de l'École Française d'Extreme-Orient, vol. 5, 1905, p. 267, no. 33.

[72] Sung-yun in *Buddhist Records*, trans. S. Beal, pp. xcii-xciii.

[73] Longhurst, p. 11, pl. X, d.

Fig. 9.15: Relief of dionysiac figure from Nāgārjunakoṇḍa. Photo from MASI, no. 54, A.H. Lonehurst, *The Buddhist Antiquities of Nāgārjunakoṇḍa*, pl. X, d.

inexpert copy of a Roman work. It seems far more likely, however, that its inspiration came not from the West but from more or less classicizing models of the Kuṣāṇa School. An indication of Kuṣāṇa presence at Vijayapurī is seen on a similar pillar relief displaying a standing warrior with spear, wearing the typical Indo-Scythian costume of a long coat, trousers, and ornamented cap.[74] The sculptor seems to have erred once more in giving this heavily clothed foreigner bare feet. It is very probable that Indo-Scythian types were employed as guards by the Ikṣvāku rulers at Vijayapurī, and that contacts such as these brought about at least some familiarity with the culture and art of north India under Kuṣāṇa domination. One inscription found near Monastery II at Nāgārjunakoṇḍa mentions the pious gift of a *patipadā* (*pratipāda*), or footprint slab, by Buddhi, sister of Moda, the Śaka.[75] Although it is impossible to find any exact counterparts for the Vijayapurī 'Dionysus' among the remains of Mathurān or Gandhāran art, it seems reasonable to suggest that the prototype must have come from this area, and that the intention was to portray the Yakṣa king Kubera with his vessel of wine.

The Yakṣa imagery of early Indian Buddhist art, particularly at Bhārhut and Sāñcī, exhibits many examples of these playful demigods producing and inhabiting vegetation (very often the lotus-vine), riding fantastic beasts, and engaged in festal drinking. In Kuṣāṇa Gandhāra, their activities are basically similar; the major difference being that the miraculous lotus has been replaced by the grapevine, and that their beverage is clearly wine. At Mathurā a compromise seems to have been achieved, since both the lotus and other indigenous vegetal motives appear along with the grapevine or actually mixed with it in the decorative repertoire.[76]

[74] Ibid., pl. X, c; cf. Rosenfield, p. 224, figs. 157-8.

[75] J.Ph. Vogel, *Epigraphia Indica*, vol. 20, p. 37; Longhurst, p. 24. Longhurst suggests that there may have been Scythian soldiers employed as a royal bodyguard, and thus a colony at Nāgarjunakoṇḍa.

[76] The Pālikhēṛā stone bowl displays a combination of grape, *aśoka*,

Viticulture most certainly thrived in the lands under Kuṣāṇa rule, and it is likely that the vine was known and cultivated in the Indo-Afghan highlands many centuries before their arrival. The earliest Indian reference to it comes from Pāṇini, who noted that a grape-wine called *kāpiśāyanī* (after the Kāpiśa region), was imported in his time.[77] Two other varieties which he mentions are the *kālikā* and *avadātikā*, probably from the Kabul valley.[78] The use of wine in Maurya times is soundly substantiated by Kauṭilya, who noted that the best known vintages were the *hārahūraka* and the *kāpiśāyanī.*[79] A taste for imported Greek wine must also have been cultivated at the Maurya court, since the Greek historian Hegesander quotes a letter from Bindusāra to the Seleucid Antiochus I requesting Smyrna figs, a Sophist, and a type of Greek sweet wine. Antiochus replied that the figs and wine would be sent, but that a Sophist, according to Greek custom, could not be given away as a gift.[80]

To the historians who documented Alexander's campaigns in Asia, the 'India' of his conquests was not a grapeless region, since viticulture had been introduced there long ages before by Dionysos himself when he had conquered India.[81] When the Macedonians reached the city of Nysa (perhaps Nagarahāra on the Kabul River), Alexander spared it in deference to its immortal founder and

---

and other motives within one vine (*vide supra*). See also Rosenfield, fig. 41 (a relief fragment showing two worshippers beside a Śaivaite *liṅgam*, next to a piece of running vine ornament with grapes and leaves, inhabited by peacocks); cf. V.S. Agrawala, 'The Vine Motif in Mathurā Art', *JISOA*, vol. 4, 1936, pp. 130-4, pl. XVII.

77 Pāṇini, *Aṣṭādhyāyī* iv.2.99. Cited by O. Prakash, in *Food and Drinks in Ancient India*, New Delhi, 1961, p. 44.

78 Ibid., v. 4. 3; Prakash, loc. cit.

79 Kauṭilya, *Arthashastra* ii.25.25; Prakash, p. 96, cf. pp. 94-5.

80 Hegesander in *Fragmenta historicorum graecorum*, ed. T. Muller, Paris, 1878-85, frag. 43, iv, p. 421.

81 *Arrian Indica* 1. 1-8; Arrian *Anabasis* v. 1; Diodorus Siculus *Bibliothekis* ii.38.4; Q. Curtius Rufus, *De rebus gestis Alexandri Magni* viii.10.

visited the shrines of the god's sacred peak, Mt. Meros.[82] Dionysos had named this mountain, so it was claimed, after the Greek word μηροζ (thigh) in honour of his second birth from the thigh of Zeus.[83] Actually, this appellation may be a Greek corruption of its true name, Mt. Meru, the fabulous Indian World Mountain, by which it was known to the local populace. On its slopes grew the laurel, ivy, and grapevine so familiar to the homesick Greeks who were allowed to linger there to attend bacchanalian celebrations.[84] We shall return to the Indian Dionysos presently; suffice to say

[82] *Anabasis* v.1.6., V.2.5-7; *Indica* 1.6. The Nysa found by Alexander is likely the Ναγαρα Διονμσοπολιζ of Ptolemy (*Geography* vii.1.43), which could only be Nagarahāra in the Jelālābād district; cf. A. Cunningham, *Ancient Geography of India*, new edn., Varanasi, 1963, p. 39. Nysa, outside its mythological associations with Dionysos in several different locations, is an old Iranian place name. According to the great Darius inscription, Nisaya was district in Media (see F.W. Konig, *Relief und inschrift des koenigs Dareios I am felsen von Bagistan*, Leiden, 193 8, p. 39 [I3], p. 69). Another Nisaya is mentioned in the *Vendidad* (i. 8). There is no reason why a region or settlement on the Kabul could not also have been given the Iranian name Nisaya or Nysa during the Achaemenid era. The Mt. Meros of Alexander, however, has been equated with the triple-peaked Mt. Koh-i-Mor in Swat (*Cambridge History of India*, vol. 1, pp. 353-4). This presents certain geographical problems, since Nysa was supposedly located at its foot. A.K. Narain supposes that Greeks, like the Branchidae, may have settled Nysa during Achaemenid times, but this cannot be proven (*The Indo-Greeks*, Oxford, 1957, pp. 2-5). Arrian mentions that the Nysaeans were shorter and fairer than the Indians, more like the Greeks, themselves (*Indica* 1.24). This could have been due to a strong admixture of non-Indian elements in the population.

[83] Ivy grew wild on Mt. Meros, as did the vine, but because of heavy rains, the grape clusters tended to fall before ripening (Strabo, *Geography*, XV.1.8). See also Pliny, *Historia* VI.22.23. According to Julius Solinus, there was a cave on Mt. Meros where Dionysos was nourished (*Collectanea* 52. 17). Polyaenos tells us that the mountain had three peaks, one called Meros, the other two, Kondraske and Korasibie (*Stratigica* I.1.2).

[84] The vine flourished in the territory of the Oxydrakai (Strabo, *Geography*, v. 8) and in the country of the Mousikanos (ibid., v.22.1).

that classical evidence strongly infers that Alexander's armies found the vine already flourishing when they descended into north-west India. This area of viticulture to the south of the Hindu Kush was probably part of a much larger complex of ancient vine-growing areas in Central Asia. The first accurate report of these was made by the Han emissary Chang-Ch'ien (*c.* 130-125 BC) who found the new and unfamiliar fruit in Ta-yüan (Ferghana) and among the An-hsi (Parthians).[85]

We may assume that the Yüeh-chih had already become acquainted with grapes and wine in Ferghana or Bactria before the establishment of the Kuṣāṇa kingdom. Subsequently, they probably not only fostered vine cultivation in their realms but also exported grapes and wine to the vineless areas of India. The demand for wine must certainly have been great, since the *Periplus of the Erythraean Sea* records imports of Italian, Laodician, and Arabian vintages at Barygaza.[86] Other wine-importing ports were Muziris, Nelcynda, Bacare, and Barbaricum, the port of Minnagara on the Indus Delta.

Although viticulture is probably less extensive in modern times, botanical surveys of the last century have demonstrated that the grape still grows in the north-west hill country, particularly around Jelālābād, Peshawar, and in the Punjab.[87] The variety abundant around Peshawar is the *vitis parvifolia*, or Himalayan wild grape, which has small leaves and small berries of a sweet

[85] B. Watson, *Records of the Grand Historian of China, translated from the Shih-chi of Ssu-ma-ch'ien*, New York, 1961, vol. 2, pp. 266-9, pp. 279-80. The inhabitants of Ta-yüan stored vast amounts of wine. Strabo relates that Margiana, Hyrcania, and Ariana produced grapes of phenomenal size (*Geography*, II.1.14); cf. B. Laufer, *Sino-Iranica*, Field Museum Anthropological Series, vol. 15, no. 3, Chicago, 1919, pp. 223, 231-3.

[86] *Periplus of the Erythraean Sea*, tr. W.H. Schoff, New York, 1912, p. 42, no. 49, p. 77, pp. 44-5, nos. 53-6.

[87] For references see G. Watt, *A Dictionary of the Economic Products of India*, London, 1893, vol. II, pt. IV, pp. 270-1.

delicate flavour and thrives in a wild or semi-cultivated state.[88] It is not impossible that this was the variety of wild grape discovered by the Greeks on Mt. Meros.

Since local traditions of Yakṣa-lore in India have their origins in the most remote antiquity of popular culture, we may suppose that the Yakṣas were not unknown in the north-west prior to the arrival of the Kuṣāṇas or perhaps even before any significant missionary activity of Buddhism in the region. With this in mind, the question inevitably arises as to whether the Yakṣa-cult of this grape growing area became associated with the vine during the Kuṣāṇa era or whether this had not taken place previously.

One of the railing pillars of the Bhārhut Stūpa bears the image of a standing warrior (Fig. 9.16) holding in his hand what appears to be a tiny vine-sprig and grape cluster, not unlike the botanical description of the Himalayan wild grape.[89] Unlike the other railing pillars on which Kubera, Yakṣas, Yakṣīs, and related beings are depicted as recognizable Indian types, the Bhārhut warrior is unusual. He wears a long sleeved tunic tied in front with cords and reaching to mid-thigh, a robe or *dhotī* falling in swallow-tail folds to the knee, high boots, and a sheathed sword hanging from his left shoulder by a strap. His head is uncovered, displaying short-cropped curly hair bound by a ribbon tied at the back with two long ends floating out behind. R.P. Chanda once suggested that this strangely attired figure might represent Vepacitta, the chief of the *asuras*, mentioned in the *Samyutta-nikāya* (I, 223-6) as wearing boots and carrying a sword.[90] Barua thinks that it might be the solar deity Mihira and associates it with the Mahila, the name of the monk who is inscribed as dedicator of the pillar.[91] Coomaraswamy calls the Warrior either Vepacitta (Virocana)

[88] Ibid., p. 360.

[89] Cunningham, *Bhārhut*, pp. 32-3, pl. XXXII, fig. 1; Coomaraswamy, *La sculpture de Bhārhut*, p. 62, pl. XVII, fig. 43.

[90] B. Barua, *Bārhut*, Calcutta, 1934, vol. 2, p. 69.

[91] Ibid., vol. 2, pp. 68-70.

Fig. 9.16: Warrior figure from Bhārhut. India Museum, Calcutta. Photo from A. Coomarawmy, *Sculpture of Bharhut*, pl. XVII, no. 43.

or Sambara, the *asura* chief as a solar divinity.[92] On the other hand, less specific suggestions have been made by Majumdar, who is undecided about the Warrior's identity but notes that the vinesprig relates the image to the north-west,[93] and by Prakash, who surmises that it might be an Indo-Greek king.[94] One can hardly imagine why an Indo-Greek king should be found in the midst of Yakṣa-types as a *stūpa* guardian, but this theory may not be too far from correct.

The Warrior's boots are characteristically non-Indian as is his sleeved jacket. Such jackets or tunics are frequently worn by the 'foreigners' depicted at Sāñcī[95] and may be associated with generally Iranian modes of costume. The particular cut of the jacket, with sleeves and ties to fasten it in front, are similar to a garment represented on the stone image of a Parthian nobleman found in Iran and tentatively dated to the second century BC.[96] The sword, which is long and broad and fitted into a scabbard with crossed thongs and a *nandipāda* pin, is probably of the *maṇḍālāgra* type known in Kauṭilya's time[97] and the same as that

[92] Coomaraswamy, loc. cit.

[93] N. G. Majumdar, *A Guide to the Sculpture in the Indian Museum*, Delhi, 1937, pt. 1, pp. 24-5.

[94] Prakash, p. 149.

[95] See *Sāñcī*, vol. 2, pl. 24, 3 (false capital on front of east end of Northern Gateway of Stūpa I showing riders wearing sleeved tunics mounted on winged lions); ibid., vol. 2, pl. 62, 4 (north end of Western Gateway of Stūpa I showing a rider with tunic boots and short hair on a winged lion); ibid., vol. 2, pl. 36 cl (inner face of west pillar of Northern Gateway of Stūpa I showing foreign musicians wearing sleeved tunics, sandals, cloaks fastened at the neck, and on their heads, round or pointed caps, or fillets).

[96] R. Ghirshman, *Iran: Parthians and Sasanians*, tr. S. Gilbert, J. Emmons, London, 1962, p. 27, fig. 36. The long-sleeved jacket has several ties in front. The hair is treated in typical Parthian style, bound by a fillet, but with long sidelocks covering the ears, unlike the Bhārhut Warrior whose hair is uniformly short in the Greek manner.

[97] Cited by M.K. Dhavalikar in *Sāñcī, a Cultural Study*, Poona, 1965, p. 29, pl. 62, 2.

described by Arrian as a sword of three cubits in length which the Indian warriors wielded with both hands in close combat.[98] The Bhārhut Warrior's headband and uncovered close-cropped hair are clearly exotic accretions, and seen together, they most closely approximate Greek fashions. The ribbon with long tails is a Greek fillet, most commonly recognizable in Hellenistic times in white *diadema* of royalty following the style set by Alexander. A preponderant number of the ruler portraits on Bactrian and Indo-Greek coins show the bareheaded profile with short curly locks bound with the *diadema*.[99] From these details of costume, all so seemingly disparate in origin, the Bhārhut Warrior is revealed as a remarkably hybrid type, combining features of dress which are Indian, Iranian and Greek.

On a false capital from the *toraṇa* or the Eastern Gateway of Stūpa I at Sāñcī, there is a pair of small figures riding fantastic winged-lions with antlers (Fig. 9.17).[100] The rider on the right side of the block wears a turban and brandishes a large lotus stalk above his head while his counterpart, who wears a sleeved-tunic and has short curly hair bound with a fillet, similarly holds a large grape-cluster. There can be no doubt that both these diminutive riders are Yakṣa-types, yet each is represented in a different costume with different attributes. The lotus, so often associated with Yakṣas in early Indian sculpture and in all periods the most auspicious vegetative life-symbol, is here juxtaposed with the alien vinestock as if both were endowed with a similar significance. In this instance, it would appear that the sculptor has shown us two culturally and geographically separate breeds of Yakṣa: one from the north-west vine country and the other an indigenous Indian type.

In regard to the Bhārhut Warrior, I would like to suggest that he too should be interpreted as a Yakṣa, like those of other pillars,

98 *Indica* 16.9.

99 See A.N. Lahiri, *Corpus of Indo-Greek Coins*, Calcutta, 1965, pp. 22-3.

100 A. Grünwedel, *Buddhist Art in India*, rev. and enl. by J. Burgess, 2nd edn., 1965, pp. 33-4, fig. 10.

Fig. 9.17: Relief from East Gateway at Sāñcī. Photo from A. Grünwedel, *Buddhist Art in India*, Fig. 10.

but one whose attire and vine-sprig attribute associate him with the north-west. Furthermore, his aspect as guardian warrior or *senāpati* together with the exotic Graeco-Iranian elements of his appearance suggest that he may have been intended to represent a prototype of the Gandhāran warlord, Pāñcika, of Kuṣāṇa times.

There is a relief on the inner face of the south pillar of the Western Gateway of Stūpa I at Sāñcī displaying a standing warrior-guardian holding a spear in his left hand.[101] He is, however, clearly an Indian type, dressed in *dhotī* and turban, with bare feet and chest adorned with heavy necklaces. Hanging from a mango tree on his right is a long sword in a scabbard bound with crossed thongs and fastened with a *nandipāda* pin. This figure was identified by Marshall and Foucher as an anonymous Yakṣa-*senāpati*, but Foucher went so far as to suggest that it might represent Pāñcika.[102] The Sāñcī *senāpati* is basically Indian in conception, without the unusual features of the Bhārhut Warrior, but his very presence and position on the Sāñcī Gateway lend

[101] *Sāñcī*, vol. 2, pl. 66, a.

[102] *Sāñcī*, loc. cit.; Foucher, vol. 2, p. 116, p. 375, fig. 470. The spear or lance is characteristic of the Gandhāran Pāñcika.

authority to an identification of the Bhārhut images as that of a proto-Pāñcika.

It seems clear that the Yakṣas of the Kuṣāṇa north-west had intimate associations with the vine and viticulture and that these connections were recognized prior to the Kuṣāṇa era, if we consider the evidence from Bhārhut and Sāñcī. A broad investigation into the antiquity of the Yakṣas in this region is not possible here, but we should not overlook the fact that Alexander's armies were said to have discovered the worship of Dionysos and his *thiasos* to the south of the Hindu Kush. Megasthenes states that the Indians of the mountains worshipped Dionysos,[103] and, according to Philostratus, Apollonius of Tyana climbed the god's sacred mountain during his visit to India and discovered there a rustic open-air shrine encircled with a thick planting of trees and vines to form a natural roof or arbour. Inside the sacred area he saw vats, baskets, and implements of viticulture of gold and silver and a white stone image of Dionysos in Indian guise.[104] It is not beyond the realm of possibility that Philostratus' description is more or less accurate (although the accoutrements of the shrine were perhaps not so splendid) and that it was a well-known place of worship in the surrounding region. Since Yakṣas, as we have seen, were linked with the vine in this area, the sanctuary could have belonged to an important Yakṣa whose image Apollonius took for Dionysos. The description is not much different, in fact, from those of early Yakṣa shrines in Indian literature since they could be, and usually were, in the open air, in groves or on mountains, within some sort of enclosure surrounding a tree or image of the deity.[105] Moreover, the whole spirit of *bhakti* worship

[103] Strabo, *Geography*, xv.1.58.

[104] Philostratus, *Life of Apollonius of Tyana*, II, 8.

[105] See Coomaraswamy, *Yakṣas*, pt. I, pp. 17-28. The abode of a Yakṣa may be outside a city in a grove of trees or on a mountain. The centre of the shrine usually included a tree with an altar or stone dais beneath, and possibly a statue. According to the *Aupapātika-sūtra*, a shrine of Puṇṇabhadde (Pūrṇabhadra) had ritual jars (*vandaṛaghade*) beside the

within theYakṣa cult – the unrestrained personal devotion of the adorants with music, dancing, pageantry, and the annointment and garlanding of the image – all these elements of Indian popular religion had much in common with the cult of Dionysos.[106] If the grapevine had been given a place of some special importance within the Yakṣa cult of the north-west prior to the advent of Alexander, it would not be difficult to see how the Greeks might have transposed its rites and shrines to those seemingly dedicated to the Asiatic Dionysos.

The most apparent reason for the presence of wine and drinking among the Kuṣāṇa Yakṣas is that these deities as well as Nāgas and other related types were considered by their devotees to enjoy offerings of *surā* (spirituous liquor). In this heterodox, non-Brahmanical form of popular religion, meat and intoxicants were the traditional offerings to all beings of the Yakṣa-class.[107] According to the *Laws of Manu* (XI.96) a Brāhmaṇa was forbidden to partake of what had been consecrated for the Yakṣas, but this prohibition probably did not include the vast majority of their worshippers. Since wine made from the grape was the most

---

entrances. It was located in a clearing in a wood around an *aśoka* tree with a stone dais beneath it. The area was enclosed by a *vedikā* or *prākāra*; cf. O. Viennot, *Le culte de l'arbre dans l'Inde ancien*, Paris, 1954, pp. 113-15.

[106] See *Yakṣas*, pt. I, p. 19. The Yakṣa shrine was a popular haunt of dancers, musicians, minstrels, and other entertainers. The Jaina *Jivāka-cintāmaṇi* tells of a drama relating the history of a Yakṣa presented on special occasions (ibid., pt. I, pp. 24-8). Yakṣa worship contains all the essential characteristics of popular Hindu worship; only the animal sacrifices and liquor offerings are peculiar to it. Correspondences between the ancient cult of the Yakṣas and the elements of a popular fertility cult surrounding the Greek Dionysos are self-evident. The presentation of a cult drama is most striking, and we should not forget that a primitive form of the god is Dionysos-*dendrites*.

[107] See *Jātakas*, no. 113, describing a Yakṣa festival with liquor offerings; no. 146, in which liquor offerings are made to Nāgas; and the *Kathāsaritsāgara* (chap. CV) where offerings of meat and wine are made to Yakṣas on the wedding day; also Rosenfield p. 315, n. 160.

common intoxicating drink in the north-west, it could easily have been used as a form of *surā*, and, as such, used in Yakṣa offerings.

We have no way of knowing whether there was any direct association between the cult of the Yakṣas and Dionysos during the Indo-Greek era, although this is a distinct possibility. The vinestock and *kantharos* were symbols of new life and ultimately of the felicity of the blessed in Roman sarcophagi. It is conceivable that the dionysiac motives of the Kuṣāṇa sculptural repertoire had similar connotations within Buddhism. In Coomaraswamy's *Yakṣas*, pt. II, we are presented with two important generalizations. First, the author recognizes that all Yakṣas, great and small, are vegetative spirits, directly controlling, and bestowing on their *bhaktas* fertility and wealth, or to use a single word, abundance. Second, Coomaraswamy points out that Yakṣas are intimately connected with the waters and water symbols, such as the conch, *makara*, lotus, or the *pūrṇaghaṭa*. Yakṣas are the veritable Lords of Life: 'The fact is that the Yakṣas control not so much the waters as mere waters, but the essence (*rasa*) in the waters which is one with the sap in trees, with the *amṛta* or elixir of the Devas, especially Agni, with the Soma, and with the seed in living beings.'[108] This *rasa* is in its purest form in the sap of plants which are the embryo of the waters (*apām garbhaḥ*) and draw it from the rain and water in the soil. Soma is the purest form of the *rasa* of plants, but it is also found in milk, rain, dew, mead (*madhu*), semen, and *surā*.[109] The Yakṣas thus symbolize the fructifying power of the Waters and protect, or actually contain within themselves the germ of creation. The whole of Coomaraswamy's Water Cosmology has its origin in the ancient popular conception of the creation of the world from the Primal Waters. From this is derived the concept of a Primal Spirit, present in or upon the Waters, out of whom all life is engendered, seen as a great Yakṣa, Varuṇa, or Viṣṇu.[110] Although there are reasonable objections to links between a vague

[108] Coomaraswamy, *Yakṣas*, pt. II, pp. 13-14.

[109] Cf. F.D.K. Bosch, *The Golden Germ*, 's-Gravenhage, 1960, pp. 59-60.

[110] See Coomaraswamy, *Yakṣas*, pt. II, pp. 25-6, 29, 35.

conception having its origin in the Vedic age and the imagery of the so-called Plant Style at Bhārhut, Coomaraswamy argues that such motives were products of a very old, but unknown, iconographic tradition.[111]

The Yakṣas of popular ancient Indian folk religion, according to Coomaraswamy, became the guardians and bearers of the fertilizing essence, the *rasa* necessary for birth and regeneration, which was ultimately the same as the heavenly *amṛta*, or Soma. In the Vedas and Brāhmaṇas the deities who fulfill this function in respect to Soma were the *gandharvas* and *apsarases*, who are considered to have their abode in trees.[112] It seems probable, as Coomaraswamy has suggested, that the original nature of the *gandharvas* and *apsarases* was transmitted to the Yakṣas who had become the popular deities of fertility.[113]

Kuṣāṇa Yakṣa images and those of Nāgas often carry the attribute of the flask, goblet, or drinking vessel of some type, which, as we have seen, also occurs in Indian art prior to the Kuṣāṇa era. Although there appears to be no standardization of these vessel types, it seems apparent that the attribute had a universally similar meaning. Yakṣas and Nāgas were believed to be great imbibers of intoxicating liquor, but it is difficult to see why this propensity alone would have caused the attribute to be so commonly repeated. The most reasonable assumption, in light of Coomaraswamy's characterization of the Yakṣas, is that these vessels were meant as containers of the *rasa* which they protected, and from which their powers as Lords of Life were derived. Although the Yakṣa cult was never connected with the Brāhmanical Soma of the *devas*, it is indeed possible that, to the pious devotees of their cult, *surā* or wine was seen not simply as an intoxicant but as an *amṛta* substance. If this is true, there is a much greater intrinsic similarity of meaning between the symbolism of the Hellenic Dionysos and that of the Kuṣāṇa Yakṣas

[111] Ibid., pt. II, p. 17.

[112] Ibid., pt. II, p. 33 (with numerous references).

[113] Ibid., pt. II, p. 34.

than has formerly been acknowledged. The grapevine, like the lotus vine, is a true *arbor vitae* in Kuṣāṇa imagery, and the flask or vessel of wine may be the *vas vitae*, conceptually akin to the *kantharos* of Dionysos.

Stacy may have been not altogether wrong in suggesting that the Silenus block originally supported a vessel for wine offerings, even if it has since been demonstrated that it was probably used within a Buddhist establishment. The use of wine offerings to Kubera or other important Yakṣas would only have been a continuation of cult practices under the aegis of Buddhism, at a time when the cult of the Yakṣas in the north-west had not been fully assimilated within the framework of Buddhist orthodoxy. It is probable, however, that later during the Kuṣāṇa era the practice was discontinued. There are, of course, a number of reported instances of the habitual offering of different types of food to tutelary Yakṣas or Nāgas within Buddhist monasteries; so this, in itself, is not unusual.[114] A late Chinese source, according to Peri, mentions outdoor altars for Yakṣa offerings made of stone in the form of an open lotus and having smooth flat tops to serve as tables.[115] The Mathurān stone vases are obviously hollow, not flat topped, but both are decorated with the open lotus motive. An additional bit of information from Coomaraswamy, offered to him by Sir Charles Elliot, is that in Japanese Buddhist temples where Gaṇeśa is worshipped, the offerings include *sake*, although, as a general rule, alcohol is forbidden in such places.[116] Since this benevolent elephant-headed deity has Yakṣa connections, this

[114] *Bali* offerings were placed before icons of Hāritī and her hungry brood each day in the refectories of monasteries. See N. Peri, *Hāritī, la mere-de-demons*, BEFEO, vol. 17, 1917, pp. III 2 (from the *Saṁyuktavastu* chap. XXXI); *I-tsing, a Record of the Buddhist Religion*, tr. J. Takakusu, Oxford, 1896, pp. 37-8. I-tsing also mentions similar offerings before images of Mahakala (Kubera) either in front of the porch or beside a pillard in the kitchen of the monastery.

[115] Peri, BEFEO, 1917, pp. 55-6.

[116] Coomaraswamy,.*Yakṣas*, pt. II, p.4.

factor seems, to Coomaraswamy to justify the offering of such liquor.[117] It may well be that this is a modern survival of heterodox practices followed by pious Buddhists in the early years of Kuṣāṇa rule at Mathurā.

If we may regard the vessels and flasks of Yakṣa and Nāga images as a form of the *amṛta-kalaśa*, and not merely as an iconographic allusion to the Yakṣas' favourite beverage, a very probable relationship exists between this attribute and the *amṛta-kalaśa* of the *bodhisattvas.*[118] In Buddhist iconography there is, however, some confusion about the name and function of this vase, since it is often called a *kamaṇḍalu*, or monastic water vessel. Actually, the shape of both the *amṛita kalaśa* and the water pot are identical in basic shape, having an ovoid body, with or without a case, a long neck, and a flared rim. The usual *kamaṇḍalu*, however, has an additional spout on one side for the purpose of adding water to the vessel.[119] During the Kuṣāṇa era this form does not appear as a *bodhisattva* attribute, and we may indeed wonder whether the flask was ever intended specifically as such. In this regard Marie-Thérèse de Mallmann, in her study of Avalokiteśvara, has justifiably observed: 'Dans l'art Kushâna de Mathur'â—ou le col du vas se distingue nettement de la panse, oui la bordure de l'orifice est retournée, et où le goulot n'est pas pointu—il ne s'agirait pas du *kamaṇḍalu*, mais du vase-à-nectar-d'immortalité, *amṛta-kalaśa*,

[117] Cf. A. Getty, *Ganeśa*, Oxford, 1936, pp. 12, 18. According to the *Mahānirvāṇa-tantra*, Gaṇeśa is offered meat, fish, and wine. His images may show him with a wine jar in his trunk.

[118] The development of the Buddha and *bodhisattva* image in the Kuṣāṇa period is a subject of the utmost complexity which cannot be dealt with here. The Mathurān Yakṣa or Nāga flask, however, is so close to that of Mathurān *bodhisattvas* that the meaning of the attribute must be essentially similar; cf. A. Coomaraswamy, 'The Origin of the Buddha Image', *Art Bulletin*, vol. 9, no. 4, 1927, pp. 303-5, figs. 48-50.

[119] This is, of course, the fully developed Buddhist *kamaṇḍalu*. It may actually have evolved from a primal *kalaśa* form, in which case the confusion would be one of terminology.

emblème des divinites royales telles que Indra et Maitreya.'[120]

Maitreya's flask, his most characteristic attribute during the Kuṣāṇa era, contains *amṛta*, but it has clearly become an abstract essence of spiritual regeneration and symbolic promise of salvation in the future. The *Lalita Vistara* (VII, 91) states: 'With the Water of life shalt thou heal the suffering due to the corruption of our mortal nature.'[121] Here the *amṛta* has lost any association with the fecundating germ of creation or propagation of life in the natural world and has emerged as the sustenance of the spirit alone.

There is, interestingly enough, one aspect of Mahāyānist iconographic development which appears to recollect the original function of *amṛta* guardianship by the Yakṣas. One of the primary triad of Mahāyāna imagery is that of the Dhyānī Buddha Amitāyus, flanked by the *bodhisattvas* Padmapāṇi and Vajrapāṇi.[122] Amitāyus holds a bowl or covered vase containing *amṛta*, and his reflex, Avalokiteśvara, in Padmapāṇi form, carries the *amṛta-kalaśa*. The third member of the triad, Vajrapāṇi, is represented with the essential *vajra* as spiritual protector. Vajrapāṇi, in fully developed Mahāyāna form, is the second Dhyāni *bodhisattva*, and reflex of Akṣobhya, but his earlier guise, before elevation to bodhisattvahood, was that of a Yakṣa whose function was to protect the Buddha throughout his earthly career.[123] This minor divinity in Gandhāran imagery, as Foucher

[120] M. de Mallmann, *Introduction a l'étude d'Avalokitecvara*, Paris, 1948, p. 266.

[121] Cited by Coomaraswamy, *Yakṣas*, pt. I, p. 31.

[122] See A. Getty, *Gods of Northern Buddhism*, Oxford, 1914, pp. 37-8. Getty mentions a Tibetan ceremony surrounding Amitāyus which is a type of communion, for the purpose of obtaining long life. Bits of dough and *amṛta* (Tibetan beer) are offered to the image of Amitāyus, consecrated, and then given to the body of worshippers. Amitāyus, in this instance, fulfils perfectly the embodiment of the deity of Eternal Life, and the *amṛta*, as Elixir of Life, is shared with his devotees.

[123] The inclusion of Vajrapāṇi is extremely frequent in Gandhāran reliefs illustrating the earthly career of the Buddha. He is always a

and others have demonstrated, has all the qualifications of a rustic Yakṣa, and in the *Mahāmāyūri* is said to be the Yakṣa of the Vulture Peak in Rājagṛha.[124] Although the *bodhisattva* Vajrapāṇi is far removed from his original character, his appearance with two *amṛita*-bearing deities as protector recalls his Yakṣa nature. Vajrapāṇi, himself, does not hold the *amṛta-kalaśa*, but his primary associations with the Water of Life have been retained within Buddhism long after their significance had been forgotten; so long, in fact, that a new mythological explanation was created to justify them. The latest and most obviously syncretic of these comes from Tibetan tradition, in a variant of the ancient cosmological myth of the Churning of the Cosmic Ocean. According to this myth, when the demons had at one time concocted a substance to poison mankind, all the Buddhas met atop Mt. Meru to devise a means of obtaining an antidote. This was accomplished by the churning of the cosmic ocean, whereby the divine nectar, *amṛta*, rose to the surface. Vajrapāṇi was set to guard it, but in a momentary lapse allowed it to be seized by the demon, Rāhu. A struggle ensued and Rahu was finally overcome, but not before the *amṛta* had been defiled by the demon's poison. As punishment, Vajrapāṇi was forced to drink the tainted *amṛta*, whereupon he turned dark blue in colour.[125] One need hardly comment on the derivative nature of this myth, except to point out that this is an excellent example of a kind of *ex post facto* myth making that incorporates elements

---

secondary figure standing guard with the ubiquitous *vajra*, and his appearance and dress could easily be that of any of a number of nameless Yakṣa types of Gandhāra sculpture. Most often, Vajrapāṇi is represented as a bearded *silenus* or pastoral type, wearing an *exomis* or *dhotī*. See Ingholt, nos. 92, 99, 100, 104, 137, 188, 189, 333, 334, 336.

124 Foucher, vol. 2, pp. 50-64; J. Ph. Vogel, *Le Vajrapāṇi gréco-bouddhique*, BEFEO, vol. 9, 1909, pp. 523-7; S. Levi, *Journal Asiatique*, 1915, p. 30, no. 3; cf. *Lalita Vistara* I, 358.

125 Getty, *Gods of Northern Buddhism*, p. 49. Vajrapāṇi is also a rain deity and patron of the Nāgas.

of diverse and half-forgotten origin, including the Yakṣa function of *amṛta* guardianship by Vajrapāṇi.

It would seem that after the final eclipse of Kuṣāṇa culture as an active force, recognizably dionysiac themes came to an end in Buddhist India, although they may have lingered for some time longer in their place of origin. Between approximately the mid-fourth and mid-fifth centuries AD the Kidara Kuṣāṇas controlled Gandhāra, and allowed Buddhism to flourish there, a fact which, in itself, implies a continuance of artistic productivity in the region.[126] Even after the destruction wrought by the Hephthalite invasion (*c.* AD 460) we cannot be sure that all forms of artistic creation came to an immediate end. The Taxila seal may be dated to the fifth century, and the Tank Bowl is probably also from the same general era of the mid-fourth to mid-fifth centuries AD. Perhaps the last visual reference to the traditions of the northwest in Indian art may be found in the representation of the Iranian-Central Asian Kubera-Vaiśravaṇa drinking in the midst of his court in the fashion of a barbarian prince, painted on the ceiling of Cave I at Ajantā.[127]

[126] *A Record of the Buddhist Kingdoms*, tr. J. Legge, Oxford, 1886, pp. 30-6. Fa-hsien, in the early fifth century, found Buddhism flourishing in north-west India. He mentions particularly the profuse patronage of the four great *stūpas* at Taxila. Sung-yun mentions the Hephthalite ravages of Gandhāra in the early sixth century, from which the Buddhist culture never revived. See Beal, vol. 1, pp. xcix-c.

[127] See A. Foucher, Lettre d'Ajantā, *Journal Asiatique*, ser. 11, vol. 17, 1921, p. 233. Foucher identified the feasting chieftan as Pāñcika. See also J. Griffiths, *Paintings in the Buddhist Cave Temples of Ajantā*, London, 1896, vol. 2, pls. 94-5. There were originally four of these scenes, three of which were well enough preserved to be illustrated by Griffiths. All are very similar in schema, showing closely related princely types in tunic and conical cap. A vase held by one of the female attendants is a rhyton-form. Perhaps, as V. Goloubew has suggested, the panels were meant to represent the Regents of the Four Directions, in which Kubera-Vaiśravaṇa would be present (*Documents pour servir a l'étude d'Ajantā, les*

Although the grapevine and dionysiac motives related to the Yakṣas disappeared in north-west India after the fifth century, numerous silver vessels of Iranian or more probably Central Asian manufacture, generally termed late-Sasanian, display the vine scroll or vine tree together with unusual variations on dionysiac themes.[128] None of these have Buddhist connections, but we may surmise that there may have been some influence upon their imagery, either directly or indirectly, from Kuṣāṇa tradition. The running vine motive is found in the architectural decoration at Pyandjikent in Sogdiana as late as the seventh century.[129] Grapes and vine tree motives also appear in Manichaean manuscript illustrations from Central Asia, and grapes, like melons, were probably considered a Fruit of Light, since they are shown together as an offering in a fragmentary illustration of what

---

peintures de la premiere grotte, Paris, 1927, pp. 19-20). The whole ceiling seems to be representative of a Yakṣa paradise, with small figures, both Indian and 'Iranian' types, drinking and carousing in the midst of lush vegetal motives. The princely drinker may be compared to Late Kuṣāṇa donor figures such as the excellent example found beside a Buddha image from Jaulian (Marshall, *Taxila*, vol. 2, p. 471, no. 181, vol. 3, pl. 139, nos. 181-181a). A very similar type of head and cap may be found on an unusual Indo-Iranian silver bowl in decorative medallions (Dalton, *Treasure of the Oxus*, pp. 59-60, no. 205, pls. XXXIV-XXXV). If Cave I may be dated *c.* 480, as Spink has postulated, the paintings on the ceiling were probably accomplished within a few decades of the initial Hephthalite invasion of Gandhāra, a relatively short period of time which was certainly not enough to obliterate the Indian image of the Kuṣāṇa lord as Kubera-Vaiśravaṇa (W. Spink, 'Ajanta and Ghatotkacha: A Preliminary Analysis', *Ars Orientalis*, vol. 6, 1966, pp. 142 ff., pl. 1).

[128] I.I. Smirnov, *Vostochnoe Cerebro*, St. Petersburg, 1909. See pl. XXXVII, 66, pl. XLIV, 77, pl. XLV, 78, pl. LII, 86, pl. LXV, 109. See especially pl. LXV, 110, and pl. LXVI, 113 (the flanges on top of the handles of both vessels show a bearded *silenus* bust with cup or rhyton, not unlike the representation on the medallion of the amphora from Khotan).

[129] A. Belenitski, *Skuptura e szevopece dryevnevo Pyandshekenta*, Moscow, 1959, pp. 121-5, figs. 20, 21, 22 and 24.

is thought to be a Manichaean Bema festival.[130] A Manichaean painting from Bäzäklik shows a fantastic tree with a triple trunk growing from a large basin, with large grape clusters hanging from its foliage, which must be a Tree of Life.[131]

In T'ang China, where the art of wine-making had been introduced from Central Asia during the seventh century, the auspicious vine is commonly found on Lion-and-Grape mirrors.[132] Within Central Asian Buddhism, however, there is little evidence for the continuity of the earlier dionysiac themes of the Kuṣāṇa era, except for the notable inclusion of the grape cluster as an attribute of Avalokiteśvara at Tun-huang.[133]

[130] A. von Le Coq, *Buddhistische Spätantike*, vol. 2, *Die manichaeischen miniaturen*, Berlin, 1923, pl. 85, a (a fragmentary illustration of a ceremony in which a bowl of melons and grapes appears as an offering); pl. 85, b (an illustration of scribes under trees with hanging grape clusters). See also G. Widengren, *Mani and Manichaeism*, London, 1961, p. 105.

[131] A. Grünwedel, *Alt-Kutscha*, Berlin, 1920, p. 176, fig. 66. J. Hackin, *Recherches archeologiques en Asie Centrale*, 1931, Paris, 1936, pp. 19-21, pls. I, XII, XIII, a and b.

[132] S. Cammann, The Lion-and-Grape Patterns on Chinese Bronze Mirrors, *Artibus Asiae*, vol. 16, 1953, pp. 265-91. Cammann sees Manichaean influence in the mirror motives. Wine making was introduced to China c. 640 AD from Turkestan; cf. B. Laufer, p. 232.

[133] See A. Waley, *A Catalogue of Paintings Recovered from Tun-huang by Sir Aurel Stein*, London, 1931, pp. 54-9, no. XXXV; A. Stein, *Serindia*, Oxford, 1921, vol. 4, pl. LXIII; *Old Chinese Art*, ed. T. Misugi, Osaka, 1961, no. 63 (a silk painting from Tun-huang of a standing thousand-armed Avalokiteśvara in the Hakutsura Museum, Kobe).

CHAPTER 10

A Parody of the Kāpālikas in the *Mattavilāsa*

*David N. Lorenzen**

The *Mattavilāsa* is a one-act comic farce written in Sanskrit and Prakrit and attributed to a Pallava ruler of south India named Mahendravarman, who ruled from his capital at Kanchi from about 600 to 630 CE. The principal character in the play is a drunken Kāpālika adept named Satyasoma.

The Kāpālikas or Kapālins are one of the earliest mentioned sectarian groups of Tāntric adepts. Unfortunately no texts survive that can unambiguously be assigned to Kāpālika authors. We have, instead, many texts written by their opponents who criticize or parody Kāpālika beliefs and practices, and a few inscriptions that record donations to or from Kāpālika adepts.

The *Mattavilāsa* is one of the oldest works that features a Kāpālika adept. As such, it has undoubtedly influenced many later portraits. One cannot, however, assume that the Kāpālikas found in Sanskrit literature are simply fictional stereotypes. The inscriptions prove that the Kāpālikas really did exist, and many elements of their literary portraits correspond to what we know about Tantric religion from other sources. Reading between the lines of parodies such as the *Mattavilāsa*, then, we can arrive at a plausible picture of the nature of Kāpālika beliefs and practices.

A central feature of Kāpālika practice was their Great Vow or

* Reprinted from D. Gordon White, ed., *Tantra in Practice*, Princeton University Press, 2000.

Mahāvrata. To fulfil this vow, the male adept would obtain his livelihood by begging for alms with a skull bowl. Since the Sanskrit word for skull is *kapāla,* this made him a Kāpālika or Kapālin, while the performance of the Mahāvrata made him a Mahāvratin. The rationale for this Great Vow is found in a myth about the gods Śiva and Brahmā. Although the details vary in different versions, the key episode is a quarrel between the two gods about who is the most powerful. Śiva, in his anger, cuts off the fifth head of Brahmā. Since Brahmā is the archetypal representative of the social class of the brāhmaṇas, this means that Śiva has committed the major crime of killing a brāhmaṇa (*brahma-hatyā*). To atone for this crime, Śiva has to wander about as a Kapālin for twelve years, using Brahmā's skull as his begging bowl.

In the *Mattavilāsa,* the action centres around the Kāpālika's attempts to find his lost skull bowl. When he falsely accuses a Buddhist monk of having stolen it, the monk displays his own bowl, which has a quite different shape and colour. The Kāpālika's female companion, Devasomā, laments that their skull—which was once 'endowed with all the auspicious marks and was as holy as the skull of Brahmā'—has become black and ugly. The Kāpālika consoles her with the thought that his penance, like that of Śiva, can make it pure again: 'Our master Śiva, who wears the crescent moon, was freed of the sin that arose when he cut off the head of Brahmā through undertaking this Great Vow.'

We have no information about how the human Kāpālikas obtained their skulls, but it is most likely that they found them in cremation grounds. In a few sources, however, Kāpālikas are said to engage in human sacrifice. This seems unlikely, but the Kāpālikas' association with cremation grounds and other inauspicious places is in keeping with the ritual practices of more extreme Tantric ascetics. The basic aim of wandering about in such places was to overcome the duality of pure and impure, and the fear of death, by constant contact with impure places and things such as cremation grounds and corpses. This constant association with impurity would also force the adepts to learn to endure the scorn and disgust of persons who were still tied to the rules of proper social behaviour.

Other social rules that the Kāpālikas and other Tantric adepts purposely transgressed concern sex and food. In literary works such as the *Mattavilāsa,* the Kāpālikas are often described as hedonists addicted to sexual play with beautiful female companions and to drinking liquor and eating meat. In the *Mattavilāsa,* the Kāpālika Satyasoma's lovely companion Devasomā is presumed to be his sexual partner and also attracts the lustful glances of the Buddhist monk and the Pāśupata ascetic. Together Satyasoma and Devasomā also enjoy the meat kabobs that they receive as alms in the skull bowl and the liquor that they drink from the same vessel.

From what we know about Tantric religion, it is unlikely the Kāpālikas were simple hedonists. Some Tantric adepts did engage in extramarital sexual intercourse and the consumption of foods prohibited to upper-caste Hindus, such as meat and liquor. Such behaviour was, however, displayed in the context of a controlled ritual, not as simple hedonistic enjoyment. In the best-known ritual, the adept took the five prohibited things whose names begin with the letter M: liquor, meat, fish, parched grain, and sexual intercourse (*madya, māṁsa, matsya, mudrā, maithuna*). The female partner in the act of sexual intercourse is usually described as a low-caste woman who is not the male adept's own wife. The basic aim of all this, as in the case of the association with cremation grounds and corpses, was to rise above the duality of the pure and the impure through the transgression of the rules of proper social conduct.

One other aspect of the ritual act of sexual intercourse is often suggested in Tantric sources. The ritual is regarded as a reenactment of the sexual intercourse between Śiva and his wife, the goddess called Pārvatī or Umā. The bliss of this union is compared to the bliss of liberation or *mokṣa*, and the Tantric adepts were expected to recreate this divine bliss in their own acts of ritual intercourse.

The theological system of the Kāpālikas is often called Soma-siddhānta, the doctrine of Soma. Several commentaries on another Sanskrit drama with a Kāpālika character gloss the Soma of Soma-siddhānta as implying 'Śiva united with Uma' (*sa-Umā = soma).* In fact, we have no way of knowing the nature of the doctrines of Soma-siddhānta, but the name appears both in literary texts and in inscriptions. In many sources, Soma-siddhāntin, like Mahāvratin, is another title given to the Kāpālikas. In the *Mattavilāsa*, the word *soma* appears in the names of both Satyasoma and Devasomā. It is also barely possible that the name also suggests some sort of connection with the ancient Brāhmanical worship of the intoxicating sacred drink called *soma.*

The physical appearance of Kāpālika adepts is only hinted at in the *Mattavilāsa,* but other sources give more detailed descriptions. One of the most interesting is from an inscription from Andhra Pradesh dated about 1050 CE. It records a donation by a brāhmaṇa (*vipra*) named Somi-bhaṭṭāraka who was the abbot of a local Śaṅkareśvara (Śiva) temple. The inscription calls him an expert in Soma-siddhanta and a Mahāvratin. He is described as 'sprinkled with ashes; adorned with the six insignia; and holding a khaṭvāṅga club, a skull (*kapāla*), damaru and mṛdaṅga drums, and a trumpet'. The six insignia are not listed, but the south Indian Vaiṣṇava theologians Yāmunācārya and Rāmānuja identify the six insignia of the Kāpālikas as two different kinds of earrings, a necklace, a jewelled crest, ashes, and the sacred thread. They add the skull and khaṭvāṅga as secondary insignia. The *khaṭvāṅga* consists of a pole about 50 to 75 cm (20-30 inches) in length, on which a complete skull is impaled.

It is impossible to know how the Kāpālikas were organized as a religious group, but their association with a specific vow, a specific doctrine, and a special dress code suggests some definite institutional tradition. By the thirteenth or fourteenth centuries, however, whatever organization they once may have had apparently had already disappeared. The Kāpālikas survived mainly in the literary and religious texts of their opponents as stereotypical villains, buffoons, or heretics.

The translation given below follows the text, *Mattavilāsaprahasana,* edited by T. Ganapati Sastri (Trivandrum: Government Press, 1917). More recent editions are available, but all seem to be based on this one. Here and there, I have added a short phrase or extra stage direction to explain things that might not be immediately obvious to readers. The translations of the numbered verses use English rhymes and/or metres to mark them off from the prose text. In the original, the women, the Buddhist, and the madman all speak in different varieties of Prakrit rather than in Sanskrit.

One additional point concerns two somewhat confusing references to the Kāpālika that appear in the text shortly after verse 20. He is called first a Great Brahman (*mahābrāhmaṇa*) and then a Great Pāśupata (*mahapāśupata*). At least one translator has assumed that these terms should refer to the Pāśupata and not to the Kāpālika. In fact, the term Great Brahman is commonly used to refer to the untouchables who help officiate during the highly polluting rite of cremation. The term Great Pāśupata is evidently a similar ironic title.

Another point easily missed is the confusion of myths and legends in the madman's speech just before verse 19. Such mixed allusions will be lost on most modern readers, but they must have amused the cultured audience of Mahendravarman's court.

FURTHER READING

A general work on the Kāpālikas is David N. Lorenzen, *The Kāpālikas and Kālāmukhas,* 2nd edn. (Delhi: Motilal Banarsidass, 1991). This also contains a chapter on the Pāśupatas. The discussion of Somibhaṭṭaraka's inscription is in Appendix A of the book. For another recent English translation of the *Mattavilāsa*, one that includes the Sanskrit text, see *Mattavilāsa Prahasana* (*The Farce of Drunken Sport*), edited and translated by Michael Lockwood and A. Vishnu Bhat (Chennai: Christian Literature Society, 1981).

MATTAVILĀSA OR DRUNKEN GAMES

Cast:

Director
Actress
Kāpālika named Satyasoma
Kāpālika's female companion named Devasomā
Buddhist monk named Nāgasena
Pāśupata named Babhrukalpa
Madman

After the verse of blessing, the Director enters.

Director:

The god who carries a skull, the divine Kapālin,
Whose languages, costumes, forms, and actions are many,
Whose dance reveals beauty through intense emotion,
Whose power moves the cosmos, of infinite wisdom,
Who is also the silent spectator watching the show,
May he grant you fame that fills the entire earth. (1)

Ah, at last I have found a suitable way to please my older wife, who has been out of sorts ever since I appointed myself a younger wife. Today the royal assembly finally appointed us to put on a public show. I must go tell her the news [*looking behind the scenes*]. My dear, please come here.

Actress: [*entering, angrily*] Have you at last come to play the drunken games of adolescents?

Director: It is as you say.

Actress: Then you should go play with her to whom you wish to make love.

Director: I want to perform it with you.

Actress: Were you told to do this?

Director: Yes, I was. What's more, if you join us you will be well paid.

Actress: You must be really pleased about this.

Director: My dear, aren't you pleased as well? If the assembly is satisfied by your performance, it will reward you generously.
Actress: [*happily*] Have I really won the honourable gentlemen's favour?
Director: I'm sure you've won it.
Actress: In that case, what favour can I offer to you?
Director: What's all this talk about favours?

My sweet love, your bright smile,
Curving eyebrow, and downy cheek,
Once I've seen your perfect face
What more is there for me to seek? (2)

Actress: What play are you about to present?
Director: The one you just mentioned, the farce called 'Drunken Games'.
Actress: It seems that my anger has spoken for me in this matter. Sir, who is the poet who has composed this work?
Director: Listen, my dear. In the lands ruled by the Pallava family there was the mighty scion Siṃhaviṣṇu-varman. Using many different tactics, he won a wide circle of vassals. In courage, he was the equal of Indra. In generosity, he outdid even the god of wealth. The author is his son, King Mahendravikrama-varman, a man who has conquered all personal vices and is dedicated to providing for the welfare of others.

Now, when the Kali Age is here,
And lofty virtues disappear,
Wisdom, compassion, and honesty,
Art, generosity, truth, and beauty,
Dignity, firmness, and modesty,
Seek refuge with this virtuous king.
As, when the universe began,
The countless fragments of creation
Sought refuge with the Primal Man. (3)

His eloquence is a mine
Of priceless gems, a presence
That brings praise to songs
Of good but lesser talents. (4)

Actress: What are we waiting for? Let the premier performance be begun.

Director:

By adding to this illustrous poet's fame,
My own humble songs have been put to shame.

[*From behind the scenes.*] My love, Devasomā!

Director:

And so, the Kāpālika, with lovely wench and skull,
Finds shame under the spell of alcohol. (5)

[*The two exit. The Kāpālika then enters with his female companion.*]

Kāpālika: [*acting drunk*] Devasomā, my love, it's true. The power of changing form at will is won by means of penance. The proper performance of the Great Vow has made you irresistibly beautiful:

Your soft laughter and gentle sighs,
Your falling garlands and flowing hair,
Your playful smiles and dancing eyes,
Your moist cheeks and lazy stare. (6)

Devasomā: My lord, you seem to be saying that it's I who am drunk.

Kāpālika: What did you say?

Devasomā: I'm not saying anything.

Kāpālika: Is it possible that I'm drunk?

Devasomā: My lord, the earth is spinning all around. I think I'm falling. Please hold me up.

Kāpālika: I've got you, my love, [*trying to support her and falling*] Somadeva, my love, are you angry at me? Every time I try to hold you up, you move away.

Devasomā: Hah! It must be this Somadevā who gets angry and moves away, even when you bow and scrape before her.

Kāpālika: Aren't you Somadevā? [*thinking*] No, you're Devasomā.

Devasomā: If you love this Somadevā so much, you shouldn't call her by my name.

Kāpālika: My dear, this was just a simple slip of the tongue. I'm drunk. No offence to you was intended.

Devasomā: How convenient that it's not you who's to blame.

Kāpālika: How can I let vile drink get control over me? All right. All right. Starting from today, I will stop being a slave of alcohol.

Devasomā: My lord, please don't interrupt your penance by breaking your holy vow because of me. [*falls at his feet*]

Kāpālika: [*happily raising her up and embracing her*] *Dhr̥rṇa dhr̥rṇa*, homage to Śiva. My love,

> Drink up until intoxication,
> Look deep into your lover's eyes,
> Wear fancy clothes from every nation:
> Long life to the god who found
> So fine a path for our salvation. (7)

Devasomā: Is it proper to speak in this way? The Jaina saints describe the path to salvation in quite another way.

Kāpālika: Dear, their views are completely mistaken.

> The Jains argue that each effect
> Resembles the cause from which it came.
> But against this they also expect
> That the bliss of our eternal salvation
> Comes from penance and its pain.
> These fools defeat this curious claim
> With their own logical argumentation. (8)

Devasomā: May their sins be ended.

Kāpālika: May their sins be ended. There is no point even to revile these sinners. They torment living beings by making them remain celibate, tear out their hair, refuse to bathe, eat only at certain hours, and wear dirty clothes. Even mentioning them makes me now want to wash out my mouth with liquor.

Devasomā: Then let's go off to another liquor shop.
Kāpālika: My love, let's do it.

[*Both walk about.*]

Kāpālika: Ah, the city of Kāñcī is incredibly beautiful. The sounds of drums mix with thunder from the clouds that sit on the top of the tall palaces; the flower markets create their own spring season; the rustle of young girls moving about announces the immanent victory of the God of Love. Likewise,

> The infinite, incomparable bliss
> That wise sages first discovered
> Is now as close as one could wish.
> For we have added a special measure,
> No need to abandon the life of a lover
> This bliss includes all sensual pleasure. (9)

Devasomā: My lord, just like the goddess of liquor, Kāñcī is irreproachably sweet.
Kāpālika: My love, just look. This liquor shop equals the majesty of the sacrificial enclosure. Here the flag pole equals the sacrificial post; the liquor equals the *soma*; the drinkers, the priests; the liquor glasses, the *soma* cups; the snacks such as meat kabobs, the various oblations; the drunken chatter, the sacrificial formulas; the songs, the sacrificial hymns; the liquor vats, the sacrificial ladles; the thirst of the drinkers, the sacrificial fire; and the owner of the shop, the sponsor of the sacrifice.
Devasomā: And the alms we get here will be the offering to Rudra.
Kāpālika: Ah, the dances of these drunken games create such a beautiful, confused uproar. The dancers move to the rhythm of the drums, gesture, shout, flirt, lift up their shirts with one hand, and lose the beat for a second as they hike up their falling garments.
Devasomā: Ah, my teacher is a true connoisseur.
Kāpālika: When poured into glasses, the goddess of liquor puts jewels to shame, reconciles angry lovers, and gives courage to youth. She is the very soul of pleasure. What more can I say?

It's just not true what they claim
About the way the fiery ray
From Śiva's eye burned to ashes
The body of our god of love.
What really happened I prefer to think
Is that Śiva's penance was so intense
The heat produced could not be controlled,
So when love came too near to the flame
He melted like wax, and ever since
Has fuelled the fire of our desire. (10)

Devasomā: This is true, my lord. Śiva is devoted to the world's welfare and would never destroy it.

[*Both drum on their own cheeks.*]

Kāpālika: Madam, please give us alms.

[From *behind the scenes.*] My lord, here are some alms. Please accept them.

Kāpālika: I accept them. My love, where is my skull bowl?
Devasomā: I don't see it anywhere.
Kāpālika: [*thinking*] Hm, I guess maybe I forgot it in the liquor shop? Oh well, we'll have to go back and see.
Devasomā: My lord, it is against our rule to not accept alms that have been offered with respect. What do we do now?
Kāpālika: We will have to resort to the rule for emergencies and accept them in this cow horn.
Devasomā: So be it. [*He accepts the alms.*]

[*Both then walk about looking for the skull bowl.*]

Kāpālika: How can it be that even here we cannot find it? [*acting depressed*] Listen, all you Māheśvaras, have any of you here seen our alms bowl? What did you say? You haven't seen it? Ay, I'm ruined. My penance is broken. How can I still remain a Kāpālika? Alas,

My spotless skull was a very dear friend.
With it in my hand I drank and was fed
And used it at night to pillow my head.
Its loss is a hurt that just won't mend. (11)

[*Falls and beats his head on the ground.*]

Let it be. The skull is merely a symbol. I can still keep the title of a Kāpālika. [*stands up*]

Devasomā: My lord, who could have grabbed the skull?
Kāpālika: My love, I suspect that it was stolen by a dog or by a Buddhist monk for the meat kabobs that were in it.
Devasomā: To find it, then, we're going to have to search the whole city of Kāñcī.
Kāpālika: So we will, my love.

[*Both walk about. Then a Buddhist monk enters with a bowl in his hand.*]

Buddhist: Ah, the house of the lay devotee and merchant Dhanadāsa provides the most magnificent charity. There I obtained these abundant morsels of all sorts of rich smelling, tasty, fish and meat. Now I'm going off to the royal monastery.

[*walking about, he says to himself*] The compassionate Lord Buddha gratified the community of monks with teachings that instruct them to live in mansions, to sleep on well-constructed beds, to eat in the morning, to take well-flavoured drinks in the afternoon, to chew betel leaves mixed with five perfumes, and to wear comfortable clothes. But what I haven't seen are the rules for taking a wife or drinking liquor. Is it possible that the Omniscient One did not envision this? I suspect that these tired, evil Buddhist elders removed the rules about women and liquor from the holy books out of their jealousy of us young folk. Where can I find an unmodified original text? If I find it, I will gratify the community by making known to all the complete words of the Buddha.

[*He walks about.*]

Devasomā: My lord, look. Look at that fellow in the red robe scurrying about in the middle of this royal road filled with crowds of happy people. He is all hunched over, looking this way and that, and moving as if he's scared of something.

Kāpālika: My love, you're quite right. And his hand is inside his robe as if he is hiding something.

Devasomā: My lord, let's go and grab him and find out.

Kāpālika: So be it. [*approaching*] Hey, monk. Stop!

Buddhist: Who's calling me? [*turning and looking*] Ay, it's the evil Kāpālika who lives at the temple of Ekāmranātha. Well, I have no intention of being the target of his drunken violence, [*goes off in haste*]

Kāpālika: Aha. My love, we've found our skull. Did you see him run away in fear when he saw me? This is clear evidence that he is the thief. [*Quickly cutting him off, the Kāpālika stops him.*] Hah! Where will you go now, you bastard?

Buddhist: Kāpālika, please don't. What's this? [*aside*] Hm, this female devotee is really beautiful.

Kāpālika: Listen, monk. Show me right now. I want to see what you have in the hand hidden beneath your robe.

Buddhist: What is there to see? It is only a begging bowl.

Kāpālika: That's precisely what I want to see.

Buddhist: No, Kāpālika, please don't. It is proper that this bowl should be kept hidden.

Kāpālika: Aha, then it was for the sake of hiding things that the Buddha first taught you to wear such ample robes.

Buddhist: This is true.

Kāpālika: This is the relative truth. But I want to hear the absolute truth.

Buddhist: Enough of this mockery! The hours for begging are over. I have to go. [*He sets off.*]

Kāpālika: Ha, bastard, where are you going? Give me the skull.

[*He grabs the end of the monk's robe.*]

Buddhist: Hail to the Buddha!

Kāpālika: What you should say is 'Hail to Kharapaṭa!' He's the one who wrote the sacred book of thieves. Or was the Buddha more an expert in this topic than even Kharapaṭa? Why's this?

> The ideas he stole, that thieving Tathāgata,
> From the Upaniṣads and *Mahābhārata,*
> He brazenly claimed as original thinking,
> While foolish brāhmaṇas stood there blinking. (12)

Buddhist: May your sins be ended.
Kāpālika: How is it possible that the sins of a well-behaved ascetic like myself not be ended?
Devasomā: My lord, you look tired. This cherished skull is not going to be easy to obtain. You should drink some liquor from this cow horn in order to recover your strength before you get into a fight with him.

[*Devasomā gives some liquor to the Kāpālika.*]

Kāpālika: [*drinks*] My love, you too should remove your fatigue.
Devasomā: Thank you, my lord. [*drinks*]
Kāpālika: This Buddhist has offended us. But sharing is the chief thing in our own doctrine. Let this teacher have the rest.
Devasomā: Whatever my lord commands. Take this, Sir.
Buddhist: [*aside*] Ha, how easy it was to get a good result. But this is so sinful, and a big merchant might see me. [*aloud*] No, no, madam. This is not proper for us. [*licks the corners of his mouth*]
Devasomā: Go to hell! What makes you so smug?
Kāpālika: My love, his mouth is watering so much that his words, so opposed to his desire, can barely be understood.
Buddhist: You still have no compassion.
Kāpālika: If I had compassion, how could I be an ascetic free of passion?
Buddhist: One who is free of passion should also be free of anger.
Kāpālika: I'll be free of anger if you give me what belongs to me.
Buddhist: And what's that?
Kāpālika: My skull!

Buddhist: How your skull?
Kāpālika: 'How your skull?' he says. But this is quite appropriate.

If you are really a son of the Buddha,
Who wrongly tried to insist
That visible things, huge and imposing,
Do not in fact exist,
Even earth, mountains, rivers, and ocean,
What could stop you from denying
The skull you hold in your fist? (13)

Devasomā: My lord, He'll never give it back with such gentle treatment. Let's just go and grab it from his hand.
Kāpālika: Let's do it, my love. [*They do their best to grab it.*]
Buddhist: Go to hell, you evil Kāpālika! [*He pushes him with his hand and kicks him with his foot.*]
Kāpālika: How's this? I've fallen.
Devasomā: [*to Buddhist*] You're a dead man, son of a slave girl! [*She tries to grab him by the hair, but since he has none, she falls.*]
Buddhist: [*aside*] How wise was the Buddha when he foresaw the need to have a shaven head, [*aloud*] Get up, sister, get up. [*He helps Devasomā to get up.*]
Kāpālika: Look at this, Māheśvaras. This evil monk named Nāgasena is grabbing the hand of my sweetheart.
Buddhist: No, brother, I'm not. Our rule is to help those fallen into distress.
Kāpālika: Is this yet another rule of the Omniscient One? Wasn't I the first one to fall? But let it be. It doesn't matter. Now your head is about to become my skull bowl.

[*All of them make a big uproar.*]

Buddhist: Help, help!
Kāpālika: Look, Māheśvaras. This evil so-called monk first robs me of my skull bowl, and then *he* calls for help. Let it be. I too can make a scandal. Sacrilege, sacrilege!

[*A Pāśupata then enters.*]

Pāśupata: Satyasoma, why are you calling for help?

Kāpālika: Ah, Babhrukalpa, this evil so-called monk Nāgasena has stolen my skull bowl and doesn't want to give it back.

Pāśupata: [*aside*] In this matter I should act like the Gandharvas and try to get the girl for myself.

> The barber's wench who I quite fancy
> This Buddhist rogue has lured his way
> Offering her coins from beneath his robe,
> As if tempting a cow with a fist of hay. (14)

But I will now defeat my rival by inciting this pimp against him. [*aloud*] Nāgasena, is it true what he said?

Buddhist: My lord, How can you say this? It is a Buddhist precept that one should abstain from taking what is not given. It is a precept that one should abstain from false speech. It is a precept that one should abstain from sexual intercourse. It is a precept that one should abstain from taking a life. It is a precept that one should abstain from eating at inappropriate times. I take my refuge in the religion of the Buddha.

Pāśupata: Satyasoma, such is their moral code. What can you reply?

Kāpālika: Well, our code is that one should not tell lies.

Pāśupata: Both these codes are quite appropriate. But how can we decide the case?

Buddhist: What possible motive can there be for one who takes the Buddha's word as his authority to grab a bowl full of liquor?

Pāśupata: A disputant cannot win a case by mere affirmation.

Kāpālika: When we have direct evidence, what is the point of disputation?

Pāśupata: What sort of direct evidence?

Devasomā: My lord, he has the skull in his hand hidden inside his monk's robe.

Pāśupata: You heard what she said.

Buddhist: This so-called skull doesn't belong to anyone else.

Kāpālika: Let us see it then.

Buddhist: There! [*He shows it.*]

Kāpālika: [*sarcastically*] Look, Māheśvaras. Look at the injustice perpetrated by the Kāpālika and the excellent conduct of this Buddhist monk.

Buddhist: It is a Buddhist precept that one should abstain from taking what is not given. [*He again recites the precepts.*]

[*Both the Kāpālika and Devasomā dance.*]

Buddhist: What's this? When he should be ashamed, he dances instead.

Kāpālika: Hah, who's dancing? [*looking all around*] He thinks he sees dancing in the display of my delight, like a flower swaying in the wind, at once again seeing my lost skull bowl.

Buddhist: My lord, why don't you take a closer look at this bowl. Tell me, what colour is it?

Kāpālika: What do you want me to say? Do you think I can't see? This skull is blacker than a crow.

Buddhist: Then you yourself admit that this is mine and not yours.

Kāpālika: What I really admit is that you know how to change its colour. Look . . .

> Once your robe was as white as chalk,
> As bright as the silk of a lotus stalk,
> And didn't you slyly make it one
> With a tint as red as the rising sun? (15)

And besides . . .

> Since you are stained, inside and out,
> With a blood-red hue,
> How could my skull not acquire
> The same stain too? (16)

Devasomā: Ay, I'm ruined! How terrible! How did this skull get such a changed condition by coming into contact with stained cloth? Endowed with all the auspicious marks, it was as holy as the skull of Brahmā. It shone like the full moon and was always full of liquor. [*She weeps.*]

Kāpālika: My love, don't cry. It will become pure once again. The sacred scriptures say that great beings have their faults removed through penance.

> Our Master Śiva, the god of the crescent moon,
> Once undertook the vow called Mahāvrata
> To free himself from the heavy sin that befell,
> When he cut-off one of the heads of the god of creation.
> Likewise, Indra, king of the thirty gods,
> Once killed the three-headed son of mighty Tvaṣṭṛ
> But managed to get the burden of his sin removed
> Through the merit of a hundred sacrifices. (17)

Babhrukalpa, is this not so?

Pāśupata: This is what the sacred Āgamas declare.

Buddhist: Sir, if I changed its colour, who made it this shape and size?

Kāpālika: Did you Buddhists not spring from the lineage of Māyā?

Buddhist: For how long do I have to curse you? Here, you take it.

Kāpālika: Did not the Buddha himself perfect the supreme virtue of generosity?

Buddhist: Now that this is over, where will I find refuge?

Kāpālika: Isn't your refuge the Buddha, the Dharma, and the Saṅgha?

Pāśupata: I am unable to decide this case. We will have to take it to the court.

Devasomā: My lord, if we do this, it's goodbye to the skull.

Pāśupata: What do you mean?

Devasomā: This Buddhist has behind him the wealth of many monasteries. He can fill the mouths of the officials of the court at will. But we are servants of the poor Kāpālika, whose wealth is merely a snake skin and ashes. With what wealth do we enter the court?

Pāśupata: This isn't so.

> The law, like the palace, has strong foundations,

Upright, solid, polished, and firm,
The one good pillars, the other good persons. (18)

Kāpālika: Enough of this! A person who obeys the law need not fear anything.

Buddhist: [*to the Pāśupata*] My Lord, you should lead the way.

Pāśupata: So be it.

[*All of them walk about. Then a madman enters.*]

Madman: This evil dog! You've grabbed the skull full of meat kabobs and run away with it. Son of a slave girl, where are you going to go? Now, he's dropped the skull and is coming running to bite me. [*looking in all directions*] I'll break his teeth with this stone. Why have you left the skull and run away? Crazy, evil dog, do you dare to get angry even with someone as brave as me? The ocean has mounted the boar of the village and flown up to the sky. It has conquered Rāvaṇa and has seized by force Indra's son Timiṅgala. Ay, castor oil tree, what did you say? 'It's not true. It's not true.' Is not this cloud, with its hands as long and wide as a club, my witness? But why should a person like me, whose bravery is renowned throughout the three worlds, need any witnesses? This is what I'm going to do. I'll eat the leftover morsel of meat that the dog bit into. [*He eats and then looks confused.*] Ay, ay, I've been killed by tears. [*He weeps and looks.*] Who is this who's beating me? [*He looks.*] Evil dog, I am the nephew of someone important, as Ghaṭotkaca was the nephew of Bhīmasena. Besides . . .

My belly is full of a hundred demons
In many guises, shapes, and sizes,
And from my mouth come flying out
Giant snakes and a hundred lions. (19)

Why are they harassing me? Be kind, be kind to me, my young lords. Don't harass me because of this morsel of meat. [*He looks ahead.*] This must be my teacher Śūranandin. I'll go up to him. [He *runs.*]

Pāśupata: Ay, this madman is coming toward me.

> His robe is tattered and secondhand,
> His hair a wild and tangled mess,
> Around his neck a withered garland,
> His body covered with dust and ash.
> Above his head are crows and hawks,
> ready to scavenge whatever they can
> It looks as though before us walks
> A garbage heap in the form of a man. (20)

Madman: I'll approach this one. [*He approaches.*] My lord, please accept this skull obtained from an excellent dog belonging to a Caṇḍāla.

Pāśupata: [*looking with disdain*] Let this be accepted by a more worthy person.

Madman: Great Brahman [*approaching the Buddhist*], please do me this favour.

Buddhist: [*indicating the Kāpālika*] This Great Pāśupata is more worthy.

Madman: [*Approaching the Kāpālika, he places the skull on the ground, circumabulates, and falls at his feet.*] Great saint, please do me this favour. This homage is for you.

Kāpālika: My skull!

Devasomā: So it is!

Kāpālika: By the grace of god I have again become a true Kāpālika.

Madman: You son of a slave girl, may you eat poison. [*He grabs the skull and goes off.*]

Kāpālika: [*chasing after him*] This servant of Death is stealing my life itself! Help me you two!

Both: As you wish. We'll be your helpers.

[*All try to stop the madman.*]

Kāpālika: Stop you, stop!

Madman: Why are they stopping me?

Kāpālika: Give me my skull and be gone.

Madman: You fool, can't you see that this is a gold bowl?
Kāpālika: Who would ever make a gold bowl like this?
Madman: I tell you, this is a gold bowl made by the bastard of a goldsmith who wears golden clothes.
Buddhist: What are you saying?
Madman: It's a gold bowl.
Buddhist: Is he a madman?
Madman: Madman . . . 'I keep hearing that word. Take this and show me the madman. [*He hands the skull to the Kāpālika.*]
Kāpālika: [*grabbing the skull*] He's over there hidden behind that wall. Go quickly and follow him.
Madman: You have been most kind.

[*The madman hastily exits.*]

Buddhist: It's a miracle! I have been saved by the success of my opponent. *Kāpālika:* [*hugging the skull*]

> Unbroken penance for years I suffered,
> And devotion to Śiva alone I offered.
> Now the madman has gone away
> And you, my skull, are back, hooray! (21)

Devasomā: My lord, when I see you today, looking like the evening reunited with the moon, my very eyes rejoice.
Pāśupata: How lucky you are.
Kāpālika: Is this not a good result for all of you?
Pāśupata: [*aside*] What's true is that those who have no fault need not fear. Today this monk escaped from the mouth of the tiger, [*aloud*] Now that I have been made happy by the success of my friend, I will go and wait for the evening worship at the eastern temple of the Lord. And starting from today. . .

> May the quarrel that once bound you two together
> Now become the source of mutual love
> As once it was when Kirāta fought with Arjuna. (22)

[*The Pāśupata exits.*]

Kāpālika: Honourable Nāgasena, if I have done you any offence, I hope you will forgive me.
Buddhist: Need you even ask? What can I do for you?
Kāpālika: If I have your forgiveness, what thing better than that can I request?
Buddhist: It is time for me to go.
Kāpālika: I hope I will see you again.
Buddhist: May it be so. [*He exits.*]
Kāpālika: Devasomā, my love, let us go also.

[*Epilogue*]

May the sacred fires always lift up to heaven
Oblations offered on the people's behalf.
May the brahmans serve the Vedas and cows give milk,
May the people be happy, each intent on his *dharma.*
May King Mahendra subdue his enemies' power
And rule for as long as the sun and moon exist. (23)

[*Both exit.*]

Here ends the farce entitled *Drunken Games.*

Contributors

F.R. Allchin (d.2010) was Professor of Archaeology, Cambridge University.

Pentti Aalto (d.1998) was a Finnish Linguist at the University of Helsinki.

Martha L. Carter has taught and curated at institutions including the Cleveland Museum of Arts and the University of Wisconsin.

M.S. Oort is Former Librarian, Kern Institute, Leiden.

Irfan Habib is Professor Emeritus, Aligarh Muslim University.

James McHugh is Assistant Professor, School of Religion, University of South California.

Jan E.M. Houben is directeur d'Études, Ecole Pratique des Hautes Etudes, Paris.

Rajendralal Mitra (d.1891) was a prominent figure of Bengal Renaissance and was the first Indian President of the Asiatic Society of Bengal.

Rajesh Kocchar, a Former Director, National Institute of Science Technology and Development Studies, New Delhi is currently Honorary Professor, Department of Mathematics, Panjab University, Chandigarh.

David Lorenzen was Professor at El Colegio de Mexico, Mexico. He is currently working on a book about the seventeenth-century Dadu Panth poet Jan Gopal.

Index